Innova   ience
of bo   ibugi
and J   *iomic*
Perfoi   *iange*
(Cam   nities
offere   vhich
have c   d use
of kno

Inn   : and
under   ogra-
phy, i   ology
studie   ading
intern   : vital
readir   rofes-
sional

DR D   earch
Coun
DR JI   ool of
Busin
JON   udies,
Birk

Innovation Policy in a Global Economy

Innovation Policy in a Global Economy

edited by Daniele Archibugi, Jeremy Howells
and Jonathan Michie

CAMBRIDGE
UNIVERSITY PRESS

PUBLISHED BY THE PRESS SYNDICATE OF THE UNIVERSITY OF CAMBRIDGE
The Pitt Building, Trumpington Street, Cambridge CB2 1RP, United Kingdom

CAMBRIDGE UNIVERSITY PRESS
The Edinburgh Building, Cambridge CB2 2RU, UK   http://www.cup.cam.ac.uk
40 West 20th Street, New York, NY 10011–4211, USA   http://www.cup.org
10 Stamford Road, Oakleigh, Melbourne 3166, Australia

First published 1999

Printed in the United Kingdom at the University Press, Cambridge

Typeset in Monotype Times 10/12 pt, in QuarkXPress® [SE]

A catalogue record for this book is available from the British Library

Library of Congress Cataloguing in Publication data applied for

ISBN 0 521 63327 3 hardback
ISBN 0 521 63361 3 paperback

Contents

List of figures   *page* ix
List of tables   x
List of contributors   xii
Foreword by Chris Freeman   xiii
Preface and acknowledgements   xv

1 Innovation systems and policy in a global economy   1
   DANIELE ARCHIBUGI, JEREMY HOWELLS AND
   JONATHAN MICHIE

PART I   National systems of innovation

2 Technology policy in the learning economy   19
   BENGT-ÅKE LUNDVALL

3 Some notes on national systems of innovation and production,
   and their implications for economic analysis   35
   GIOVANNI DOSI

4 Technology, growth and employment: do national systems
   matter?   49
   MARIO PIANTA

PART II   Regional, national and global forces

5 Regional systems of innovation?   67
   JEREMY HOWELLS

6   Global corporations and national systems of innovation: who
    dominates whom?   94
    KEITH PAVITT AND PARIMAL PATEL

7   Globalisation and financial diversity: The making of venture
    capital markets in France, Germany and UK   120
    MICHAEL F. KLUTH AND JØRN B. ANDERSEN

8   Patterns of national specialisation in the global competitive
    environment   139
    PAOLO GUERRIERI

PART III   Globalisation and economic performance

9   The political economy of globalisation   163
    MICHAEL KITSON AND JONATHAN MICHIE

10 The geographical sourcing of technology-based assets by
    multinational enterprises   185
    JOHN H. DUNNING AND CLIFFORD WYMBS

11 Innovation as the principal source of growth in the global
    economy   225
    JOHN CANTWELL

12 The policy implications of the globalisation of innovation   242
    DANIELE ARCHIBUGI AND SIMONA IAMMARINO

    Index   272

Figures

4.1 Globalisation, national system of innovation and their
     economic impact   *page* 52
4.2 Total R&D and investment per employee   55
4.3 Product innovation sectors and employment change, 1989–94   58
4.4 Process innovation sectors and employment change, 1989–94   59

Tables

6.1 Nationalities of the top 20 firms in US patenting in eleven
broad technological fields, 1985–90   *page* 95
6.2 The source of large firms' patenting in the USA, according to
their principal product group, 1985–90   96
6.3 The source of large firms' patenting in the USA, according to
their country of origin, 1985–90   97
6.4 Large firms in national technological activities, 1985–90   100
6.5 National performance in basic research (mean citations per
paper) and in technology (business-funded R&D as
percentage of GDP)   102
6.6 Qualifications of the workforce in five European countries   103
6.7 Trends in business-funded R&D as percentage of GDP   105
6.8 Own R&D expenditures by world's 200 largest R&D
spenders (1994)   106
6.9 Sectoral patterns of revealed technological advantage;
1963–8 to 1985–90   109
8.1 Weights of the sectoral groups in total exports   141
8.2 Shares of intra-regional trade of the three regional groupings
(percentage)   143
8.3 Patterns of trade specialisation: United States, Japan and
the EU   148
8.4 Patterns of trade specialisation: Germany, France and the
United Kingdom   151
8.5 Patterns of trade specialisation: Sweden, Italy and Spain   153
9.1 Growth of world output and world trade, 1870–1990
(annual % growth rates, calculated peak to peak)   165
9.2 The growth and volatility of world output and world trade,
1870–1990   166

9.3   GDP shares of world capitalist countries (% benchmark
       years)   170
9.4   Export shares of world capitalist countries (% benchmark
       years)   171
9.5   Exports: shares of world exports of manufactures (%)   172
9.6   Shares of OECD trade in manufactures (%)   173
10.1   Distribution of 150 leading industrial MNEs by sector,
       1994–5   188
10.2   Distribution of 150 leading industrial MNEs by region or
       country of origin, 1994–5   189
10.3   Percentage of R&D undertaken outside home country by
       technology grouping   191
10.4   The sourcing of technological advantage of sample firms by
       industrial sector   194
10.5   The sourcing of technological advantage of sample firms by
       industrial sector and degree of multinationality of sales and
       assets   196
10.6   The sourcing of technological advantage of sample firms by
       industrial sector and degree of multinationality of R&D   198
10.7   The sourcing of technological assets of sample firms by
       country and degree of multinationality (a) sales and assets   200
10.8   The sourcing of technological assets of sample firms by
       country and degree of multinationality (b) R&D   201
10.9   Importance of FDI as a means of accessing foreign
       technological advantage, 1994–5   202
10.10 Importance of alliances as a means of accessing foreign
       technological advantage, 1994–5   203
10.11 Importance of trade as a means of accessing foreign
       technological advantage, 1994–5   204
10.12 Assets by mode of sourcing   213
12.1   A taxonomy of the globalisation of innovation   244
12.2   The regimes of the globalisation of innovation – interactions   247
12.3   The regimes of the globalistion of innovation – implications
       for the national economies   249
12.4   Public policies' targets and instruments for the globalisation
       of innovation   256

Contributors

JØRN B. ANDERSEN	Danish Agency for Development of Trade and Industry, Copenhagen
DANIELE ARCHIBUGI	Institute for Studies on Scientific Research and Documentation, Italian National Research Council, Rome
JOHN CANTWELL	University of Reading
GIOVANNI DOSI	Department of Economics, University of Rome 'La Sapienza'
JOHN H. DUNNING	University of Reading and Rutgers University
PAOLO GUERRIERI	Faculty of Economics, University of Rome
JEREMY HOWELLS	PREST, University of Manchester
SIMONA IAMMARINO	University of Reading and ISRDS-CNR, Rome
MICHAEL KITSON	St Catharine's College and ESRC Centre for Business Research, University of Cambridge
MICHAEL F. KLUTH	Roskilde University, Roskilde
BENGT-ÅKE LUNDVALL	Aalborg University, Aalborg
JONATHAN MICHIE	Birkbeck College, University of London
CHRIS FREEMAN	University of Sussex
PARIMAL PATEL	SPRU, University of Sussex
KEITH PAVITT	SPRU, University of Sussex
MARIO PIANTA	Institute for Studies on Scientific Research and Documentation, Italian National Research Council, Rome, and University of Urbino
CLIFFORD WYMBS	Rutgers University

Foreword

This is a brilliant set of papers. Unlike many such collections by diverse authors, the standard is uniformly high and even more surprisingly, there is a clear common theme which links them together despite the lack of common authorship. That theme is the elucidation of just what is meant by 'globalisation'. As Archibugi and Iammarino observe, this is a catch-all concept which is used indiscriminately to describe many diverse phenomena.

In particular, the book concentrates on the ways in which globalisation affects and is affected by technical change and systems of innovation. Over the last decade or so many authors have used the expression 'national system of innovation' to describe and analyse those networks of institutions and activities, which in any country, initiate, modify, import and diffuse new technologies. Some of the authors have attributed the origin of this concept to me. This is not accurate. To the best of my knowledge the expression was coined by Lundvall, who contributes the first chapter in this book in which he argues cogently that what matters most is *learning*, rather than knowledge itself. In any case, as I am sure he would agree, and as several of the chapters point out (e.g. Dosi and Kluth and Andersen) there is a long tradition in economic thought of this combined approach to technical innovation and institutional change, going back at least to Count Serra in Naples.

As this discussion has unfolded, it has become apparent that both the international ('global') and the sub-national ('regional') dimensions of innovative activities merit investigation and debate as well as the national dimension. This book explores all three of these and contributed substantial new theoretical insights and empirical evidence at each level. It would be invidious to single out individual chapters in a book where the overall standard is so high but for reasons of space it is not possible to discuss them all in a brief preface. I therefore just comment on a few points which are of exceptional interest.

The chapter by Jeremy Howells provides an outstandingly good review and analysis of regional systems of innovation. He points out, with a wealth of illustrations, the necessity of an historical as well as a geographical approach to this topic. The example of Scotland illustrates very well his point that what were once 'nations' may become 'regions' and *vice-versa*. This leads to the conclusion that an historical 'multi-layered' approach is essential.

This conclusion is just as relevant for the global/national level which is the main focus of most of the chapters. Patel and Pavitt sustain their well-known position that the domestic national home base of multi-national corporations continues to be the main platform for most of their innovative activities. However, Dunning and Wymbs provide interesting new evidence of the increasing efforts of many MNCs to extend their sources of information and new ideas through the activities of their subsidiaries abroad. It is especially welcome to see the contributions to this volume from John Dunning and John Cantwell from Reading University. John Dunning pioneered the programme of research at this university which made it a leading centre in Europe for the study of MNCs, and it is good to see that he is still an active source of inspiration for this work about 40 years later.

Perhaps it is not too far-fetched to suggest that this is a small example of that type of sustained and cumulative learning by research (in this case in the academic world), which underlies institutional trajectories and in the industrial sphere leads to the 'strickness' of the patterns of specialisation, which many of the chapter authors observe. It is to be hoped that the editors continue their own collaboration in promoting this research trajectory which has produced such fruitful results. The cohesion of the book should be attributed to their sustained efforts, as well as to the fascination of the topic and the work of the authors. All of them merit warm congratulations and a wide circulation for this excellent publication.

Chris Freeman
University of Sussex

Preface and acknowledgements

All the chapters in this book were commissioned specifically for this volume and draft versions were discussed at a working conference in April 1996 in Rome. This conference marked the second in a series of Euroconferences entitled 'The Globalization of Technology: Lessons for the Public and Business Sectors' co-funded by DGXII of the European Commission as part of the Human Capital Mobility (HCM) Programme (Grant no. ERBCHECCT940230), organised by the three of us.

The overall Euroconference initiative has a number of objectives, but a key aim is to help inform, involve and support young scientists and researchers in the field of industrial innovation and technology policy. The Rome conference therefore sought to bring together an informal group of some young and some not so young researchers working in this field. The result was a lively and interesting debate surrounding the issues of national innovation systems and of the globalisation of technology which is of such crucial strategic importance to both private and public sectors alike.

Obviously a vital role was played by all the conference presenters, many of whom have subsequently become contributors to this book. We would therefore like to thank Jørn Andersen, Giovanni Dosi, Paolo Guerrieri, Simona Iammarino, Michael Kitson, Michael Kluth, Bengt-Åke Lundvall, Keith Pavitt and Mario Pianta for presenting papers and participating in the discussions. We would also like to thank John Cantwell, John Dunning, Pari Patel and Clifford Wymbs for their contributions.

We are grateful to the Institute for Studies on Scientific Research and Documentation of the Italian National Research Council for hosting the Conference in Rome.

Special thanks go to Carol Jones, Shay Ramalingam, Enza Moretti and Cinzia Spaziani for helping to organise the event and for ensuring it ran smoothly.

Our thanks go to Ashwin Rattan of Cambridge University Press for his assistance at every stage of commissioning and producing this book; to Marcela Bulcu and Cinzia Spaziani for help on various stages of the manuscript; and to Chris Freeman for contributing the Foreword.

Our personal thanks go respectively to Paola, Clara and Orlando; to Jane, Katherine, Mark and Louisa; and to Carolyn, Alex and Duncan.

Daniele Archibugi
Jeremy Howells
Jonathan Michie

1 Innovation systems and policy in a global economy

DANIELE ARCHIBUGI, JEREMY HOWELLS
AND JONATHAN MICHIE

New technologies are a fundamental part of modern economic life. Economists and engineers, no less than politicians and public opinion, are devoting increasing attention to understanding why, how and where technological innovations are generated. This book is devoted to discussing two separate, but closely connected bodies of literature on the sources and nature of new technologies. The first set is focused on the similarities and differences in the organisation of innovative activities at the national level, whilst the second group is centred on the role of globalisation in shaping technological change.

The first body of literature stresses that a proper understanding of technological developments, and their dissemination throughout the economy and society, requires us to also understand the social fabric that shapes these developments. Over the last decade, the notion of systems of innovation, either local, regional, sectoral or national, has been widely used to map and explain the interactions between agents that generate and use technology.

The second body of literature has studied how innovation interacts with economic and social globalisation. The debate on globalisation has flourished over the last decade and a large number of themes connected to it have been investigated. Trade, production, finance, culture, media and many other fields have been scrutinised from the viewpoint of globalisation. The issue of technological change has been at the core of these debates on globalisation, and rightly so. On the one hand, technology is a vehicle for the diffusion of information and knowledge across borders; on the other hand, technological developments have themselves been stimulated by the globalisation of markets.

This book is devoted to studying the interplay between these national and global forces shaping technological change; it builds on three previous books that have analysed related issues (Archibugi and Michie eds., 1997;

Howells and Michie eds., 1997; Archibugi and Michie eds., 1998). This introductory chapter sets out the key concepts addressed in more detail in the subsequent chapters. The first part is devoted to outlining the origin of, and latest developments in, the systems of innovation approach; we then turn to consider more specifically the implications of globalisation for systems of innovation.

The origin of the 'system of innovation' approach

The 'systems of innovation' approach has developed and evolved since its initial appearance in the form of the 'national systems of innovation' (NSI) studies presented by Freeman (1987, 1988, 1995), Lundvall (1988), Lundvall ed., (1992) and Nelson ed. (1993). Chris Freeman (1987) was among the first to use the concept to help describe and interpret the performance of Japan over the post-war period. He identified a number of vital and distinctive elements in its national system of innovation to which could be attributed its success in terms of innovation and economic growth (Freeman, 1988, p. 338). It has subsequently been applied in a number of different contexts, many of which have been outside the original focus of a national setting. Thus, although the national focus remains strong, and rightly so, it has been accompanied by studies seeking to analyse the notion of systems of innovation at an international (or pan-national) level and at a sub-national scale.

Studies have also examined the systems of innovation approach within the context of a sectoral or technology perspective. Thus Bo Carlsson has developed what has become termed the 'technological systems' approach, indicating that systems can be specific to particular technology fields or sectors (Carlsson ed., 1995). Sectors and technologies do matter and have their own dynamic. But as argued by Nelson, it is also the case that 'nationhood matters and has a pervasive influence' (Nelson, 1993, p. 518). Sectors and technological systems within a nation have a powerful shaping influence on the structure and dynamic of a national innovation system, whilst national contexts have important influences on sectoral conditioning and performance. Thus, prior institutional endowments of a national system may help or hinder innovative activity and performance within particular sectors of a national economy (Howells and Neary, 1995, p. 245). The concepts of national (or spatially bounded) systems of innovation and technology systems (or sectoral innovation systems) should not be seen as mutually exclusive. Indeed, establishing the interrelationships between the two can yield valuable insights into the wider systems of innovation approach (Archibugi and Michie, 1997, p. 13).

Some definitions and concepts

Much of the literature on systems of innovation, and more especially on national systems of innovation, has been covered in an excellent review by Edquist (1997), which draws on earlier valuable discussion and reviews by Lundvall (1992a), Nelson and Rosenberg (1993) and Freeman (1995). However, certain preliminaries in terms of definitions and concepts are useful here for two reasons. Firstly, they form the basis of the subsequent discussion within this chapter and in the rest of the book, and, secondly, such a discussion highlights areas that may prove particularly profitable in terms of future work within the 'systems of innovation' research area.

Chris Freeman (1987, p. 1) defined the concept as 'the network of institutions in the public and private sectors whose activities and interactions initiate, import, modify and diffuse new technologies'. Lundvall (1992a, p. 12) makes a distinction between a narrow and broad definition of a system of innovation. His narrow definition would include 'organisations and institutions involved in searching and exploring – such as R&D departments, technological institutes and universities'. His broader definition would include 'all parts and aspects of the economic structure and the institutional set-up affecting learning as well as searching and exploring – the production system, the marketing system and the system of finance present themselves as sub-systems in which learning takes place'.

In respect of the 'national' element, Lundvall (1992a, pp. 2–3) stresses that this is not as clear-cut as is often assumed. The concept of 'national systems of innovation' has two dimensions: the national-cultural and the Étatist-political. The ideal, abstract nation state where these two dimensions coincide controlled by one central state authority is difficult, if not impossible, to find in the real world. Moreover, this nationally bounded view, at least in geographical terms, has been loosened over time. The approach has now been widened and developed to include systems of innovation that are sectoral in dimension and those that are at a different geographical scale, both above in terms of what Freeman (1995) coined 'upper' regions ('triad' and continental regions), and below in relation to regional[1] and local systems.

Regarding the term 'innovation', Edquist (1997, p. 10) has stressed the ambiguity and wide variation in its use. Thus, Nelson and Rosenberg (1993) and Carlsson and Stankiewicz (1995) have tended to adopt narrower definitions, mainly (though not wholly) centred on technological innovations, whilst Lundvall (1992a) seeks to include non-technological innovations, in particular institutional innovations (this point is further developed in his chapter in this volume). In his analysis of the Japanese innovation system, Freeman (1988, pp. 339–41) also emphasised the role of social and educational innovations, whilst Carlsson and Stankiewicz (1995, p. 28), in adopting Dosi's (1988) definition of innovation would also seem to include the emergence and development of new organisational set-ups.

Lastly, discussion of the term 'system' has been strangely limited. Lundvall (1992a, p. 2) is the most specific here although still brief. Thus he makes a short reference to Boulding's (1985) definition of a system as 'anything not in chaos' as well as noting that a system 'is constituted by a number of elements and by the relationships between these elements' (p. 2). Little reference is made to earlier work on systems theory, or to how this literature originally defined, or perceived, a system (see, for example, Hall and Fagen, 1956).

The evolution and development of the concept

Edquist (1997) reviewed the different elements and perspectives of the systems of innovation literature, in particular concentrating on the commonalities of the different approaches. More specifically, he outlines nine common characteristics of the systems of innovation approach and their advantages and problems. These core characteristics of systems of innovation approaches are: innovation and learning; their holistic and interdisciplinary nature; the natural inclusion of a historical perspective; differences between systems and non-optimality; their emphasis on inter-dependence and non-linearity; the incorporation of product technologies and organisational innovations; the central role of institutions in the systems of innovation approach; their conceptually diffuse nature; and the focus of the systems of innovation literature on conceptual constructs rather than on a more deeply rooted theoretical framework (Edquist, 1997, pp. 16–29).

Edquist's contribution is important because it seeks to determine common foundations of a 'systems of innovation' approach and seeks to build common frames of reference. It also highlights the high degree of diversity of approaches. While at one level this diversity is problematic, it might also explain why the approach has provoked such interest and pro-duced such a rich vein of inter-disciplinary work. Seeking to harmonise and more closely delimit definitions and concepts may now be necessary if the research programme is to develop further; on the other hand, it is impor-tant to avoid the danger of foreclosing on ideas too early on. The following sections focus on a number of these ideas and key issues in current systems of innovation thinking.

The role of learning in an innovation system

Although Lundvall noted the role that learning played in binding together production and innovation in a national system of innovation (Lundvall, 1988, p. 362) and sought to further emphasise the importance of learning in his 1992 discourse on the notion of national systems of innovation (Lundvall, 1992a, pp. 9–11), it has been only recently that he has sought to develop the role of learning and to put it at the core of the national systems of innovation construct (Lundvall, 1995; Lundvall and Johnson, 1995; see also his chapter in this volume). In these latter works he has stressed the role of learning in new and competitive national systems of innovation and especially the process of interactive learning (Lundvall, 1995, p. 39).

Learning is important in Lundvall's conception of systems of innovation because it is a key element in both the *dynamic* of the system and as a key agent in *binding* the whole system together. Thus, 'many different sectors and segments of the economy contribute to the overall process of inter-active learning and the specificity of the elements, as well as the linkages and modes of interaction between them, are crucial for the rate and direction of technical change' Lundvall (1995, p. 40).

Learning thus plays a major role in the development of the system, whilst forming the key element in its connectivity. In this framework learning takes place at all levels from the individual, through to the firm and organisation, on to inter-firm and inter-organisational learning, institutional learning (Johnson, 1992), cross institutional learning, and on through to the whole system – the 'learning economy'. Obviously the learning process involves a clear interactive and collective dimension. There are also inter-firm and more general institutional routines that can be set up through this interactive learning process (Hodgson, 1988). However, it is much harder to ascribe collections of firms, organisations and institutions as having a single, clear cognitive process, involving both a decision-making and memory function. The notion that what is learnt will be exactly the same for each individual, firm, organisation and institution is difficult to accept (see Antonelli, 1994).

The evolutionary nature of systems of innovation

There have been important attempts recently to develop the latent evolutionary aspects of the national systems of innovation concept. This has been done by outlining the value of evolutionary concepts in providing a stronger theoretical underpinning to the national systems of innovation model (Saviotti, 1997) and also by highlighting the utility of evolutionary concepts in helping to define what is meant by a national system of innovation (McKelvey, 1997).

Although such evolutionary approaches have, a posteriori, helped to explain the dynamic aspects of systems of innovation they have provided very little, if any, predictive insights into how national systems of innovation might develop in the future. While Galli and Teubal (1997, pp. 345–64) have outlined what they see as paradigmatic changes and structural adjustments of national systems of innovation since the late 1970s, this approach does not directly draw upon an evolutionary perspective, nor does it suggest what new transition stages will appear or when. The lack of any predictive element within systems of innovation thinking is a reflection of the fact that it represents a partial model rather than claiming to be a complete formal theory (Edquist, 1997, pp. 28–9). As yet, although the systems of innovation approach stresses historical processes, it has yielded few insights into the dynamics of the innovation process.

Systems as flows, links and networks

Although there is a general stress on 'interaction' and more specifically 'interactive learning' by Lundvall (1992a; see also Lundvall and Johnson, 1995) and on knowledge flows by, for example, David and Foray (1995; 1996) there are very few references to, let alone analysis of, the specific nature of these interactions in terms of flows and linkages connecting the actors in a network. This neglect of linkages and flows is strange, given that networks form one of the cornerstones in defining a system (Saviotti, 1997, pp. 193–5).

There are, of course, notable exceptions. An important analysis of the flows within and across systems of innovation is supplied by the literature on inter-industry technology flows (see Scherer, 1982; Pavitt, 1984; Archibugi, 1988; DeBresson ed., 1996). This literature has managed to map to what extent certain industries benefit from the innovations generated by 'upstream' suppliers which in turn has indicated the degree of sectoral integration amongst industries. This body of literature has also had the notable advantage of being able to quantitatively map these flows. However, this approach has so far not been specifically integrated into the framework of innovation systems.

As discussed above, the concept of innovation systems is much wider than inter-industry technology flows. Firstly, because it includes also flows which are not necessarily inter-sectoral, such as knowledge and information flows that occur within firms belonging to the same industry. Secondly, because it takes into account also the transfer of tacit and non-codified knowledge (Howells, 1996), which is not captured by the indicators that have so far been used to map inter-industry technology flows. Thirdly, because the innovation systems approach also considers flows which occur between different types of organisations and institutions, including firms, agencies and government establishments.

One attempt to take into account an extended framework is provided by Galli and Teubal (1997, pp. 347–8), who briefly mention linkages in their commentary on the main components of systems of innovation. Another is the analysis by Andersen (1992, 1996; Andersen and Lundvall, 1997) of innovation systems using firstly, 'primitive graph techniques' (see, for example, Andersen and Lundvall, 1997, p. 243, and for an earlier attempt, Santarelli, 1995) and, secondly, simulation modelling to describe vertical relationships in innovations, although as yet these techniques outlined by Andersen have not been empirically applied or tested (Andersen and Lundvall, 1997, p. 253).

This relative under analysis of linkages and flows within the systems of innovation literature represents an important barrier to the further conceptual development of the approach for three key reasons:

1   Firstly, the way that networks and, in turn, systems are usually defined is by the volume and characteristics of the linkages that bind them together. In short, systems are made up of the interactions between the actors or nodes in a system. Without any interaction between actors and nodes it is difficult to accept that a system exists.
2   Following on from this, flows and linkages in a system are also critical in defining an innovation system, and the way in which it functions and operates.
3   Lastly, a key element in gaining an adequate dynamic and evolutionary perspective on a system is by analysing the changing flow and linkage patterns between the actors and institutions that compose a system. Although the nature of the actors and institutions can change and forms an essential dynamic in itself, this change is also reflected and altered by the changing relationships between such actors and institutions.

Thus, growth in a system can be characterised in a number of different ways. In relation to an innovation system, growth could be confined within the individual elements or actors (the firms or other organisations), or it could result from increased flows between the elements of the system. Similarly, all the growth in a system could reside within the system if it was fully 'closed' but could flow out of it, to varying degrees, if it was an 'open' system. Even changing these two simple dimensions, in relation to growth and linkages within an innovation system, can alter its growth characteristics and dynamics radically. The fact that these aspects are as yet relatively under researched may reflect the 'youthfulness' of the systems of innovation research programme, and also the relative difficulty of trying to measure such innovation flows and linkages in a dynamic context. Nevertheless, a more detailed analysis of innovation flows and linkages is certainly required if an adequate model (or set of models) of innovation systems is to be provided.

Systems as innovation 'task environments' for firms

Another rich seam for future research within the systems of innovation literature is a bottom–up perspective of how national/sectoral systems of innovation may condition and influence the innovation decision making and behaviour of firms. The systems of innovation approach tends, by its very nature, to take a 'top–down' view of firms' innovative activity (see Howells, this volume). There is still much to be learned regarding how firms respond to, and interact with, the innovation system (national, sectoral or otherwise) at any point in time.

Much of the discussion that does indirectly refer to firm-level action, *de facto* considers *individual* firms as simply reacting to changes that are occurring within the wider system – or within the more specific network or at the institutional level. There has been little discussion about firm behaviour and technology strategy in terms of their relationship with systems of innovation approaches, even though firms represent important actors within the innovation system. Exceptions include Carlsson and Stankiewicz (1995, pp. 25–6) who consider the issue of individual firm behaviour in their outline of a technology system.[2] Ehrnberg and Jacobsson (1997, pp. 320–6) also discuss firm-level strategy, although mainly within the context of a firm's response to technological discontinuities.

The key issue here is how much the presence (or indeed absence) of a national or sectoral system of innovation may affect the innovation behaviour, actions and outcomes of firms. Yet the systems of innovation research programme has, as yet, had little impact on the technology strategy and management literature. Certainly an empirical analysis of the innovative performance of firms in weak and strong national and/or sectoral systems of innovation might provide an interesting new avenue of research.

The empirical analysis of systems of innovation

Archibugi and Pianta (1992) and Patel and Pavitt (1994) set out a list of indicators that might be used to 'measure' a national system of innovation, and these have been taken up to varying degrees by a number of subsequent studies (see, for example, Gassler *et al.*, 1996). In this volume, a valuable set of empirically based studies, using aggregate data sets on a national and international basis, outline national patterns of innovative activity and performance (see the chapters by Guerrieri, and by Pavitt and Patel).

However, on a more micro, firm or organisational level, most acknowledge that there remains a gap between theoretical developments and empirical analysis (Saviotti, 1997) and researchers are still at the stage of discussing and defining which analytical tools and methods might most profitably be used in empirical studies to bridge this gap. The work by Andersen, noted above, using graph techniques and simulation modelling appears to be a promising avenue of empirical work along these lines (Andersen and Lundvall, 1997). However, more certainly needs to be done to review, systematise and apply existing empirical studies covering these issues to systems of innovation work.

Perhaps the biggest task that remains in the development of the systems of innovation approach remains in providing a better linkage between the more aggregate, macro level studies and the micro level analysis of firm relationships and behaviour. In terms of the conceptual framework of the approach it is at this 'meta' level where the role of institutions and wider organisational networks is crucial, and where further empirical work beckons.

What is globalisation?

It is certainly telling that the debate on national innovation systems has developed in an age when the forces of globalisation are transforming economic life. It seems that the pressures of globalisation have generated a new concern regarding the role played by nation-specific factors. The term 'globalisation', however, has been used and abused. The recent literature has used the concept in, at least, two different ways.[3]

The first is related to the mapping of global factors in economic and social life. Global factors have always influenced the performance of local and/or national communities, but the reason why we talk about globalisation in this age is based on the assumption (right or wrong) that the importance of world-wide relations has increased both quantitatively and qualitatively. To map the resulting global transformations requires the ability to identify the dynamic context which is leading, according to some authors, to a dramatic increase of cross-border flows of information, knowledge, commodities and capital.

The second meaning of globalisation is linked to policy analysis. For example, the term 'globalisation' is often used implicitly, if not explicitly, as equivalent to the term 'liberalisation'. This is however inappropriate since globalisation is mainly a descriptive concept while liberalisation has a prescriptive meaning. In a related context, the debate on globalisation has

often collided with the assessment of the effectiveness of government policies (see Michie and Grieve Smith eds., 1995). It has been argued that
globalisation is reducing the impact of certain policy instruments, for
example interest rate changes, since all national public policies act under
international constraints. Certainly, globalisation is putting new pressures
on nation states which often lead to unwelcome outcomes. However, to
influence these outcomes, a different mix of policies may be needed. While
certain traditional macroeconomic policies, such as those based on
exchange rates and interest rates, may have lost a significant part of their
effectiveness, other kinds of policies, such as industrial policies, may be
becoming increasingly important if governments are to pursue their own
objectives.

Policies directed towards competence (such as those favouring training,
education, the acquisition of managerial skills and encouraging technological change) become crucial instruments to allow national communities to
face the processes of globalisation. Thus several of the subsequent chapters
argue that policies aimed at the creation of technological competence are
needed to strengthen national competitiveness and to preserve local well-
being (see, for example, the chapters by Lundvall, by Pavitt and Patel, and
Archibugi and Iammarino).

The boundaries of innovation systems in a global economy

Technological change provides a privileged viewpoint from which to understand the dynamics of globalisation. New technologies have always been
international in scope; the transmission of knowledge has never respected
states' borders. There is a complex interplay between technological change
and globalisation. On the one hand, new technologies act as a powerful
vehicle for the diffusion of information across distant communities. For
example, it would be difficult to imagine the current globalisation of
financial markets without the existence of the new information and
communication technologies, since they have made it possible to obtain
instant transactions across the world. On the other hand, the process of
generating and diffusing new technologies has been moulded and strengthened by the flows of individuals, commodities and capital. This has created
a circular process whereby technology has facilitated globalisation and vice
versa.

The focus of several chapters in this book is on the following questions:
(i) If the globalisation of technological innovation is occurring, will it lead
to the eventual dissolution of national systems of innovation?[4] (ii) Will
national systems of innovation converge towards more similar structures

because of the forces of globalisation? (iii) Is globalisation eroding the importance of innovation policies carried out at the national level?

It is often argued that globalisation is making spatially bounded systems less relevant. This implies that technology-based innovation systems (such as semiconductors) will be dominated by common technological regimes, regardless of the spatial location in which the connected production will take place. It is therefore possible to compare two approaches: the first stresses the importance of spatially bounded (local, regional or national) innovation systems, but which pays less attention to the differences between neighbouring firms operating in different industries. The second approach stresses instead the role of global factors in the making of innovation systems, but has the consequent danger of overlooking location-specific aspects of this process.

As already stressed, we need to go beyond an either/or debate and try to identify the relative role of regional, national, sectoral and global factors in shaping innovation systems (see Howells, this volume, within the context of regional innovation systems). The innovation systems concept is itself flexible enough to allow us to take into account the relative importance of each of these factors; some criteria can be identified in order to assess when and how local or global factors will prevail and how they will interact.

First, globalisation makes easier the transmission of best-practice techniques across countries. Semiconductors, antibiotics and new materials are based upon similar and shared knowledge across the globe. This, however, does not imply an automatic process of acquisition of knowledge since learning is neither instant nor automatic (see Lundvall's chapter, this volume).

Second, globalisation does not act only as the vehicle of best-practice techniques; it is also a vehicle for the international flow of goods and services. In order to survive in a competitive environment, firms are forced to find their own market niches where they can exploit their own competitive advantages. Often these niches rely heavily on endogenous capabilities. The problem that firms and nations have to face is not simply in being able to access the basic knowledge for semiconductors, new molecules or materials, but also to be able to use this knowledge to generate competitive products.

Third, there are location-specific advantages which have not lost their importance. Foreign direct investment by multinational corporations is increasingly sensitive to exploiting the locality-specific advantages associated with certain areas or regions. These growing capital flows are directed at picking out the best-practice conditions in specific countries (this is an issue discussed in this volume by Dunning and Wymbs). Cantwell (this volume) stresses that globalisation has made even more important the role of nation-specific assets for multinational corporations.

Fourth, there is increasing evidence that the international distribution of production and of technological capabilities is becoming more sectorally differentiated (see Archibugi and Michie eds., 1998; and Guerrieri, this volume). The process of international integration is leading to an increased division of labour and this implies that each country is focusing on selected industries and relying on trade for others. Even if the manufacture of semiconductors, for example, is becoming increasingly similar across countries, this does not imply that all countries are active in semiconductor production.

The role of multinational corporations in the global economy

Multinational enterprises have a major influence on national systems of innovation. Several chapters in this book discuss the interplay between large firms and nation-specific factors (see in particular Pavitt and Patel, and Dunning and Wymbs). Do large multinational firms have more influence on a national system of innovation, or do more nationally oriented, medium-sized companies that are more strongly embedded in the national system? Valuable work on this issue has been undertaken by Chesnais (1992) and more recently by Barré (1995) in his analysis of the relationship of multinational firms' strategies and national innovation systems. However, as Barré (1995, p. 218) admits, his work has been restricted by the nature and availability of the data that could be deployed and the assumptions behind their use.

Pavitt and Patel (this volume) provide significant evidence on three aspects of the innovative behaviour of large firms: first, multinational corporations are rather reluctant to locate technological activities in host countries. Core competences, including R&D and innovation centres, are still heavily concentrated in the companies' home countries. Second, traditional industries are, in proportion, more internationalised than high-tech industries. This result is certainly significant since it indicates that knowledge-intensive productions are more dependent on territorially bounded competences. Third, when companies decide to move part of their R&D and innovation centres abroad, they generally select the fields of excellence of the host countries. In other words, companies are more likely to go abroad to exploit the national capabilities of the country they are invading rather than to expand their own core competences. This last point is confirmed by the survey results reported by Dunning and Wymbs (this volume), which documents how firms augment their technological advantages from foreign sources.

Conclusions

We live in a turbulent world dominated by an increasing rate of technological change. Economic agents, including firms and governments, are forced to adapt to technological change in order to survive in a competitive environment. This book is an attempt to identify some of the emerging patterns in the resulting organisation of innovative activities. The notion of innovation systems proves to be a hugely useful tool in understanding how innovative activities are generated and disseminated, and what their impact is on economic and social life. This book thus makes an attempt to evaluate the notion of innovation systems in the context of current trends in the globalisation of economic, as well as technological, activities. We have suggested that globalisation does *not* make local, regional or national systems redundant; it is however relevant to identify how location-specific factors are transformed by global relations. We began our enquiry with the hypothesis that technological change is a factor in globalisation and, at the same time, one of its most important outcomes. The chapters in this volume seek, from a variety of viewpoints, to shed some light on this complex interconnection.

Notes

1 Freeman (1995, p. 21) defines these as 'nether' regions to avoid the confusion of some commentators who use the world 'region' to denote triad or continental regions.
2 However, this is only within the context of variety and diversity. Also they appear to rather downplay the point by citing Alchian's (1951) argument that attention should be paid to distributions of economic behaviour rather than to the behaviour of the individual (see also Metcalfe 1989, pp. 59–66).
3 Paul Streeten (1996) has, half in jest, provided a long list of different definitions of the term globalisation.
4 See, for example, the conclusions presented on this by Saviotti (1997, p. 196).

References

Alchian, A. 1951. Uncertainty, evolution and economic theory, *Journal of Political Economy*, 68: 211–21.
Andersen, S. E. 1992. User–producer relationships, national systems of innovation and internationalisation, in Lundvall (ed.) 1992.
    1996. From static structures to dynamics: specialization and innovative linkages, in DeBresson (ed.).
Andersen, E. S. and Lundvall, B.-Å. 1997. National innovation systems and the dynamics of the division of labor, in Edquist (ed.) 1997.

Antonelli, C. 1994. *The Economics of Localized Technological Change and Industrial Change*, Boston, Kluwer Academic Publisher.

Archibugi, D. 1988. In search of a useful measure of technological innovation, *Technological Forecasting and Social Change*, 34: 253–77.

Archibugi, D. and Michie, J. 1997. Technological globalisation and national systems of innovation: an introduction, in Archibugi and Michie (eds.) 1997.

Archibugi, D. and Michie, J. (eds.) 1997. *Technology, Globalisation and Economic Performance*, Cambridge, Cambridge University Press.

1998. *Trade, Growth and Technical Change*, Cambridge, Cambridge University Press.

Archibugi, D. and Pianta, M. 1992. *The Technological Specialization of Advanced Countries*, Dordrecht, Kluwer.

Barré, R. 1995. Relationships between multinational firms' technology strategies and national innovation systems: a model and empirical analysis, *STI Review*, 15: 201–22.

Boulding, K. E. 1985. *The World as a Total System*, Beverly Hills, CA, Sage.

Carlsson, B. (ed.) 1995. *Technological Systems and Economic Performance: The Case of Factory Automation*, Dordrecht, Kluwer.

Carlsson, B. and Stankiewicz, R. 1991. On the nature, function and composition of technological systems, *Journal of Evolutionary Economic*, 1: 93–118.

1995. On the nature, function and composition of technological systems, in Carlsson (ed.).

Chesnais, F. 1992. National systems of innovation, foreign direct investment and the operations of multinational enterprises, in Lundvall (ed.) 1992.

David, P. A. and Foray, D. 1995. Accessing and expanding the science and technology knowledge base, *STI Review*, n.16: 13–68.

1996. Information distribution and the growth of economically valuable knowledge: a rationale for technological infrastructure policies, in M. Teubal, D. Foray, M. Justman and Zuscovitch, E. (eds.) *Technological Infrastructure Policy: An International Perspective*, Dordrecht, Kluwer.

DeBresson, C. (ed.) 1996. *Economic Interdependence and Innovative Activity: An Input-Output Analysis*, Cheltenham, Edward Elgar.

Dosi, G. 1988. Sources, procedures and microeconomic effects of innovation, *Journal of Economic Literature*, 36: 1126–71.

Dosi, G., Freeman, C. Nelson, R. Silverberg, G. and Soete, L. (eds.) 1988. *Technological Change and Economic Theory*, London, Pinter,

Dosi, G., Giannetti, R. and Toninelli, P. A. (eds.) 1992. *Technology and the Enterprise in a Historical Perspective*, Oxford, Oxford University Press.

Edquist, C. 1997. Systems of innovation approaches. Their emergence and characteristics, in Edquist (ed.) 1997.

Edquist, C. (ed.) 1997. *Systems of Innovation: Technologies, Institutions and Organizations*, London, Pinter.

Edquist, C. and Johnson, B. 1997. Institutions and organizations in systems of innovation, in Edquist (ed.) 1997.

Ehrnberg, E. and Jacobsson, S. 1997. Technological discontinuities and incumbents' performance: an analytical framework, in Edquist (ed.) 1997.

Foray, D. 1997. Generation and distribution of technological knowledge: incentives, norms and institutions, in Edquist (ed.) 1997.

Freeman, C. 1987. *Technology Policy and Economic Performance: Lessons from Japan*, London, Frances Pinter.

1988. Japan: a new national system of innovation?, in Dosi *et al.* (eds).

1995. The National System of Innovation in historical perspective, *Cambridge Journal of Economics*, 19: 5–24. Reprinted in Archibugi and Michie (eds.) 1997.

Galli, R. and Teubal, M. 1997. Paradigmatic shifts in national innovation systems, in Edquist (ed.) 1997.

Gassler, H. Fröhlich, J. and Kopcsa, A. 1996. Selective information on the National System of Innovation as an important input for the technology management of firms, *International Journal of Technology Management*, 11: 329–42.

Håkansson, H. 1989. *Corporate Technological Behaviour: Cooperation and Networks*, London, Routledge.

Hall, A. D. and Fagen, R. E. 1956. Definition of system, *General Systems Yearbook*, 1: 18–28.

Hodgson, G. 1988. *Economics and Institutions*, Cambridge, Polity Press.

Howells, J. 1996. Tacit knowledge, innovation and technology transfer, *Technology Analysis & Strategic Management*, 8: 91–106.

Howells, J. and Michie, J. (eds.) 1997. *Technology, Innovation and Competitiveness*, Cheltenham, Edward Elgar.

Howells, J. and Neary, I. 1995. *Intervention and Technological Innovation: Government and the Pharmaceutical Industry in the UK*, Basingstoke, Macmillan.

Johnson, B. 1992. Institutional learning, in Lundvall (ed.) 1992.

Johnson, B. and Gregersen, B. 1995. Systems of innovation and economic integration, *Journal of Industry Studies*, 2: 1–18.

Lundvall, B.-Å. 1988. Innovation as an interactive process. From user-producer interaction to National Systems of Innovation, in Dosi *et al.* (eds.).

1992a. Introduction, in Lundvall (ed.) 1992.

1992b. User-producer relationships, national systems of innovation and internationalization, in Lundvall (ed.) 1992.

1992c. Explaining inter-firm cooperation. The limits of the transaction cost approach, in Grabher, G. (ed.) *The Embedded Firm: On the Socioeconomics of Industrial Networks*, London, Routledge.

1995. The global unemployment problem and national systems of innovation, in O'Doherty, D. P. (ed.) *Globalisation, Networking and Small Firm Innovation*, London, Graham & Trotman.

Lundvall, B.-A. (ed.) 1992. *National Systems of Innovation: Towards a Theory of Innovation and Interactive Learning*, London, Pinter.

Lundvall, B.-Å. and Johnson, B.A. 1995. The learning economy, *Journal of Industry Studies*, 1: 23–41.

McKelvey, M. 1994. How do National Systems of Innovation differ? A critical analysis of Porter, Freeman, Lundvall and Nelson, in G. Hodgson and E. Screpanti (eds.) *Rethinking Economics. Markets, Technology and Market Evolution*, Aldershot, Edward Elgar.

1997. Using evolutionary theory to define systems of innovation, in Edquist (ed.) 1997.

Metcalfe, J. S. 1989. Evolution and economic change, in Silberston, A. (ed.) *Technology and Economic Progress*, London, Macmillan.

1995. Technology systems and technology policy in an evolutionary framework, *Cambridge Journal of Economics*, 19: 25–46. Reprinted in Archibugi and Michie (eds.) 1997b.

Michie, J. and Grieve Smith, J. (eds.) 1995. *Managing the Global Economy*, Oxford, Oxford University Press.

Nelson, R. R. 1993. A retrospective, in Nelson (ed.) 1993.

Nelson, R. R. (ed.) 1993. *National Innovation Systems: A Comparative Analysis*, New York, Oxford University Press.

Nelson, R. R. and Rosenberg, N. 1993. Technical innovation and national systems, in Nelson (ed.) 1993.

Niosi, J. and Bellon, B. 1994. The global interdependence of National Innovation Systems: evidence, limits and implications, *Technology in Society*, 16: 173–97.

Patel, P. and Pavitt, K. 1994. National Innovation Systems: why they are important, and how they might be measured and compared, *Economics of Innovation and New Technology*, 3: 77–95.

Pavitt, K. 1984. Sectoral Patterns of Technical Change, *Research Policy*, 13: 343–73.

Santarelli, E. 1995. Directed graph theory and the economic analysis of innovation, *Metroeconomica*, 46: 111–26.

Saviotti, P. P. 1997. Innovation systems and evolutionary theories, in Edquist (ed.) 1997.

Sachwald, F. 1993. Mondialisation et systems nationaux, in F. Sachwald (ed.) *L'Europe et la globalisation. Acquisitions et accords dans l'industrie*, Paris, IFRI-Masson.

Scherer, F. M. 1982. Inter-industry technology flows in the US, *Research Policy,* 11: 227–45.

Streeten, P. 1996. Governance of the global economy, paper presented at the International Conference 'Globalization and Citizenship', United Nations Research Institute for Social Development, Geneva, 9–11 December.

PART I

National systems of innovation

2 Technology policy in the learning economy

BENGT-ÅKE LUNDVALL

There has been a major change in the perspectives on technology policy in the last couple of years. Most importantly it has been explicitly recognised that the key resource is knowledge and that it is the learning capabilities of people, firms and and national systems which dictate their relative economic success. In 1993, the European Commission in its White paper on 'Growth, competitiveness and employment' gave high priority to the need to reinforce the knowledge base and to invest in information infrastructures (CEC, 1993, p. 10 et passim). At the G7-meeting in Detroit in March 1994 president Clinton and his advisors emphasised the need to create new high quality jobs through a strengthening of the knowledge base and investing in education, research and innovation.[1]

As a follow-up to this meeting the OECD secretariat was asked to analyse the role of technology and technology policy in relation to productivity and employment. The first major report responding to this request (OECD, 1996a) takes the shift in perspective one step further by arguing explicitly that OECD countries are in the midst of entering a new growth regime where knowledge and learning has become crucial for economic performance. It is also stated that in this new growth regime technology policy, including policies related to information and communication technology, becomes more important than before. Part of the reason why OECD governments have begun to take these areas more seriously is that the room for manoeuvre and effectiveness within other policy areas such as macroeconomic policy and labour market policy are becoming increasingly reduced. But it is mainly because knowledge, learning and information play an ever important role in economic development. In this chapter I will highlight two implications for industrial and technology policies.

The first is that today industrial and technology policies must be devised more broadly than has previously been the case – the societal framework is imperative for the effects of the policy. Learning is necessarily an interactive and socially embedded process. Without a minimum of social cohesion the capability to learn to master new technologies and new and more flexible forms of organisation will be weak.

Conversely the societal consequences of these policies must be considered more than previously. What is perhaps the most serious current threat to the well-being of the OECD societies – the growing polarisation in labour markets – has as one major explanation an acceleration of the rate of innovation and change. Traditionally industrial and technology policies have been thought of as having a single aim to accelerate innovation and economic growth. In the new context the social and distributional impact of industrial and technology policies must be taken into account. This is why technology policy and industrial policy now have become more important also in relation to issues related to employment and income distribution and why they have to be integrated, or at least coordinated, with policies relating to infrastructures, social justice and not least education and training.

The second main point is that investment in technology which neglects user competence, social needs and the need for organisational renewal can do more harm than good in the context of the learning economy. Technology is an instrument and not a goal in itself. As with other instruments, the positive impact will depend on the skill of those who use it. There is no point in acquiring a Steinway before we have learned to play the piano.

The 'learning economy'

The title of this chapter refers to 'the learning economy'. This concept emphasises that we today find ourselves in an economy in which the competitiveness of individuals, firms and entire systems of innovation reflects the ability to learn.[2] Part of the reason for speaking about the learning economy today is new trends in production and in the labour market. Changes in the structure of the labour market and production show how the economy is to an increasing extent becoming knowledge based. This naturally means that knowledge building and learning are becoming more and more crucial for economic growth and competitiveness.[3]

This is reflected in developments in the labour market where there is a growing demand for wage-earning and salaried employees with skills, competences and qualifications; whereas it is those with the poorest education who are particularly hard hit by unemployment and falling real incomes. This trend can be seen in all the large member countries of the OECD and was the most striking outcome of the OECD Job's Study completed in the summer of 1994 (OECD, 1994a, pp. 22–3).

The analysis also showed how this shift in the demand for labour reflects two types of changes in industrial composition occuring simultaneously. Firstly, within each sector, there is an increase in the proportion of qualified labour, and, secondly, there is a tendency that employment growth is most rapid within those sectors that are most intensive in their use of highly skilled workers.[4]

In addition, an increasing proportion of output is knowledge and information. This obviously applies to new growth areas such as software and entertainment, but it in fact also applies to many traditional product areas. For instance, cars and ships are to an increasing extent equipped with large quantities of in-built knowledge in the form of information technology with associated software programs.

Underlying this move towards an increasingly knowledge-based economy are two phenomena. Firstly, it reflects intensified and increasingly global competition which makes it more difficult for firms in high-income countries to survive simply by producing traditional products using unskilled labour.[5] The second phenomenon is of course the dramatic advances in information and communication technology. Information technology is drastically reducing the price of data and simple information at the same time as its diffusion gives rise to an increase in demand for new skills and qualifications – not least those which are related to the ability to sift through and utilise the more and more copious but also more and more overwhelming and complex supply of information.

It is tempting to follow the terminology increasingly adopted by OECD (OECD, 1996a and OECD, 1996b) and use the concept 'knowledge-based economy'. I strongly prefer 'the learning economy' for a number of reasons. First, you do not have to argue that knowledge is much more important today than it has been. The hypothesis behind the 'learning economy' is rather that the rate of change and therefore the need for rapid learning has increased. Second, and this follows from the first point, what matters for economic performance is not so much the knowledge possessed by agents and organisations at a certain point of time but rather the capability to learn (and forget). Finally, it is only by focusing on learning that the most important implications for how the economy works in the new context can be brought out. Learning, and especially learning new skills and competences, is necessarily a social and interactive process which cannot flourish in a pure market economy. The learning economy-perspective clarifies why the social dimension has to be brought into the analysis of modern economic development.

How should the traditional view of the economy be adjusted to the fact that the economy is more and more about learning, i.e., about the generation, transfer and distribution of knowledge? What does it mean that a growing part of the trade taking place is the trading of knowledge and information? These are some of the questions to be addressed in the first part of the article.[6] In concluding, I will summarise some of the lessons to be drawn with respect to industrial and technology policies.

Rethinking economics and policy making

One of the things which serious economists normally agree upon is that the pure market cannot as a matter of course deal with the trading of knowledge. Nobel prize winner Kenneth Arrow, who is adept at reducing complicated matters to apparently simple paradoxes, has observed that people will only pay for knowledge they do not have – but that, on the other hand, it is difficult to assess how much to pay when you do not know what you are getting for your money (Arrow, 1973).

Added to this is the fact that the right to private ownership of knowledge is problematic. If I sell my knowledge, it is difficult to prevent the purchaser from selling it on to others who are my potential customers. On the other hand, I do not lose access to the knowledge just because I have sold it. All this is discussed from time to time as the problem associated with intellectual property rights and often in connection with software in particular, but the problem is much deeper and wider in the learning economy.

A third characteristic of knowledge is that it is not a scarce resource in the same manner as raw materials. It is true that the supply of economically useful knowledge is less than demand and that privately controlled information may lose in value when distributed to others (as in the case of giving a license for utilising a specific patented technology). But it is also true that, normally, individuals and organisations have access to much more information than they can utilise and that to sort out what is relevant is often the major problem. Even more fundamental is that the more individuals and organizations use their knowledge, the more knowledge they acquire. This is of special importance since the allocation of scarce resources has been at the very core of mainstream neoclassical economic theory for more than 100 years.

These specific properties mean that economic theory as it is taught at our universities is becoming less relevant than it has been. Uncertainty, unequal access to information, dynamic economies of scale and other difficulties which economists normally present as phenomena of marginal importance are gradually becoming the rule rather than the exception. This also means that the ways in which society and the economy are organised must be seen in a new light and reassessed in order to see to what extent they are at all adequate for stimulating learning processes. There is no obvious reason why the form of organisation which promotes efficient resource allocation would also be ideal when it comes to promote learning.

The social dimension

An important consequence of this new perspective is that social cohesion and trust play a growing role in determining the long-term performance of the economy. One reason is that transaction costs are high when information is to be exchanged in the market place. When great uncertainty exists in the market – and this applies perforce in the learning economy – the different parties can of course endeavour to protect themselves against it by using complex and extensive contracts which attempt to take into account everything that can go wrong. This is particularly the case in Anglo-Saxon countries, and not least in the USA where the legal system is extensively used as a regulatory mechanism. In real life this is an expensive option. It demands many 'lawyer-hours', and these are by no means cheap. It would be far more efficient if agents could trust each other, i.e., that they normally assume that if anything goes wrong, the burden of the unforeseen costs would be shared. Such solutions where mutual trust is established appear to be common in Japan and other East Asian countries in particular, but historically, favourable conditions also exist for them in the Nordic region.

Even more important are the difficulties in connection with the transfer of know-how and with learning tacit knowledge. Certain elements of knowledge – such as statistical facts and mathematical formulae – have been translated into universal codes and therefore they can be produced and communicated in the form of bits and this is a kind of knowledge which we can call 'information'. At a pinch, it is possible to imagine that information can be bought and sold on a market. But other types of knowledge are acquired via processes which have very little to do with market transactions. As a rule, what enables some people (and organisations) to earn more money than others is that they have access to knowledge which does not readily lend itself to codifying – they have access to tacit knowledge. This type of knowledge, which is associated with any kind of professional activity, can generally only be acquired by means of an apprentice–master relationship and by practical experiences gained in a close interaction with colleagues. Here it is absolutely imperative that a minimum of respect and mutual trust exists for the transfer of knowledge to take place.[7]

In principle, it is possible to imagine highly efficient local communities within which trust relationships flourish while those outside the communities are socially marginalised and excluded from the 'club' or the 'tribe'. This could be true for mafia-like organisations as well as for associations of professionals with a common background and the development of trans-national and knowledge intensive networks may actually be promoting such patterns of inclusion and exclusion. But there are also tendencies in the learning economy which challenge the sustainablity and efficiency of such tribal societies. First, the need for flexibility and rapid innovation can only be fulfilled by organisations where the leadership can delegate responsibility to a majority of the employees. Second, organisations increasingly have to open their borders in order to get access to knowledge through an interaction with external agents. Third, permanent exclusion of parts of the labour force will undermine the flexibility firms can obtain by hiring and firing skilful workers. Finally, extreme social polarisation fosters criminal behaviour and it is difficult if not impossible to avoid spillovers from the criminal sector to the regular sector of the economy. In certain respects the learning economy might be more vulnerable to crime and sabotage than any other economy (cf. for computer crime, etc.).

The fact that the relatively stable and homogenous Nordic welfare states have succeeded in asserting themselves in international competition is perhaps not due so much to their forests, mineral resources and agriculture as to a social cohesion which has made it possible to adapt to international competition and to learn things quickly. Conversely, the economic crisis which characterises the rich countries today may have its roots in, among other things, social polarisation. It may be difficult to establish shared norms of behaviour and trust in a society where at one pole there is ready access to fast speculative gains and at the other increasing poverty and insecurity.

Like knowledge, trust is difficult to incorporate in an economic analysis. Once more it is Kenneth Arrow who has expressed it most lucidly. He says 'trust cannot be bought; and if it could, it would have no value whatsoever' (Arrow, 1971). In making the choice between different economic and political strategies one must consider not only the immediate economic effects but also how it affects coherence in society. Thatcher's policies in England were perhaps in the short-term effective in reducing the rate of inflation, but they had the decisively negative side-effect of breaking down the solidarity necessary in society for involving workers, public servants and business leaders in mutual learning processes.

The fact that an acceleration of learning and the rate of change – for instance through policies giving more free play for competition – tends to lead to social polarisation is now recognised by policy makers and policy analysts (see for instance CEC, 1993, p.12 and OECD, 1996b, p. 236). The fact that this constitutes a major threat to the sustainability of the new growth regime remains to be fully taken into account.[8]

Plan versus market – a dead issue?

Another important consequence of this new perspective is that the traditional distinctions between pure market or centrally planned economies have to be rethought in completely new terms. In connection with the collapse of the planned economies in the Soviet Union and Eastern Europe, new-right economists have proclaimed the ultimate victory of the pure market economy. This might be a perilous misinterpretation.

The problem with the planned economies was not so much that too little market resulted in a poor utilisation of existing resources but rather that learning and innovation processes came to a standstill. This had different causes. Part of the explanation was the absence of democracy and the extreme degree of centralisation of economic decision making. In a rapidly changing world it is necessary to give those who execute activities a minimum of discretion. This has to do both with lacking incentives to engage in change and with lacking access to information and knowledge in order to act swiftly and intelligently.

Another, but related, reason for the weak capability to learn and to innovate was the centralisation of activites related to research and technological development, which primarily took place in large state-owned institutes separated from the production firms that were expected to use the output of the institutes. More generally, the users of technology were, with the exception of the military, poorly placed, and this meant that product development and quality control either ceased or foundered.

In the learning economy pure markets can only thrive on the fringes of the system where standardised products with stable traits are bought and sold. In all areas where new products are developed and new user needs evolve markets will be characterised by a mixture of market relationships and social relationships supporting interactive learning between producers and users. The closest we get to pure markets is perhaps the market for financial assets such as shares and government bonds. There are many indications that the neo-liberal philosophy primarily has its social roots among those who trade in financial assets. Engineers, development and production managers do not have quite so many illusions about the blessings of the pure market. They see the necessity for removing markets through vertical integration or at least for stabilising them by establishing close cooperation with both suppliers and customers.

The general conclusion is that when shaping industrial and technology policy in the learning economy a pragmatic and practical approach should be adopted. It is pointless to latch on to ideological simplifications and opt for a pure planned economy or a pure market economy. The learning economy is perforce a mixed economy where the markets can only function if they are firmly anchored in a functioning social context and if they are supported by organisational elements. In the most dynamic product areas buyers and sellers communicate continuously, and not just about prices. One of the most important prerequisites for successful product development is that the users are involved in the innovation process.

Increased competition may under certain circumstances stimulate innovative activities and promote economic growth and this is why deregulation and privatisation may have positive long-term effects.[9] But there are also instances where the destructive effects of increased competition are stronger than the creative ones and the very rate of change may become so high that the capability to learn among consumers, workers and managers becomes insufficient. To strike the right balance in this respect is far from a simple task and it is dangerous to get caught by ideological gimmicks which lead to a neglect of the fact that also in this area there are trade-offs to be considered.

Competence and social equality

Another area where there is a need for reassessment is social and distribution policy. In the Nordic region it has been a cardinal belief that education is a prime instrument for creating social equality. The Tocquevillian perspective is that, at least, all citizens should have the same opportunities to start with. Today, developments in the OECD labour markets make this perspective topical in a new and dramatic way. At the same time as the proportion of well-educated people in the workforce is increasing, those who have no education are becoming more and more poorly placed; either they become unemployed such as in Germany, France and Italy, or their incomes fall below the poverty line such as in the USA. Japan is experiencing this problem to a lesser degree while on the other hand the English neo-liberal strategy has managed to combine these two evils, i.e., record-high unemployment among the unskilled and a brutal reduction in their relative earnings (OECD, 1994a, p. 23).

This is the negative aspect of the learning economy. An accelerating rate of change in terms of technology and organisation places heavy demands on the ability of the individual to learn. Empirical analyses show that this particularly applies in connection with the introduction and application of information technology. The consequences will be worst felt in those societies with rigid and anti-social education systems. However, these appear to be general tendencies.

In addition, it becomes increasingly difficult to compensate for these disparities once they have arisen by income redistribution schemes. Fiscal policy can and should be used, but the results are less than encouraging.

Large government budget deficits and a high tax burden place restrictions on the extent to which this method can be applied. This advances the need for preventive measures by ensuring a more equal distribution of knowledge and competence, and it is necessary to seek part of the solution in an expansion of the existing education system.

There are, however, two important limitations to such a strategy. One is that only young people can be reached through the ordinary school system. Here, one should remember that each year only a small proportion of the total workforce emerges directly from youth education, and that it will therefore take several decades before the entire workforce has been renewed in this way.

The other problem relates to pedagogical principles. The methods used in teaching today result in a large number of both young people and adults falling by the wayside in the process. Radical new thinking which places learning, including learning through practice, in a more central role in peoples' working lives and which also opens up a range of unconventional measures with respect to the structure and content of the teaching is necessary in order to tackle these problems.

To tackle the first limitation much more energetic and large-scale initiatives in the field of adult education must be taken. One such initiative could have as its starting point present schemes in Denmark and Finland which give employees who take leave in order to participate in education financial support and a guarantee that they can come back to their original workplace. The advantage of these schemes is that they, at least to some degree, involve recruitment of the formerly unemployed who get a chance to learn-by-doing while the ones they stand in for learn-by-studying. But these schemes could be made much more selective and aim explicitly at the unskilled as well as give stronger incentives both to the workers and the employers involved.

In general it is difficult to see how to solve the inherent contradictions in the dynamics of the learning economy without giving firms – both private and public – a much more important role in enhancing the qualifications of their employees. This can be done within the individual firm or through cooperation between several firms. The public sector must create an incentive system and an institutional set-up which makes it attractive for firms to move in this direction. This is one of the most important areas for policy making and institutional design in the learning economy.

Fundamental principles for industrial and technology policy

The OECD monitoring of the development of the technology and industrial policies of its member countries provides a unique viewpoint on the most recent developments (OECD, 1993; OECD, 1994b; OECD, 1996b). The latest editions of these reports show that more and more countries are beginning to shape their policies to take into account factors which characterise a learning economy.

Firstly, it can be seen that the actual distinction between industrial policy and technology policies is becoming less and less pronounced. The technology policy is tending to become the main cornerstone of any industrial policy strategy. In continuation of this lies a policy which aims to influence all the factors which promote technological innovation. In this context it is interesting to note that more and more OECD countries are now in the process of carrying out analyses of what the OECD describes as 'the national system of innovation'.[10] This reflects a growing recognition that learning is a cumulative process – in attempting to further technological innovation, one must start with the existing knowledge base and in the given institutional context.

Secondly, greater notice has been taken of the wide-ranging internationalisation of technological development and implementation. The ability to incorporate technology developed outside a country's borders is becoming a decisive factor of competition. Firms increasingly get involved in international cooperation involving the development and use of new technologies but especially firms of limited size have difficulties in following what is going on in these respects. Therefore there is a new task for government institutions to support firms through technology forecasting and through establishing international rules for the sharing and protection of intellectual property rights. The rapid advances in information and communication technology also mean it is becoming ever more imperative to be able to absorb elements of this in production.

Thirdly, a clear tendency can be seen away from sector-specific subsidies and equivalent industry-specific arrangements. Learning is an interactive process which takes place in the form of interplay between firms and industries. Where a particular part of the economy continues to be made the object of industrial policy, it is more a case of development blocks which consist of several mutually related sectors or branches (Carlsson and Henriksson eds., 1991). It is becoming increasingly common to focus on how services and other non-industrial activities are linked to different parts of industry.[11] There is a general tendency to recognise that services are becoming more important also in relation to innovation and learning and that the borderlines between services are gradually becoming less and less clear (OECD, 1996b).

Fourthly, there is a growing recognition that new technology alone will not solve the problems. Learning and knowledge are tied to people, and if the people cannot keep pace, there is little point in having access to advanced machinery or advanced computer programs. Not least experience from the implementation of information technology has shown that without employee training and without organisational renewal, the implementation of technology can lead to dramatic reductions in efficiency. A very clear illustration of this can be seen in Denmark. In the middle of the 1980s during which time there was a massive surge of investment in information technology, productivity in the manufacturing sector was falling (Næss Gjerding *et al.*, 1990). Recent analyses in connection with the Danish welfare commission have shown that these difficulties in achieving productivity gains through the utilisation of information technology continue to affect Danish firms (Nyholm, 1995). The need to stimulate investments in human resources and organisational change at the level of the firm is becoming more and more widely recognised (OECD, 1996a, p. 24).

Finally, a change in focus has occurred with respect to the development of technology from the supply side towards the demand side. Given that innovation and learning processes are interactive and involve both technological knowledge and knowledge of user needs, it is natural that the one-sided focus of technology policy on the producer side must be abandoned in favour of a more balanced approach. The technology policies which seem to provide the most visible and positive results are those which place most importance in development projects on the users. In practice, this may entail supporting measures to improve user competence, promoting cooperation projects which comprise both producers and users, or providing development support directly to the users who in turn via cooperative purchasing mechanisms stimulate the producers to develop new and better products. Among other things, this has resulted in distinct advantages in the energy sector in terms of more efficient and ecologically better solutions (Westling, 1994).

Six steps in the formulation of a knowledge-based and knowledge-oriented technology policy

In somewhat simplified terms these new tendencies can be translated into six steps which should be incorporated in the shaping of an adequate industrial and technology policy.

Step 1: Analyse the system of innovation seen as a whole. Where are its strengths? How does the institutional framework around the processes of innovation and learning compare with other countries or regions? Where are the most important interfaces in the system? Where are there missing linkages?

Step 2: Focus on the ability of the system to absorb knowledge developed elsewhere and in particular foreign technology and information technology. Introduce new elements and institutions in a way which takes into account the characteristics of the existing system of innovation.

Step 3: Analyse the economy in terms of development blocks which comprise primary, secondary and tertiary production as well as the relevant parts of the knowledge-producing institutions. Analyse market perspectives for these blocks and localise weak links.

Step 4: Focus on the user side when shaping the part of the technology policy aimed at product development and quality improvements. Give the users – which can be private or government organisations – competence, power and resources in connection with the development of new products and systems.

Step 5: Focus on the human resources. In the case of programmes aimed at improving productivity and efficiency in production, encourage the implementation of new process technology only after seeking organisational solutions. Programmes for promoting the implementation of new process technology must be accompanied by support for organisational development and in particular by the improvement of employee qualifications.

Step 6: Take into account the impact of the policy strategy on the social cohesion of the economy as a whole. Is the speed-up of change compatible with the capability to learn and adjust? What supplementary policies should be developed to make the trade-off between accelerating change and polarisation more attractive?

Summary

The message I have tried to convey is that industrial and technology policy today must more than ever before be seen as an important part of an overall economic strategy aimed at creating employment and good jobs. Therefore, it must be coordinated with other policy areas. The connection with education policy is obvious, but given that we find ourselves in a learning economy, such coordination must also include other policy areas. For instance, it is today an illusion to believe that unemployment can be eliminated through a combination of macroeconomic policy and labour market and income policies. Crucial to the growth in demand for labour will be the creative side of economic development. Without strong initiatives to enhance the qualifications of employees and firms, it is difficult to see how anything resembling full employment can once more be achieved. A prerequisite for the creation of new firms and the emergence of new products in existing firms, which then lead to new jobs, is that the ability to learn is strengthened in all parts of the economy.

I have also tried to show how growing inequality in our society is a threat to the ability to create economic renewal. At the same time, it is a fact that this inequality partly stems from technological advances. The technology and education policies of the future must address this issue in a completely new and more aggressive manner if efforts to further innovation and progress are not to undermine coherence in society. If this should happen, it would ultimately rebound in the form of a weakening of the national system of innovation. The learning economy can hardly thrive in a social-Darwinist climate where a large and growing section of the population become in effect excluded from the economic life.

Finally, I have tried to show that in the learning economy the primary task of industrial and innovation policies will be to promote learning processes involving an interaction between sub-systems, organisations and individuals. This involves, among other things, ensuring good communication between knowledge producers such as universities and schools on the one hand, and firms, on the other. But it is even more important that firms, both on an individual basis and in an interplay with each other, invest in knowledge creation. It is also of crucial importance that the knowledge created in one firm is used to stimulate innovation in other firms. Particularly with respect to organisational renewal, it is imperative that firms are encouraged to learn from each other.

Notes

This is a revised version of a paper published in Danish, in the Festschrift for Reinhard Lund (Danish title: 'Teknologipolitik og konkurrenceevne i "the Learning Economy"' in Jørgensen, H. and Rasmussen, J. G. (1995), *Samarbejde – Festskrift til Reinhard Lund*, Aalborg University Press, Aalborg.

1 The emphasis given to knowledge and the formation of skills is reflected in the speech given by Clinton in February 1994 to the American Council on Education: 'Once the principal source of wealth was natural resources. Then it was mass production. Today it is clearly the problem-solving capacity of the human mind – making products and tailoring services to the needs of people all across the globe.'

2 For a more detailed definition and analysis of 'the learning economy', see Lundvall and Johnson (1994) and Foray and Lundvall (1996).

3 The fundamental role of technical progress for economic growth was recognised already by the growth theorists of the 1950s. The most recent contributions to new growth theory and to innovation theory reinforce these results by emphasising the advent of a new growth regime characterised by the existence of increasing returns to the production and use of knowledge (OECD, 1996a).

Technology in the narrow sense (understood as information about sets of production techniques) is only part of the economically important knowledge base, however, and it must be seen as being complementary to the development of human ressources.

4 Recent analysis of the structure of skills in the labour force shows that the main factor behind the upskilling of the whole workforce is growing skill intensity in all sectors rather than shifts in the weight of sectors (OECD, 1996b, p. 43). This observation illustrates that it would be misleading to understand the learning economy as rooted in hi-tech sectors. The need for rapid learning is economy wide and involves a majority of the workers, including many unskilled workers.

5 The relevance of the learning economy perspective is not limited to the most developed OECD countries. The two NIC countries (South Korea and Taiwan) with the highest growth rates during recent years have specialised in knowledge-intensive products, such as computers, etc. Moreover, today they recruit a greater proportion of school leavers into tertiary education in the areas of natural science and technology than any other OECD member country (Dosi *et al.*, 1993).

6 'Learning' is not an unfamiliar concept in economic theory, but it is normally given a quite specific and limited definition depending on the theoretical context. Often it refers to agents getting more accurate information about a given state of the world and normally it does not incorporate what is at the core of what non-economists mean by learning: the acquisition of skills and competencies. For the Austrian School, learning processes are closely tied to the market and to transactions (Hayek, 1978). Arrow (1962) introduced learning-by-doing in analyses of economic growth and Rosenberg (1982) introduced learning-by-using in connection with the use and production of complex technological systems. The analysis of 'the learning economy' can be seen as a follow-up and extension of their analyses and of how knowledge and competence emerge in a process of learning-by-interacting, i.e., in an inter-play between firms or between individuals (Lundvall, 1988).

7 It is important to note that tacit knowledge is not limited to actual craftsmanship. In fact, Polanyi, who developed the concept 'tacit knowledge', bases his work on an analysis of research in the field of natural science and shows how tacit knowledge also plays a fundamental role in this context (Polanyi, 1958/1978).

8 There might now be a growing understanding of the fact that the conflict between rapid learning and social polarisation is inherent in and undermines the learning economy. In the OECD G7 report on technology, productivity and employment one of the main headings in the policy conclusions is 'The key challenge is to boost productivity and growth through increased knowledge-intensive activities, while maintaining social cohesion' (OECD, 1996a, p .9).

9 It is interesting to note that increased competition tends to make cooperation within and between firms even more important (new data from a project on the Danish Innovation System in Comparative Perspective). This reflects that in a highly competitive environment the need to communicate and interact is strong

since communication and interactive learning is a key to flexibility and innovativeness. This mixture of competition and cooperation presents policy makers with a complex task of institutional design where a single-minded emphasis on promoting individualistic instrumental rationality may not be the full answer.

10 There is a fast-growing volume of literature (see Lundvall ed., 1992; Nelson ed., 1993; Freeman, 1995) concerning this concept developed at the end of the 1980s in connection with a book project concerning technology and economic theory (see contributions by Freeman, Lundvall and Nelson in Dosi *et al.* eds., 1988).

11 Denmark, Portugal, Austria and France have all moved in this direction and defined industrial clusters or business areas as part of the policy process (OECD, 1996b, pp.106f.) In Denmark the entire economy has been divided into eight so-called resource areas. Connected to each of these is a panel of industrialists, experts and policy makers who are expected to develop policy recommendations specially designed to the area (Danish Ministry of Industry and Coordination, 1994).

References

Archibugi, D. and Michie, J. (eds.) 1997. *Technology, Globalisation and Economic Performance*, Cambridge, Cambridge University Press.

Arrow, K. J. 1962. The economic implications of learning by doing, *Review of Economic Studies*, 29: 155–73.

    1971. Political and economic evaluation of social effects of externalities, in Intrilligator (ed.).

    1973. *Information and Economic Behaviour*, Stockholm, Federation of Swedish Industries.

Carlsson, B. and Henriksson, R. H. G. (eds.) 1991. *Development Blocks and Industrial Transformation*, Stockholm, The Industrial Institute for Economic and Social Research.

Commission of the European Communities 1993. *Growth, Competitiveness and Employment*, Bulletin of the European Communities, Supplement 6/93.

Danish Ministry of Industry and Coordination, 1994. Erhvervsredegørelsen, *Industry Review,* Copenhagen.

Dosi, G., Freeman, C., Nelson, R., Silverberg, G. and Soete, L. (eds.) 1988. *Technical Change and Economic Theory*, London, Pinter Publishers.

Dosi, G., Fabiani, S., Freeman, C. and Aversi, R. 1993. On the process of economic development, CCC-Working paper No. 93–2, Center for Research in Management, University of California at Berkeley.

Foray, D. and Lundvall, B.-Å. 1996. The knowledge-based economy: from the economics of knowledge to the learning economy in OECD, *Employment and Growth in the Knowledge-based Economy*, Paris, OECD.

Freeman, C. 1995. The national system of innovation in historical perspective, *Cambridge Journal of Economics*, 19(1): 5–24. Reprinted in Archibugi and Michie (eds.).

Hayek, F. A. 1978. Competition as a discovery procedure, in Hayek, F. A., *New*

Studies in Philosophy, Politics, Economics and the History of Ideas, Chicago, University of Chicago Press.

Intrilligator, M. (ed.) 1971. *Frontiers of Quantitative Economics*, Amsterdam, North-Holland.

Jorghensen, H. and Rasmussen, J. G. (eds.) 1995. *Samarbejde – Festskrift til Reinhard Lund*, Aalborg, Aalborg University Press.

Lundvall, B.-Å. 1988. Innovation as an interactive process – from user–producer interaction to the national system of innovation, in Dosi *et al.* (eds.).

Lundvall, B.-Å. (ed.) 1992. *National Systems of Innovation: Towards a Theory of Innovation and Interactive Learning*, London, Pinter Publishers.

Lundvall, B.-Å. and Johnson, B. 1994. The learning economy, *Journal of Industrial Studies*, 1(2): 23–42.

Næss Gjerding, A. *et al.* 1990. *Den forsvundne produktivitet* [The missing productivity], Copenhagen.

Nelson, R. R. (ed.) 1993. *National Systems of Innovation. A Comparative Study*, Oxford, Oxford University Press.

Nyholm, J. 1995. Information technology, organizational changes and productivity in Danish manufacturing, paper prepared for the Conference on 'Effects of Advanced Technologies and Innovation Practises on Firm Performance', Washington, DC, 1–2, May 1995.

OECD 1993. *Industrial Policy in OECD Countries: Annual Review*, Paris, OECD.

1994a. *The OECD Jobs Study. Facts, Analysis, Strategies*, Paris, OECD.

1994b. *Science and Technology Policy, Review and Outlook*, Paris, OECD.

1996a. *Technology, Productivity and Job Creation*, Vol. 1 Highlights, Paris, OECD.

1996b. *Science, Technology and Industry Outlook*, Paris, OECD.

Polanyi, M. 1958/1978. *Personal Knowledge*, London, Routledge and Kegan Paul.

Rosenberg, N. 1982. *Inside the Black Box: Technology and Economics*, Cambridge, Cambridge University Press.

Westling, H. 1994. Conference Documentation for the Conference on 'Market-pull activities and co-operative procurement of innovative technologies', organised by NUTEK and IEA, Paris, 29–30 November.

3 Some notes on national systems of innovation and production, and their implications for economic analysis

GIOVANNI DOSI

1 Introduction

In these short notes it is certainly impossible to provide any fair assessment of the wealth of research which has gone over the last decade into the analysis of national systems of innovation (and, relatedly, national systems of production). Hence, in the following, I will limit myself to some rather telegraphic remarks and propositions concerning, first, the empirical background of such studies; second, the relations among (partly different) interpretative perspectives on the subject; and, third, their implications also for other domains of economic analysis – including the theory of the firm and growth theory. Finally, I shall briefly hint at some policy implications, especially with reference to the European case. In doing all that I will raise more questions than provide answers: however, a few of the propositions that follow are empirically testable, and thus may provide some inspiration for further research in the area.

2 Persistent asymmetries across firms and countries

The general historical background of the discussion of 'national systems', as I see it, is the observation of non-random distributions across countries of:

 (i) corporate capabilities;
 (ii) organisational forms;
(iii) strategies; and ultimately
(iv) revealed performances, in terms of production efficiency and inputs productivities, rates of innovation (however measured), rates of adoption/diffusion of innovation themselves, dynamics of market shares on the world markets, growth of income and employment.

Note that the patterns defined by the latter indicators, when measured at the level of sectors and countries, tend to display relatively high degrees of persistence over time, despite a somewhat higher inter-company variability. So, for example, one is likely to observe a higher variability in the technological and market performance of individual German machine-tool companies than in the German aggregate position in the machine-tool sector, etc.

Relatedly, one observes also a relative stability of lags and leads in innovative patterns across countries within the same sector, and of 'revealed' technology and trade advantages across sectors within the same country, or the same region (cf. among others: Archibugi and Pianta, 1992, and 1994; Archibugi and Michie eds,, 1997; Dosi, Pavitt and Soete, 1990; Pavitt and Patel, 1988).

In a nutshell, one of the points of departure of the investigation on national systems are the 'stylised facts' concerning the limited convergence in economic performances across countries, the equally limited convergence in technological capabilities – even among developed countries, and more so regarding developing ones – and the growing evidence on the role of technology as determinant of competitiveness and growth (within a vast literature, see, e.g., Dollar and Wolff, 1993; Dosi, Freeman and Fabiani, 1994; Fagerberg, 1994; Nelson, 1996; Verspagen, 1993).

3 From firms to location-related heterogeneity

A long series of questions stems naturally from these observed patterns, related to the factors shaping innovation and diffusion, and their economic exploitation. Indeed, at least part of the answer to these questions rests upon location-related heterogeneity in the opportunities and constraints facing individual economic agents. Needless to say, this heterogeneity has to be more profound than that postulated by classical and neoclassical theories of comparative advantage (e.g., Costa Rica producing and exporting more 'sun-intensive' products than Norway . . .). Rather, the issue more fundamentally concerns:

  (i) different abilities of generating and absorbing new knowledge;
 (ii) equally different abilities to put it to a productive use and economically exploit it;
(iii) different behavioural patterns *vis-à-vis* innovation and market growth even when facing similar notional opportunities (this last point might be harder to swallow for economic theorists committed to 'hyper-rational' agents, but easy to accept for business economists and practitioners alike).

It is important to notice that the rates and directions of knowledge accumulation of each society display both a microeconomic dimension and a collective, institutional, one. After all, even many commonly accepted but rarely checked statements, with far-reaching policy implications relate to this domain of analysis. Think, for example, of propositions such as '. . . the advantage of the US in many high-tech industries derives from the quality of its university/industry links . . .', or '. . . it derives from the ability of venture capital to support innovative entrepreneurs, while Japanese firms are better suited to answer flexibly to changing market demands . . .'; but, also, '. . . Singapore or US firms build on the differential flexibility of their labour markets in order to adjust to market changes . . .', or, conversely, 'rather sticky bank/producer/user relationships support differential learning skills of German or Scandinavian firms . . .'; and many more. What all these propositions have in common is the intuitive idea that the institutional context matters in shaping what firms do and how successfully they do it.

But still there is a lot to learn about the processes through which this occurs. For example, what is the influence of particular forms of organisation of production, innovative search and market competition upon the competitive performance of individual firms (measured, say, in terms of profits, market shares, or growth)? Do differences in individual corporate organisation/strategies or performances carry an impact also upon the collective performance of whole countries in terms of, e.g., GDP growth, employment or whatever other proxy for collective 'welfare' is chosen? But, if there is at least some circumstantial evidence that the answer to the latter question might be positive, what accounts for the purely non-random distributions of apparently 'better' organisations and strategies across countries? Or, in a stronger version, why do firms and, by implication, countries, not quickly converge to the most efficient 'way of doing things'?

In turn, were one to assess significant and persistent differences across countries and major socio-economic entities (such as the EU, the USA, Japan, etc.) in both corporate characteristics and aggregate performances, what determines them? To what extent is this due to the institutional context of origin (or of location) of the firms? And, conversely, what is the extent of discretionality of strategic managerial decisions? Moreover, if indeed there appear to be systematic links between corporate characteristics, context-specific institutions and collective socioeconomic outcomes, what are the forms of these relationships? For example, in which respects is it fruitful to enlarge the notion of 'competitiveness' from individual firms to whole countries? How far can we safely go in explaining different aggregate performances in terms of degrees of 'institutional inertia'? Are there diverse patterns of matching/mismatching between microeconomic traits and institutional set-ups yielding roughly similar macroeconomic performances, or, conversely, can one unequivocally identify any one 'best way' to which both institutions and corporate strategies should swiftly adapt? And, finally, lurking in the background of all these questions, there are even larger ones, concerning the relationships between 'competitiveness', growth and employment; the role of firms' organisations and strategies in all that; and, the ability of policy making in shaping long-term patterns of industrial change.

Needless to say, in these short notes it is impossible to provide any fair account of what we know about the answers to these long list of questions (which admittedly, in my view, is not very much). For the purposes of this chapter, let me just note that it is in the context of the discussion of these questions that the notion of national systems of innovation and, I would add, of production ought to show their heuristic values.

4 National systems of innovation and production: antecedents and current approaches

Among several available definitions, let us start with the quite general albeit slightly vague one put forward by Francois Chesnais (1995), namely that:

the notion of national systems of innovation may be viewed as a way of encompassing these numerous facets (of the relationship between technology, trade and growth) so as to suggest that the performance of national economies depend on the manner in which organizational and institutional arrangements and linkages conducive to innovation and growth have been permitted to thrive in different countries (Chesnais, 1995, p. 23).

In the contemporary debate, the notion of a national system of innovation was introduced, as known, by Christopher Freeman (1987) while analysing the specificities of the Japanese patterns of technological learning, and further explored by Lundvall ed. (1992) and Nelson ed. (1993), in a comparative perspective, across sectors and countries. I shall come back shortly to the empirical insights of recent investigations on the properties of 'national systems'. However, well beyond the current achievements of (sometimes naive) investigations in the field, this very perspective highlights in my view a major underlying divide dating far back into the history of economic thought. It is straightforward that if the whole world were a general equilibrium, national systems of innovations would hold little importance as determinants of the 'wealth of nations'. Conversely as Freeman (1995), points out, there is another, largely forgotten, tradition dating back at least to F. List (1841) which, in short, one could call increasing returns, institutionally focused, alternative to good parts of A. Smith and most of Walras – just to name funding symbols of the currently dominant *weltanshauung* (on 'List vs. A. Smith' see also McCrow, 1997). And amongst forgotten ancestors one might mention, among others, Reverend Tucker, Count Serra of Naples, Ferrier and Hamilton. There are certainly many good reasons why the 'Smith–Walras' story became the dominant one, including the enormous gap in the alternative tradition between the richness of historical/institutional intuitions and the poverty of analytical instruments (in this respect, compare on the contrary the relative balance of contemporary works in somewhat similar respects, such as Krugman, 1991). Come as it may, the resurgence of 'national systems' is also associated with rapidly expanding interests on the economics of innovation and the related increase in respectability of the view that, after all, knowledge accumulation might be indeed: (a) a primary engine of long-term growth; (b) unevenly distributed across countries; and (c) fundamentally shaped by national institutions (on the first two points, one should certainly be thankful also to the success of 'New Growth' theories).[1]

From other camps, some 'system' notions have been quite central in development literature (cf. Gerschenkron) and in the French tradition of industrial economics (see, for example, the emphasis on filières – i.e., more or less industrial clusters) originally put forward by de Bernis and Perroux, among others. Here the emphasis is on the specificities of inter-sectoral linkages, seen as both carriers of demand impulses and of technology flows. And, in a similar perspective, Dahmen (1988) has suggested the notion of 'development blocks'.

Contemporary analyses of 'national systems' while not at all inconsistent with earlier insights, place a much more explicit emphasis on the processes by which particular institutional contexts foster (or hinder) location-specific patterns of innovation. In this respect one may distinguish some, indeed highly complementary and overlapping, approaches to 'national systems'.

At first one focuses upon the specificities of national institutions and policies supporting directly or indirectly innovation, diffusion and skills accumulation (for sake of illustration, think for example of the role of university research and of military/space programs in the US 'national system' or of training institutions in the German one . . .). In this vein, see especially the contributions in Nelson ed. (1993).

A second approach emphasises especially the importance of users–producers relations and the associated development of collective knowledge bases and commonly shared behavioural rules and expectations: cf., in particular, the works in Lundvall ed. (1992).

Third, Patel and Pavitt, among others, have stressed the links between national patterns of technological accumulation and the competencies and innovative strategies of a few major national companies. Note that this holds under the hypothesis for which there is rather robust evidence that, with few exceptions, even multinational companies perform most of their innovative activities in the home country: see Patel and Pavitt (1991; and their chapters in this volume) and, for some qualifications, Cantwell (1989) and (1997).

Fourth, Amable, Barré and Boyer (1997), and from somewhat different angles Soskice (1993) and Zysman (1994), focus upon the specificities of national institutions including, for example, the forms of organisation of financial and labour markets, training institutions, forms of state intervention in the economy, etc.

5 Some common underlying hypotheses

The four perspectives mentioned above are largely consistent with each other and indeed share some basic underlying hypotheses. In my view they include (or ought to include) the following:

1) Knowledge is much more sticky and context dependent than information. Moreover, notwithstanding the increasing communication possibilities based on information technologies and the increasing codification that the latter allow, tacit and 'local' forms of knowledge are likely to continue to play a major role in most economic activities. Hence, as Soete (1996) puts it in relation to services (but I believe this applies also to manufacturing):

The codification process will even only rarely reduce the importance of tacit knowledge in the form of skills, competencies and other elements . . . rather than the contrary. It is in these latter activities which will become the main value of the service activity . . . while part of this might be based on pure tacitness, such as talent or creativity, the largest part will depend closely on continuous new knowledge accumulation – learning – which will typically be based on the spiral movement whereby tacit knowledge is transformed into codified knowledge, followed by a movement back where new kinds of tacit knowledge are developed in close interaction with the new pieces of codified knowledge. Such a spiral knowledge is at the very core of individual as well as organizational learning. (Soete, 1996, p. 11).[2]

2) Self-reinforcing mechanisms of reproduction of knowledge are to a good extent location specific although sometimes partly external to individual firms (the competencies associated with 'industrial districts' are only the clearest example).

3) With globalisation of markets and production activities, accumulation might even increase diversity across nations and regions if local knowledge

externalities outweigh the diffusion of knowledge 'carried' by globalised firms.

In sum, it is my general conjecture that national (and regional) systems of innovation are there to stay, even in a more globalised world, and that they will continue, albeit in different forms, to shape the growth possibilities of different geographical areas and institutional entities. As mentioned earlier, a lot of work has recently gone into the analysis of the specificities of technological learning but, in my view, a lot needs to be done to understand in greater detail the co-evolution between technologies and business organisations.

6 A closer look within business organisations

There is a step that a few of us have been urging for and have begun to scientifically pursue: in analogy, and together with 'opening the technological blackbox',[3] one needs also to better understand the ways organisations learn 'how to do things' and improve/modify these capabilities over time.

Hence, the first point: since a fundamental dimension of business firms (as well as other organisations) is the coordination of distributed knowledge (including of course technological knowledge), in order to perform collective problem-solving tasks, one needs to look at the specificities of the American, or Japanese or European ways (almost certainly more than one) of doing things, and their revealed outcomes.

Second, one ought to look in particular depth at the influence that the social embeddedness of corporate routines and strategies exert upon the directions and rates of accumulation of problem-solving knowledge.[4] By 'social embeddedness', in brief, I mean also the ways corporate behaviours are shaped by socially specific factors such as the nature of the local labour markets, workforce training institutions, financial institutions, mechanisms governing the birth and finance of new firms, etc.

Third, if knowledge – as argued above – is a fundamental determinant of competitiveness, it is important to achieve a better understanding of the ways replications and transferability of organisational capabilities are constrained by the idiosyncratic and tacit nature of knowledge underpinning problem solving and by the difficulty of separating highly interrelated tasks and pieces of knowledge. So, for example, part of the answer to the question as to why firm A is more 'competitive' than firm B is likely to rest upon the differential knowledge firm A incorporates. But what does 'organisational knowledge' exactly mean? Where does it reside? And how can firm B acquire it, too?

Fourth, and equally important (as one argued in more detail in Coriat and Dosi, 1994; expanded upon in Nelson and Winter, 1982) the specific forms of corporate organisation and routines involve equally specific modes of governance of potentially conflicting interests. By that, we mean that the 'ways of doing things' of an organisation go together with a specific incentive structure for the members of the organisation itself, and with mechanisms for controlling, punishing, rewarding, etc. In turn, the latter influence how an organisation learns over time and the effectiveness by which it exploits its competitive advantages. Moreover, modes of learning and modes of governance co-evolve in ways that are likely to be specific to national and regional institutions. So, for example, the rules for corporate information-sharing, internal training, workforce mobility, etc. typically have to match the ways labour market and industrial relations are organised. Similarly, strategic management orientations have to match the patterns of financing and corporate governance specific to any one financial system.

Consider as an illustration the European case.

With respect to all the above points Europe presents a rich variety of organisational and institutional arrangements. Just for the sake of illustration think of the differences between an 'archetypical' German firm with its bank-based mode of financial governance, its training system, its participating labour relations, etc. versus the much more 'market based' British archetype versus an Italian district. The analysis of such variety, and the related performances, is not only interesting from a scientific point of view, but of course entails major policy issues. For example, to what extent can national systems learn from each other within the Union? Will they all remain viable within the emerging super-national institutional framework? How can one make a collective European asset out of such a diversity?

7 From technology and corporate organisations to national/regional competitiveness and employment

In an extreme synthesis, our general conjecture is that the nature of business organizations, their capabilities and strategic orientations – embedded as they are in specific national institutions – are a crucial, albeit often overlooked, ingredient of competitiveness of nations and regions. Consider again the European case. The conjecture put forward here is that, the organisational and institutional dimension might help in explaining also what has been discussed in Andreasen *et al.* (1995) under the heading of the 'European paradox'. In essence, it is the following. Most indicators of scientific and technological output[5] show European performances broadly in line with the other major international players, the USA and Japan, although with the remarkable exception of microelectronics/information technologies, where Europe appears to significantly lag behind. However, a general point of European weakness appears with regard to the 'transformation capabilities' of scientific and technological knowledge into growth, export and employment opportunities (cf. Amable and Boyer, 1995; and Coriat, 1995).

A plausible conjecture (as argued in Coriat, 1995) is that in fact good parts of the European system of corporate organisation display major weaknesses and lags in tapping novel avenues of research, inertia in adjustment, inefficient use of human resources and 'strategic myopia'.

In summary, this perspective highlights the crucial importance of, jointly (a) technology, or more broadly knowledge generation and diffusion, and (b) organisational forms and strategies in shaping long-term competitiveness.

It also has remarkable implications in terms of the underlying determinants of growth and employment rates. Pushing it to a caricatural extreme, there are two distinctly different views here. First, the conventional one says more or less that unemployment appears only as a consequence of some market malfunctioning, including those rigidities which prevent input prices setting at their market clearing levels. Conversely, in what we could call a knowledge-centred view of competitiveness and growth, employment (and income) generation are seen as ultimately driven by the rates of accumulation and exploitation of knowledge in the society. Related claims are that: (a) knowledge and physical capital accumulation go intrinsically hand-in-hand (more technically they are 'dynamically coupled' through positive feedbacks) and, (b) income distribution and market conditions, of course, do matter a lot, but they do so primarily through the influence they exert upon the patterns of collective learning, on the one hand, and on the 'dynamic contestability' on any rent-earning position, on the other[6] (in the latter we include the easiness of entry of new competitors, the financial constraints to their possibility to grow, etc.).

Let me be more concrete with reference to current diagnoses of the competitiveness–growth–employment links. The bottom line of the conventional view is that all three augment monotonically with the 'blood, sweat and tears' that a society (or most likely a part of it) is ready to put up. So, for example, an almost exclusive emphasis is put upon downward adjustment in input prices as the solution to most problems of insufficient competitiveness and stagnating employment. And any failure of the cure is seen as just revealing this inadequacy of the doses of blood, etc. extracted. The other view is somewhat more sophisticated (and, possibly also for that reason, less appealing: after all it would be easier if all diseases could be cured with a single drug). It partly overlaps with the former in identifying market competition (and, in primis, the easiness of entry conditions) as a highly desirable requirement for economic dynamism.[7]

So, for example, both views are likely to share the conclusion that quite a few institutional arrangements in Europe are major culprits for, together, monopolistic rent extraction, consumer maltreatment and innovative inertia. However, given reasonable conditions of competition, and incentive compatibility in both product and labour markets, the two views are likely to depart in terms of priority prescriptions in order to foster employment growth. The conventional one would be inclined to claim that again, in an extreme caricature – 'blood is what it takes . . .'.

Conversely, in the conjecture put forward here, technological and organisational learning might be a major collective positive-sum game[8] whereby, under certain institutional and micro-organisational conditions, knowledge accumulation couples with investment opportunities which couples with labour demand which couples with market growth. In the contemporary case at hand, for example, a possible achievable scenario, albeit by no means the only predictable one, is precisely a renewed path of self-sustained income growth characterised, to a major extent, by an increasingly diffused access to information-processing competences, 'intangible investments', and rapid development of the related infrastructures.

8 Some conclusions

On purpose I have presented the foregoing notes ridden of question marks, hinting at a sort of ambitious research agenda directly related to the micro-organisational and institutional foundation of national/regional systems of innovation and production.[9] Let me conclude by mentioning, even more telegraphically, some other issues impinging on the 'national systems research program'. One of them certainly concerns the processes by which such systems emerge and the identification of possible invariances which hold across different countries.[10] Second, a better understanding is needed of the relationship between national and sectoral systems of innovation (with the latter I mean sector-specific institutional set-ups which possibly recur across countries). Third, from a theoretical point of view a lot might be learnt also from modelling efforts which explicitly account for the local and path-dependent features of knowledge accumulation and their impact upon growth patterns.[11]

With regards to policy I have tried above to sketch some normative implications deriving from 'the national systems' approach. In a sense, historical comparative analyses in this perspective may help in identifying the 'seeds' already present in the current socio-economic environment allowing different options for 'institutional engineering', for science/technology/ industrial/ competition policies, and for strategic management orientations. As I see it, transition across discretely different regimes of knowledge accumulation and social governance present major 'windows of opportunity' as Paul David puts it,[12] and equally major opportunities for disasters. These are the times where managerial and policy discretionality is the highest and where also 'sticking to old ways of doing things' may produce irreversible losses.

Notes

Support for the research upon which this chapter is based by the International Institute of Applied System Analysis (IIASA) and the Italian National Research Council (CNR) is gratefully acknowledged. Part of the argument below was summarised in 'The new socio-economics of organisations, competitiveness and employment', Seville, IPTS Report, June 1997.

1 Still at theoretical level the central role of knowledge as determinant of growth has long been emphasised by Pasinetti (1993).
2 However, for a rather different view on codification trends, cf. David and Foray (1995).
3 Cf. Rosenberg (1982), and complementarily, among others, on the economic analysis of the generation and diffusion of technological change, Freeman (1982 and 1994), Dosi (1988).
4 More on this point in Nelson (1996), Zysman (1994), Dosi and Kogut (1993).
5 As measured in terms of, for example, international scientific publications, patents, etc.
6 A less telegraphic presentation of these points is in Dosi (1996).
7 Although not always attainable due to the rather widespread existence of so-called in the economists' jargon, 'market failures' externalities, natural monopolies, dynamic increasing returns, fuzzy definition of property rights, etc.
8 This paraphrases the title and the spirit of Landau and Rosenberg eds. (1986).
9 Indeed some of these questions are addressed in a research project that the author is beginning to coordinate under the auspices of the European Commission (Targeted Socio-Economic Research, Directorate-General Science, Research and Development).
10 Such an issue is obviously crucial also for development theory and policy: for preliminary discussion, cf. Bell and Pavitt (1997).
11 An attempt to model in an evolutionary spirit the interaction among multiple learning economies in Dosi *et al.* (1994); a sort of reduced form growth model accounting for path-dependent learning is in Bassanini (1997).
12 More generally, on the interplay between 'historical lock-ins' and purposeful strategic discretionality, cf. David (1988).

References

Amable, B., Barré, R. and Boyer, R. 1997. *Les Systèmes d'Innovation à l'Ere de la Globalisation*, Paris, Economica.

Amable, B. and Boyer, R. 1995. Europe in the world technological competition, *Structural Change and Economic Dynamics*, 6: 167–83.

Andreasen, L., Coriat, B., den Hartog, F. and Kaplinsky, R. (eds.) 1995. *Europe's Next Step*, London, Frank Cass.

Archibugi, D. and Michie, J. (eds.) 1997. *Technology, Globalisation and Economic Performance*, Cambridge, Cambridge University Press.

Archibugi, D. and Pianta, M. 1992. *The Technological Specialization of Advanced Countries*, Boston, Kluwer.

1994. Aggregate convergence and sectoral patterns of specialisation in innovation, *Journal of Evolutionary Economics*, 4: 17–33.

Bassanini, A. P. 1997. Localized technological change and path-dependent growth, IIASA Report, Laxenburg.

Bell, M. and Pavitt, K. 1997. Technological accumulation and industrial growth: contrasts between developed and developing countries, in Archibugi and Michie (eds.).

Cantwell, J. A. 1989. *Technological Innovation and Multinational Corporations*, Oxford, Basil Blackwell.

1997. The globalisation of technology: What remains of the product cycle model?, in Archibugi and Michie (eds.).

Chandler, A. D., Amatori, F and Hikino, T. (eds.) 1997. *Big Business and the Wealth of Nations*, Cambridge, Cambridge University Press.

Chesnais, F. 1995. Convergence and divergence in technology strategies, in Hagerdoorn (ed.).

Coriat, B. 1995. Organizational innovation: the missing link in European competitiveness, in Andreasen *et al.* (eds.).

Coriat, B. and Dosi, G. 1994. Learning how to govern and learning how to solve problems, IIASA Working Paper WP-95–06, Laxenburg, Austria.

Dahmen, E. 1988. Development blocks in industrial economics, *Scandinavian Economic Review*, 1: 3–14.

David, P. 1988. Path-dependencies: putting the past into the future of economics, Stanford, Institute for Mathematical Studies in the Social Sciences, Technical Report 533.

David, P. A. and Foray, D. 1995. Accessing and expanding the science and technology knowledge base, *STI Review*, 16: 14–68.

Dollar, D. and Wolff, E. N. 1993. *Competitiveness, Convergence and International Specialization*, Cambridge, MA, MIT Press.

Dosi, G. 1988. Sources, procedures and microeconomic effects of innovation, *Journal of Economic Literature*, 26: 1120–71.

1996. The contribution of economic theory to the understanding of a knowledge-based economy, in Foray and Lundvall (eds.).

Dosi, G., Fabiani, S., Aversi, R. and Meacci, M. 1994. The dynamics of international differentiation: a multi country evolutionary model, *Industrial and Corporate Change*, 3: 225–42.

Dosi, G., Freeman, C. and Fabiani, S. 1994. The process of economic development: introducing some stylized facts and theories on technologies, firms and the institutions, *Industrial and Corporate Change*, 3: 1–45.

Dosi, G. and Kogut, B. 1993. National specificities and the context of change: the coevolution of organisation and technology, in Kogut (ed.).

Dosi, G., Pavitt, K. and Soete, L. 1990. *The Economics of Technological Change and International Trade*, Brighton, Wheatsheaf/Harvester Press and New York, New York University Press.

Fagerberg, J. 1994. Technology and international differences in growth rates, *Journal of Economic Literature*, 32: 1147–75.

Foray, D. and Lundvall, Å-B. (eds.) 1996. *Knowledge, Employment and Growth*, Paris, OECD.

Freeman, C. 1982. *The Economics of Industrial Innovation*, London, Francis Pinter, 2nd edition.

1987. *Technology Policy and Economic Performance: Lessons from Japan*, London, Francis Pinter.

1994. The economics of technical change, *Cambridge Journal of Economics*, 18: 463–514.

1995. The 'National System of Innovation' in historical perspective, *Cambridge Journal of Economics*, 19(1), pp. 5–24. Reprinted in Archibugi and Michie (eds.) 1997.

1997. The 'national system of innovation' in historical perspective, in D. Archibugi and Michie (eds.).

Hagerdoorn, J. (ed.) 1995. *Technical Change in the World Economy*, Aldershot, Edward Elgar.

Kogut, B. (ed.) 1993. *Country Competitiveness. Technology and Reorganization of Work*, Oxford/New York, Oxford University Press.

Krugman, P. R. 1991. *Geography and Trade*, Cambridge, MA, MIT Press.

Landau, R. and Rosenberg, N. (eds.) 1986. *The Positive Sum Strategy. Harnessing Technology for Economic Growth*, Washington, DC, National Academy Press.

List, F. 1841. *The National System of Political Economy*, English edition, London, Longman, 1904.

Lundvall, B.-Å. (ed.) 1992. *National Systems of Innovation. Toward a Theory of Innovation and Interactive Learning*, London, Francis Pinter.

McCrow, T. K. 1997. Government, big business and the wealth of nations, in Chandler *et al.* (eds.).

Nelson, R. R. 1996. *The Sources of Economic Growth*, Cambridge, MA, Harvard University Press.

Nelson, R. R. (ed.) 1993. *National Innovation Systems*, Oxford, Oxford University Press.

Nelson, R. and Winter, S. 1982. *An Evolutionary Theory of Economic Change*, Cambridge, MA, The Belknap Press of Harvard University Press.

Pasinetti, L. L. 1993. *Structural Economic Dynamics. A Theory of the Economic Consequences of Human Learning*, Cambridge, Cambridge University Press.

Patel, P. and Pavitt, K. 1991. Large firms in the production of the world's technology: an important case of 'non-globalization', *Journal of International Business Studies*, 22: 1–21.

1994. 'Uneven (and divergent) technological accumulation among advanced countries. evidence and a framework for explanation', *Industrial and Corporate Change*, 3: 759–87.

Pavitt, K. and Patel, P. 1988. The international distribution and determinants of innovative activities, *Oxford Review of Economic Policy*, 4: 35–55.

Rosenberg, N. 1982. *Inside the Black Box,* Cambridge, Cambridge University Press.

Soete, L. 1996. The challenges of innovation, Seville, IPTS Report, September.

Soskice, D. 1993. Innovation strategies of companies: a comparative institutional explanation of cross-countries differences, Berlin, Wissenschaftszentrum, Working Paper.

Verspagen, B. 1993. *Uneven Growth between Interdependent Economies. An Evolutionary View on Technology Gaps, Trade and Growth*, Aldershot, Avebury.

Zysman, J. 1994. How institutions create historically rooted trajectories of growth, *Industrial and Corporate Change*, 3: 243–83.

4 Technology, growth and employment: do national systems matter?

MARIO PIANTA

Much of the research on national systems of innovation has focused on their institutional aspects, on the relationships between firms, universities and government agencies and on the science and technology activities carried out by such actors. Less attention has been paid to the economic outcomes, in terms of growth and employment performances, of the operation of national systems of innovation and of their interaction with the production system.

In this chapter first an analytical framework is proposed, linking some key aspects of national systems of innovation with the globalisation of technology, and with the outcomes in terms of economic growth and employment. The dominance of product or process innovations in the operation of firms and of national systems is identified as a key discriminant for assessing the possible outcomes for growth and job creation. Such a distinction appears to be crucial both in conceptual and empirical terms. On the one hand it allows us to identify two distinct trajectories of technological change, with specific impacts on innovation and economic performance; on the other hand, these outcomes can be empirically examined using a number of appropriate proxies for innovation efforts which can be related to growth and employment patterns.

Second, an empirical analysis is carried out with a cross-country comparison, where the orientation of national innovation systems towards product innovations is proxied by R&D intensitites, and the orientation towards process innovations is proxied by aggregate investment intensities; the impact on growth performances is also assessed.

Third, the sectoral structure of manufacturing industry in the more advanced countries is considered, grouping industries on the basis of the dominance of product or process innovations, as emerged from the recent European Community Innovation Surveys. The impact of such characteristics of national innovation (and production) systems on growth and employment dynamics is investigated.

Finally, in the conclusion the relevance of differences in the structure and orientation of national innovation systems is pointed out, assessing the possible contribution of alternative sources to long-term growth.

1 National systems of innovations and their performance

The concept of 'national systems of innovation' has been developed to explain national specificities in technology (and growth) as a result of particular institutional contexts, firms' organisation, patterns of innovative activity and the role of the public sector (Lundvall ed., 1992; Nelson ed., 1993; Freeman, 1995). The role of national innovation systems has to be seen in the context of the current process of technological change; the key issues shaping the impact of innovation systems on economic performance can be briefly summarised as follows.

1.1 The nature and direction of technological change

A new technological paradigm based on information and communication technologies (ICTs) has emerged, with a radical change in the nature and trajectories of innovations, in the forms of production and organisation and in the operation of national innovation systems. Firms' strategies have struggled to cope with such changes, leading to a variety of efforts to introduce new ICT-based products, to adapt and incorporate the new technologies in the upgrading of established production, or to restructure traditional processes. The employment effects of such innovation patterns has been increasingly problematic, with some evidence of a negative impact (see Freeman, Clark and Soete, 1982; Science Technology Industry Review, 1995; OECD, 1996b).

1.2 The globalisation of technology

The rapid international diffusion of innovations and the increasing competition on more open markets are changing the shape of the innovation and production systems found within national boundaries. The ability of firms and public organisations to benefit from the technological opportunities offered from globalisation is crucial for the upgrading of the capabilities of national innovation systems. Conversely, globalisation can erode the production and employment base of advanced countries (see Archibugi and Michie eds., 1997; Amable, Barré and Boyer, 1997).

1.3 The structure of the economy

The strains of change on national economies are higher the greater is the extension of traditional industries facing restructuring or decline. Growth opportunities are higher in countries where new fast growing sectors, in both manufacturing and services, are more important. The sectoral structure of economies is therefore an important factor which can help explain differences in national economic performances. Its weight is emphasised by the process of globalisation which exacerbates competition and makes more evident the relative advantages associated to 'structural' competitiveness and the disadvantages associated to traditional industries (see Pianta, Evangelista and Perani, 1996).

1.4 The importance of new demand

In the current context of slower growth and sluggish demand, a dramatic mismatch is now found between the high potential of new ICT-based products, offering more various and 'personalised' goods and services, and the lack of emergence of new large markets with strong demand. The slow learning processes in consumption, the need for social innovations (particularly in the use of time) required to 'match' the opportunities of technological innovations, the lack of appropriate institutions and public policies managing such problems are all factors which may explain such a mismatch. But a more direct economic factor is also important, associated to the current distribution of incomes with the reduction of the wage share. The strong polarisation pattern, most extreme in the US, but clearly present also in Europe, has reduced the aggregate demand effects and has prevented the emergence of a large demand for new ICT-based products from wage-earners (see Applebaum and Schettkat, 1996; Petit, 1995; Pini, 1995).

The effectiveness of national innovation systems in sustaining growth and employment can be assessed on the basis of their ability to address and benefit from these major processes.

Figure 4.1 points out the web of relationships linking the national systems of innovations with the process of globalisation of technology, leading to specific growth and employment outcomes.

First, the national systems of innovation, with the parallel activity of firms and institutions, shape the nature and direction of technological change, whose main aspect considered here is the distinction between product and process innovations.

Process innovations (introduced mainly through new investment) and product innovation (based on internal innovative activities as well as on new intermediate or capital goods) lead to the well-known contrasting

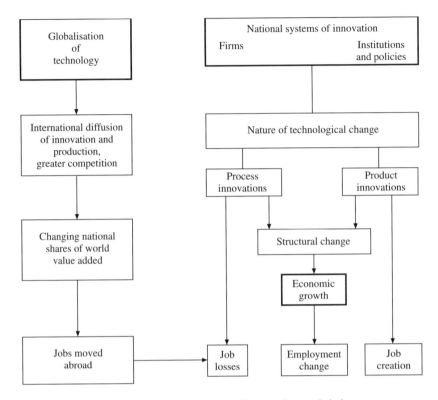

Figure 4.1 Globalisation, national system of innovation and their
economic impact

effects of increasing productivity and replacing labour, on the one hand,
and of creating new markets, demand and production, on the other hand,
through different compensation mechanisms (see Vivarelli, 1995; Vivarelli,
Evangelista and Pianta, 1996; Edquist, 1997).

In a context of globalisation of production and markets, however,
innovations have a rapid international diffusion. The result is greater
competition and a new international division of labour, both in terms of the
sectors of a country's activity and of the different phases of production
localised in each nation.

This process changes countries' shares in the value added of global production. Greater competition reinforces the pressure to increase productivity, giving a greater role to specialisation advantages. This, together with the
emergence of new innovation-led fields of activity, leads to the increased
pace of structural change, resulting in a different sectoral composition of
national economies.

These developments on the supply side do not act alone. The growth and employment outcome is the result of the interaction with the demand side, shaped by the same institutions and policies relevant for the national systems of innovation, by the macroeconomic context and by specific industrial strategies.

The direct impact on employment is therefore the net result of:

(a) job losses due to the direct labour-displacing effect of innovations (mainly in processes) and to the decline of particular sectors, associated to the shift abroad of production and jobs and/or to weak demand patterns, and

(b) job gains due to the employment-creation effect of technological change (mainly product innovations) and of the growth of expanding sectors, supported by a growing demand.

The indirect effects on employment emerge through the variety of compensation mechanisms which cannot be investigated without complex models of the whole economy.

The empirical analysis of the next sections makes it possible to identify the different outcomes that the processes outlined above may have. In section 2 the analysis is carried out in aggregate terms, while in section 3 the focus is on manufacturing industry, due to the availability of data and to the relevance of the internal generation of know-how as a source of technological change, while in the rest of the economy the dominant pattern is the adoption of innovations generated elsewhere.

Far from being a deterministic process, the economic and employment outcomes of technological change are the result of social processes, where institutions, government policies and social relations play a major role, alongside the developments in technology and the strategies of firms. Therefore we expect to find different patterns and performances across countries, rooted also in the differences of their national systems of innovation.

Drawing from this analytical framework, the empirical analysis tries to make operational a distinction among national systems of innovation in terms of the dominant nature of the technological change they sustain. In the next section an analysis will be carried out using R&D expenditure as a proxy for product innovations and fixed investments as a proxy for the relevance of process innovations. In section 3 the findings of a detailed study based on the results of the Eureopean Community Innovation Survey make it possible to develop a definition of industries dominated by product or process innovations and such a sectoral classification leads us to assess the growth and employment performances of a group of more advanced countries.

2 R&D-based and investment-based innovation systems

The relationships between technology and growth can be conceptualised as a 'virtuous circle' of cumulative causation, where research and innovation sustain a country's technological capability, contribute to its capital accumulation (together with other factors affecting investment), leading to economic growth. In turn, growth provides the resources and incentives for further advances in both research and investment (Lundvall ed., 1992).

Two key technological factors stand out in this process: first, the innovative activity centred on the generation of new knowledge, mainly oriented towards the development of new products and services (and therefore linked to technological activities of a 'disembodied' nature) which can be proxied by data on R&D expenditure; second, the role of capital accumulation, development of new processes, the diffusion and use of innovations and of the technology embodied in new plants and machinery which can be proxied by data on investment. This distinction between the embodied and disembodied aspects of innovative activities is one of the key factors characterising the different national systems of innovation. While some countries have developed a strong research system, either in the private or public sector, with a large generation of inventions, other countries have largely relied on the rapid diffusion of innovations embodied in investment and often originated in other countries and sectors.[1]

The impact of these two factors on countries' growth, proxied by GDP per capita, is investigated here with a description of national patterns. The variables considered are the following:

Total R&D expenditure per labour force, measuring the intensity of the resources used as inputs for the formalised part of innovative activities;[2]

Gross fixed capital formation per labour force, measuring the investment intensity, which is also an indirect indicator of the introduction of innovations embodied in capital goods;[3]

GDP per capita, measuring the level of income, and a proxy for productivity.

All three variables have been calculated using purchasing power parities.

Data for 20 OECD countries have been collected for four five–year periods, 1971–5, 1976–80, 1981–5, 1986–90.[4] Over these two decades OECD countries have moved from strong differences in their level of development to more similar aggregate performances, while strong differences persist in their research efforts. Over the four periods considered the coefficients of variation show a moderate convergence in GDP per capita in the 1970s and a stable distribution in the 1980s; a moderately

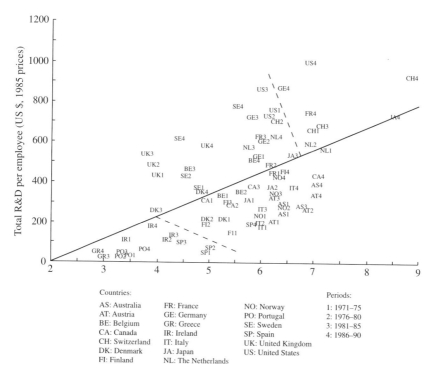

Figure 4.2 Total R&D and investment per employee

increasing divergence since the mid 1970s in the (relatively similar) levels of investment per employee; a significant convergence in the technology variables (where countries' differences however remain high).[5]

In another study (Pianta, 1995) the pattern of relationships among several technological and economic indicators has been investigated, suggesting that the link between technology and growth can hardly be expressed in terms of general regularities, as assumed by mainstream economic models, and can be identified only within particular boundaries of time, country sets and groups of sectors, with frequent exceptions due to the specificities of national innovation systems.

The relationship between R&D and investment intensities is highlighted by figure 4.2, which shows the distribution of the 20 countries in the four periods, together with the regression line based on the pooling of all observations.

The diversity of national patterns and positions is evident in the figure, with four broad groups of countries which can be identified:

A first group is the *high R&D, high investment* cluster, including the US, Switzerland and the positions of France, Germany and Japan at the end of the 1980s.

A second group is the *high R&D, low investment* cluster including the UK, Sweden, The Netherlands, with Belgium and Denmark moving into this group in the 1980s and France and Germany leaving it at the end of the period.

A third group is the *low R&D, high investment* cluster including Italy, Austria, Finland, Norway, Australia and Canada, with Japan, Belgium and Denmark moving out in the 1980s and Spain joining the group in the late 1980s.

Finally, a fourth group is the *very low R&D, low investment* cluster including Ireland, Greece and Portugal, as well as Spain until the last period, countries with higher investment than R&D intensities but with a continuing large gap with the rest of OECD countries.

A strong persistence of the 'specialisation' of national innovation systems either in R&D or in investment intensity, relative to the OECD general pattern, can be identified; the path of a country's growth mostly remains within a particular cluster, while the existing 'mobility' follows a standard path from the fourth to the first cluster.

The different national patterns suggest that in most countries economic development in the last two decades has mainly relied upon one of the two 'engines of growth' offered by technology: either the generation of knowledge and innovation of a disembodied nature (proxied by the R&D intensity) or the use of technology embodied in investment (proxied by capital formation per employee). While at first marked differences existed, with countries mainly focusing either on the creation of know-how (through R&D) or on the diffusion of innovations (through investment), as a result of growth itself and under the pressure of renewed international competition, greater complementarities between research and investment appear to have emerged. National innovation systems appear to have somewhat reduced their diversity in institutional and macroeconomic terms, while preserving the differences in their sectoral specialisations.

Turning to the impact on economic performance (measured in terms of rates of growth of GDP per capita) we can identify different groups of countries on the basis of the *rates of change* of the R&D and investment intensities. A first group combines above-average increases in R&D and investment intensities with the fastest growth rates of GDP per capita in the OECD group. It includes Japan, Finland and Ireland, followed by Italy and Austria (Norway is close to this group but its growth rate is largely affected by the new exploitation of natural resources).[6] Only Japan however has clear above-average growth in both variables, while most other countries have concentrated their efforts in one direction only, usually catching up in R&D intensities.

Still, a strong technological effort is a necessary but not a sufficient condition for strong growth, as is shown by the performance of Spain and Sweden which have also increased strongly their R&D intensities, but have registered below-average growth rates in GDP per capita.

Another group of countries, including the core European nations, had a growth performance close to the OECD average. The technological efforts of this group have been concentrated either in R&D or in investment. With relative improvements in one variable and relative decreases in the other, the performances of these countries in terms of GDP per capita have remained broadly in line with the OECD average.

Finally, a group of high-income countries, including Australia, The United States, The Netherlands and Switzerland, show a below-average growth in all indicators.[7]

While countries' long-term growth of GDP per capita is affected by a variety of factors other than technology, the evidence shows how difficult it has been for most OECD countries to improve at the same time both their R&D and investment intensities, using two key aspects of innovation as combined engines of growth.

This evidence suggests that national innovation systems have a strong persistence in their fundamental characteristics (see figure 4.2), shaped by the given economic structure and research infrastructure, but they can also change and imitate one another in the institutional arrangements and in the sources of their dynamism. The best performances in terms of GDP per capita growth have been associated to the ability of national innovation systems to evolve more rapidly and integrate the need for different and increasingly complementary sources of technological change and learning.

3 The employment performance of product and process innovation industries

Another way of investigating empirically the nature and economic performance of national innovation systems is to look beyond the aggregate indicators of the previous section, at the sectoral structure of innovation and production activities.

The European Community Innovation Survey has recently gathered important information on the nature and patterns of technological change in manufacturing industry in most EU countries (see Archibugi and Pianta, 1996). From the survey it is possible to identify the dominance of product or process innovations in each industry, and a recent study (Pianta, 1997)

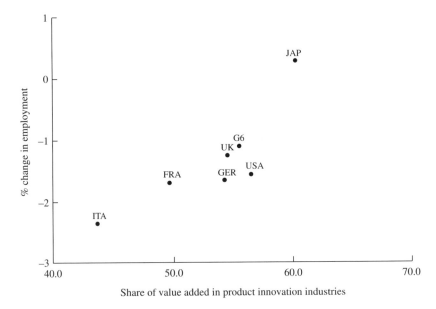

Figure 4.3 Product innovation sectors and employment change, 1989–94

has contrasted the growth and employment performances of the two groups of industries in the case of five European countries.

In this section the definition of 'product innovation industries' and 'process innovation industries' is generalised to the six more advanced economies (G6: the US, Japan, Germany, France, the UK and Italy), in order to test whether different economic performances can be identified as a result of the different orientation of national innovation and production systems.[8] The impact is assessed on the employment change in each of the two groups of sectors, consistently with the argument made in section 1 on the diverging consequences on job creation and job destruction of product and process innovations.

In figures 4.3 and 4.4 the relevance of product- and process-based industries (measured by the shares of value added in total manufacturing in 1994) is plotted against the employment change in the same group of industries (average annual growth from 1989 to 1994).

The well-known structural differences among the national innovation systems of the six countries lead to a clear ranking; on the basis of the share of manufacturing value added in industries based on product innovation, Japan is the leader, followed by the US, the UK, Germany, France and Italy. The reverse order is obviously found for the share of process innovation-based industries. This ranking is broadly consistent with the evidence of the

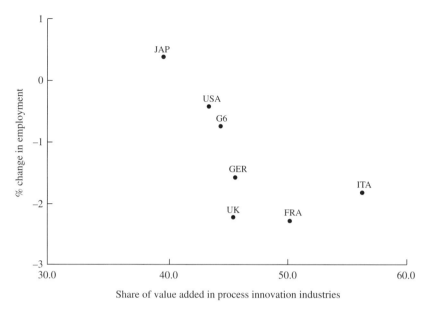

Figure 4.4 Process innovation sectors and employment change, 1989–94

previous section on the different R&D and investment intensities of countries and with the particular sectoral specialisations shown by each country (see Archibugi and Pianta, 1992). In terms of employment change in total manufacturing in the 1989–94 period, the ranking of countries is basically the same, with only Japan showing a moderate 0.33 per cent annual growth and all others reducing manufacturing jobs at rates ranging from –1 per cent in the US to –2 per cent in Italy.

These aggregate outcomes in employment change are the result of different industry dynamics, shown in the two figures. A positive relation is found between the dominance of product innovation industries and employment change in figure 4.2, while a clear negative link emerges between the importance of process innovation industries and employment change in figure 4.4; the same contrasting relationships are found also for the 1975–89 period. The more a country was 'specialised' in product innovation industries, the better the employment performance has been in these industries, while the opposite holds for process innovation industries. The aggregate outcomes, with the better employment performances of Japan and the US than in European countries, are clearly associated with the different orientation of the national innovation and production systems.

A national innovation system geared to the generation of new knowledge and new products in industries characterised by higher R&D intensities and disembodied technological change turns out to be an industrial structure where product innovation-based industries dominate and are able to sustain employment growth, or at least to limit job losses, as is the case for most countries in the early 1990s.

Conversely, national innovation systems mainly relying on the acquisition of foreign know-how and technology, on investment in machinery and on new production processes turn out to be an industrial structure where more traditional industries are important, but their use of process innovations to sustain international competitiveness (mainly based on cost advantages, rather than on product changes) has led to greater job losses. The nature and content of the 'specialisation' of national innovation systems has therefore strongly different economic and employment outcomes, and increasingly so with greater competition and globalisation.

4 Concluding remarks

While more systematic investigations are needed in this direction, consistent evidence suggests that national innovation systems, and in particular their orientation towards either R&D activities, product innovations and disembodied technological change, or investment, process innovation and embodied techological change are associated with alternative patterns of evolution and with contrasting perfomances in employment. The nature of national innovation systems and their interaction with the industrial structure do matter for the economic and employment performances of advanced countries.

Obviously the contrast between product and process orientation should not be taken too far. Both types of innovations are always needed and we have seen that the better performances in terms of GDP per capita growth are found where the integration of the two aspects is greater. The choice of periods under study also matters. The post-war decades of generalised rapid growth in OECD countries offered opportunities for good performances in a variety of innovative systems. In the 1990s, marked by greater competition, stagnant markets and sluggish demand, the different nature of innovation systems has a more direct impact.

In the long-term dynamics of growth over the past decades, considerable scope for catching up among OECD countries existed, making strong economic and employment growth possible, with an orientation towards investment intensive, process innovation-based sectors. Countries starting with the lowest levels of GDP per capita, R&D and investment per employee have generally shown a rate of growth higher than the OECD average, leading to a moderate convergence among the 20 countries. In spite of such aggregate convergence countries have maintained their relative 'specialisation' in the levels of either R&D or investment intensity compared to the OECD pattern.

A possible interpretation of this pattern is that at first the scope for catching up was so large that countries could 'specialise' either in the production of innovations, reaching high R&D intensities, or in the diffusion and use of technology through higher investment per employee.

However, after the recession of the early 1990s, with slower growth of world markets and increasing international competition, the economic and employment outcomes of the different models of innovation systems have started to diverge again. The contrast emerged in the 1990s between Japan and the US, on the one hand, and European countries, on the other, in terms of growth rates, and job creation has its roots also in the different orientations of national innovation systems and in the vulnerability of European economies due to their greater reliance on process innovation-based industries, where international cost-based competition has become stronger.

For the future evolution of national innovation systems, good economic performances are more likely to be achieved with a more balanced development of the different 'engines of growth', with increasing complementarities between the different aspects of national technological activities. When countries have achieved high-income and productivity levels and are closer to the technological frontier, a more complex set of relationships between technological factors and economic performance operates. A greater role is played by factors such as knowledge, learning processes, human capital, quality of research, immaterial investment, organisational innovations, favourable institutional conditions; these are the dimensions summarised in the concept of national systems of innovation, and therefore they may need to take up some aspects of one another and become moderately more similar.

The policy lessons from this evidence are that the distinction between models of technological change oriented towards product or process innovations plays an important role in shaping the economic and employment outcomes, and should inform analysis and policy in this field.

With innovations in all industries dominated by the new information and communication technologies, the use and adaptation of innovations developed elsewhere, and changes in processes and organisations may acquire particular importance, leading to the emergence of new forms of flexible organisation which tend to be 'unfriendly' to employment growth. On the other hand, the development of new products based on the new technologies has so far failed to create large markets, often due to the lagging behind of new demand in these new fields.

A reassessment of innovation and technology policies is therefore needed, and the strong differences that characterise the technology–growth–employment links across industries suggests that new forms of sector-specific policies are needed. The current incentives to ever-greater labour-saving process innovations might be limited, and efforts concentrated on creating and organising new markets with greater potential for growth and job creation. Such demand-oriented policies might also emphasise the role of users (actual and potential ones), especially in the new fields of ICT and services, replacing the old industrial policy of 'picking winners' with a new one 'empowering the users'.

Notes

1 A large literature has addressed the theoretical and empirical problems of linking technology and growth. See in particular Dosi *et al.* (1988), OECD (1992), Fagerberg (1994), Archibugi and Michie (1998).
2 Across the 20 OECD countries, this variable shows a very high association to other key indicators such as total R&D as a share of GDP, industry-financed and performed R&D as a share of GDP, researchers and scientists as a share of the labour force.
3 Unfortunately data for investment in machinery and equipment only, which would be a better indicator, are not available for all countries and years; when comparisons were possible, the variable used appeared to be a good proxy.
4 Data have been transformed in constant 1985 prices and then converted in US dollars using 1985 purchasing power parities (from OECD, Main Science and Technology Indicators, 1993). The averages for the five-year periods have been calculated in order to avoid annual fluctuations and offer a more satisfatory picture of interactions which include lagged effects.
5 For GDP per capita the coefficients of variation (standard deviation divided by the mean) in the first and last periods are 0.27 and 0.24; for investment per employee values are 0.20 and 0.24; for R&D per employee values are 0.54 and 0.43.
6 For this group of countries the real growth of GDP per capita between the average in 1971–75 and 1986–90 has ranged between the 60 per cent for Japan and the 41 per cent for Austria. The average growth for the 20 OECD countries was 36 per cent. Spain and Sweden had growth slightly below 30 per cent.
7 Their growth of GDP per capita has ranged from 27 per cent for Australia to 17 per cent for Switzerland.
8 The Community Innovation Surveys provide data on the shares of R&D related to product or process innovations, which are rather consistent across countries and with other indicators of the prevalence of either form of innovation available for particular countries. Data in this section are drawn from the OECD STAN database, 1996.
   The sectors dominated by *process innovations* include: food, beverages, tobacco, textiles, wearing apparel, leather, wood products, paper, printing and

publishing, petroleum refineries, petroleum and coal products, pottery and china, glass, non-metallic products, iron and steel, non-ferrous metals, metal products.

Sectors dominated by *product innovations* include: footwear, furniture, industrial chemicals, other chemicals, rubber products, plastic products, non-electrical machinery, electrical machinery, shipbuilding, motor vehicles, aircraft, other transport equipment, professional goods, other manufacturing.

References

Amable, B., Barré, R. and Boyer, R. 1997. *Les systèmes d'innovation à l'ère de la globalisation*, Paris, Economica.

Appelbaum, E. and Schettkat, R. 1996. Product demand, productivity and labour demand in a structural model, Paper for the TSER conference 'Technology, economic integration and social cohesion', Cepremap, Paris, 22–23 November.

Archibugi, D. and Michie, J. 1997. The globalisation of technology: a new taxonomy, in Archibugi, D. and Michie, J. (eds.) *Technology, Globalisation and Economic Performance*, Cambridge, Cambridge University Press.

Archibugi, D. and Michie, J. (eds.) 1998. *Trade, Growth and Technical Change,* Cambridge, Cambridge University Press.

Archibugi, D. and Pianta, M. 1992. *The Technological Specialization of Advanced Countries*, Dordrecht, Kluwer.

1996. Innovation surveys and patents as technology indicators: the state of the art, in OECD, 1996a.

Dosi, G., Freeman, C., Nelson, R., Silverberg, G. and Soete, L. (eds.) 1988. *Technical Change and Economic Theory*, London, Pinter.

Edquist, C. 1997. Product versus process innovation: a conceptual framework for assessing employment impacts, in *Creativity, Innovation and Job Creation*, Paris, OECD.

Fagerberg, J. 1994. Technology and international differences in growth rates, *Journal of Economic Literature*, 32: 1147–75.

Freeman, C. 1995. The 'national system of innovation' in historical perspective, *Cambridge Journal of Economics*, 19: 5–24. Reprinted in Archibugi and Michie (eds.) 1997.

Freeman, C., Clark, J. and Soete, L. 1982. *Unemployment and Technical Innovation*, London, Pinter.

Lundvall, B.-Å. (ed.) 1992. *National Systems of Innovation*, London, Pinter.

Nelson, R. (ed.) 1993. *National Innovation Systems: A Comparative Study*, Oxford, Oxford University Press.

OECD 1992. *Technology and the Economy. The Key Relationships.* Paris, OECD.

1996a. *Innovation, Patents and Technological Strategies.* Paris, OECD.

1996b. *Technology, Productivity and Job Creation.* 2 vols. Paris, OECD.

Petit, P. 1995. Technology and employment: key questions in a context of high unemployment, *Science Technology Industry Review*, n.15. 13–47.

Pianta, M. 1995. Technology and growth in OECD countries, 1970–1990,

Cambridge Journal of Economics, 19: 175–87. Reprinted in Archibugi and Michie (eds.) 1998.

1997. Patterns of innovation, demand and employment in Europe, paper for the TSER conference 'Technology, economic integration and social cohesion', Cepremap, Paris, 17–18 October.

Pianta, M., Evangelista, R. and Perani, G. 1996. The dynamics of innovation and employment: an international comparison, *Science, Technology Industry Review*, n.18: 67–94.

Pini, P. 1995. Economic growth, technological change and employment: empirical evidence for a cumulative growth model with external causation for nine OECD countries, 1960–1990, *Structural Change and Economic Dynamics*, 6: 185–213.

Science, Technology, Industry Review, 1995. Special issue on technology, productivity and employment, n.18, Paris, OECD.

Vivarelli, M. 1995. *The Economics of Technology and Employment*, Aldershot, Elgar.

Vivarelli, M., Evangelista, R. and Pianta, M. 1996. Innovation and employment in Italian manufacturing industry, *Research Policy*, 25: 1013–26.

PART II

Regional, national and global forces

5 Regional systems of innovation?

JEREMY HOWELLS

Introduction

This chapter explores the possible existence and form of regional systems of innovation (RSI). Christopher Freeman has defined a national system of innovation (NSI) as the network of institutions in the public and private sectors whose activities and interactions initiate, import, modify and diffuse new technologies (Freeman, 1987, p. 1). Although this definition was applied at a national level it can arguably be equally applied at a regional or local level. This chapter will seek to explore these issues, not suggesting that regional systems of innovation should be seen in some way as supplanting national systems of innovation, but rather should be viewed as providing another layer or conceptual lens to the whole system of innovation. In so doing, it seeks to develop in a geographical sense at least part of Metcalfe's (1995, p. 41) view that the national unit may be too broad a category to allow a clear understanding of the complete dynamics of a technological system and instead focus should be on 'a number of distinct technology-based systems each of which is geographically and institutionally localised within the nation but with links into the supporting national and international system'.

More specifically, therefore, this analysis will examine whether the broad definition of *national* systems of innovation can also be applied at a regional level. Do, or can, regions offer distinct systems of innovation that are worthy of study? If they do exist, in what ways are they different from national systems of innovation? If the concept is relevant, is it becoming more or less applicable over time? What more general lessons can be learnt from the study of regional systems of innovation? This analysis will therefore seek to explore these questions and posit the discussion within the wider framework of the systems of innovation debate.

Regional systems of innovation versus national systems of innovation: an historical perspective

At one level it can be argued that as many regions are former nations, and indeed that many former regions have become nations, systems of innovation at a regional scale can exist as proto forms of national systems of innovation. Thus in the case of the UK, Scotland was a former nation which had quite a distinct system of innovation and science before Scotland was eventually absorbed into Great Britain in 1707. Moreover, up until the end of the seventeenth-century Scotland had a clear lead over England in terms of scientific and medical discoveries (Wood, 1992, pp. 266–7). This was because of a high number of factors. Firstly, Scots studied in universities abroad and there was a free flow of ideas between Scotland and other European countries. Secondly, there were a number of key institutional innovations in Scotland, such as the establishment of the Royal College of Physicians of Edinburgh in 1681, which provided a strong formal and informal impetus to scientific discovery and innovation. Lastly, there was a highly developed patronage system for funding science, almost unique anywhere in the world at that time. As a result, by as early as the mid 1680s, an institutional innovation infrastructure was already in place which would later facilitate the meteoric rise of the prominence of the Scottish scientific and medical base in a world sphere (Wood, 1992, p. 267). This pre-eminence and distinctiveness of the Scottish lasted long after union with England, so that even by 1789 Scotland and Edinburgh in particular was seen to have a unique place in science within Britain and the rest of the world, and this distinction continues, particularly in areas such as medical science. Indeed Scotland still has a different educational and university system from England and Wales as well as a separate legal system and a distinct innovation infrastructure.

However this example is perhaps part false. What is described perhaps can better illustrate the resilience and persistence of a former national system of innovation; NSIs are slow in dying. Even if it perhaps cannot be formally defined as a national system of innovation it still remains a quasi-national system of innovation. Alternatively it only serves to emphasise the issue of how the nation state should be defined. Many in Scotland would still assert that Scotland is, and always has been, a separate nation from the rest of Britain and now with devolution is likely to regain more fully many aspects of a full nation state. Both arguments and viewpoints are plausible here, but the discussion here should not become weighted down with the particular analysis of the Scottish innovation system. What it does serve to illustrate is the importance of a historical perspective, particularly in the evolution of the institutional structures which make up a system of innovation.

Other historical studies, however, have also served to highlight the formation and development of quite distinct regional systems of scientific and industrial endeavour. Thus, Nye (1986) has outlined the important and distinctive nature of scientific communities in the French provinces between 1860–1930. Far from the conventional wisdom that the most important scientific work in France occurred in Paris and that Paris dominated the science scene in France, Nye emphasises the lively, open and diverse scientific networks of the French provinces and concludes Provincial scientists were often leaders and innovators, not followers of Parisian scientific culture and values. Provincial university science frequently was more open and innovative than Parisian science (Nye, 1986, p. 8). What Nye emphasises in particular is the uniqueness of the different provinces, based on the different context of their university science and above all on close contact and support of local industry which in turn shaped the scientific and engineering specialisation of the university science base in the regions. Thus, for example, Nancy specialised in programmes that sought to develop chemistry, brewing, electricity and metallurgy; the Pyrenees and French Alps specialised in electrical physics and industrial chemistry, whilst Lyon concentrated on scientific research into textiles and chemicals (Nye, 1986, p. 7).

What this and other studies raise is how far national systems of innovation can be considered as homogenous systems. However, this homogeneity is not only based on the distinctive nature of regions or areas in terms of scientific and technological specialism, but also on their absolute and relative performance in relation to a national norm regarding innovative activity. There has been a whole series of studies which have sought to emphasise the highly uneven geographical pattern of innovative activity (see, for example, Feller, 1973; Oakey, Thwaites and Nash, 1980; Malecki, 1985). Core and/or metropolitan regions have been seen as being much more innovative than more peripheral areas or regions. Much depends on how centralised national territories are, but even countries with fairly uniform rates of innovation geographically can hide quite marked disparities on a local or regional level. Again these disparities can be traced back a long way. Thus Carlton and Coclanis (1995) have tried to analyse what factors were behind the lack of inventive activity in the South (defined as the Old Confederacy, plus Oklahoma, Kentucky and West Virginia) of the United States between 1870 and 1920 compared to the rest of the country. Studies that stressed the role played by the creation of a highly integrated national economy in furthering growth in the United Sates have largely ignored the major disparities in industrial and technological performance at the region or state level (Carlton and Coclanis, 1995, p. 302).

These regional differences persist today. Treating national systems as implying homogenous spatial systems of innovation can be dangerous.

Studies have shown that there are highly significant regional differences in research and technical activity and in the technological specialisation of different regions within a national territory (see later). For example, the UK exhibits a high degree of specialisation in the pharmaceutical and biomedical sector dating back to the 1970s and beyond (Archibugi and Pianta, 1992, p. 97) and research and technical orientation is continuing to grow according to the OECD STAN/ANBERD database which shows that private sector UK expenditure (Business Expenditure on Research and Development (BERD) expressed in purchasing power parity) on pharmaceuticals relative to total BERD was proportionately much higher than that of the US or the EU (as a whole) between 1973 and 1990 (Howells and Neary, 1995, p. 89). As an indication, private sector pharmaceutical expenditure on R&D relative to total expenditure on R&D grew from 5.38 per cent in 1973 to 13.81 per cent by 1990 compared to, for example, 3.28 per cent to 4.31 per cent over the same period for the USA. However, within this national specialisation, the industry is highly *uneven* in its spatial distribution regionally. The second largest UK region in terms of manufacturing jobs, the West Midlands, has negligible involvement in the drugs industry, whilst Wales, the South West and East Anglia also have limited involvement in such a core sector of the UK (although this now may be changing in the case of East Anglia). All these regions, and in particular the West Midlands, are effectively isolated or detached from what is happening within the broader UK national system of innovation in terms of this key sector. At a more detailed level, how far the UK pharmaceutical industry operates within a meaningful national system of innovation, neglecting what are arguably strong sectoral and distinct regional systems of innovation, is open to debate.

Regional systems of innovation: a top–down perspective

The previous section has sought to put forward the argument of the possible existence of a regional system of innovation, but how would this be defined? What are its characteristics? In attempting to unravel the different spatial levels of the systems of innovation approach, this section outlines a top–down perspective of regional systems of innovation. In particular, can the essential components of national systems of innovation be found existing and operating at a regional level? If so, in what way? Are regional systems of innovation really just a national system of innovation writ small?

Both Freeman, Lundvall and Nelson have provided definitions of national systems of innovation (although it should be noted that though these definitions do display much commonality, they are based on somewhat different conceptions of national systems of innovation; McKelvey,

1994). A broad definition by Freeman has already been outlined above, stressing (not unexpectedly in a system) the network and interactive qualities of an innovation system. Lundvall ed. (1992, p. 13) breaks down the components or elements of a national system, that in turn differentiate them from each other. These core elements are:

the internal organisations of firms;
the interfirm relationships;
the role of the public sector;
the institutional set-up of the financial sector; and
R&D intensity and R&D organisation.

Lundvall argues that the focus on the *national* level is associated with the fact that national economies vary according to their production system and their institutional framework and these differences are in turn strengthened by different historical experiences, language and culture. Nelson and Rosenberg (1993, pp. 4–5) have a similar concept in mind when they define a national innovation system as involving 'a set of institutions whose interactions determine the innovative performance . . . of national firms'. The systems concept portrayed by Nelson and Rosenberg is somewhat different from that of Freeman's and Lundvall's and seeks to emphasise the role of a set of institutional actors, which together play a major role in influencing innovative performance.

Although a number of commentators have tried to determine differences between the definitions and differences in emphasis, the purpose here is to identify whether out of the broad definitions whether these elements of the system of innovation model could in part or in total be applied at the regional level. Certainly most economic geographers and regional economists would have no difficulty in identifying significant regional variations in the components identified by Lundvall above, and indeed such an integrated systems view of regions can be traced back a long way in geography, in particular the highly influential French school of regional geographers in the late nineteenth and early twentieth centuries. Moreover, all the key proponents of the national systems of innovation concept have indeed accepted that there could also be other types of systems of innovation which operate at a sectoral, transnational or indeed regional level (Nelson and Rosenberg, 1993, p. 5; Lundvall ed., 1992, p. 3; Freeman, 1995, p. 21; see also in particular Carlsson and Stankiewicz, 1991; in relation to their discussion of technological systems).

Thus on a sectoral level, Nelson and Rosenberg (1993, p. 5) highlight intra-national diversity by indicating that there may be very little overlap between sectors within a nation in the systems of institutions supporting innovation, say between aerospace and pharmaceuticals. This echoes

Kitschelt's (1991, pp. 443–5) earlier work on the importance of 'sectoral governance structures' in helping to shape, as well as being influenced by, national systems of innovation. This can help explain why some industries prosper in certain countries, but not others. The continued growth of the pharmaceutical industry in the poorly performing UK innovation system, and its languishing in the generally highly successful Japanese innovation system is a case in point here (Howells and Neary, 1995).

Equally on the basis of Lundvall's definition of a national systems of innovation it can be argued regions within nations can also display distinct or idiosyncratic systems of innovation which depart from the national norm and in turn are different from other regions. Obviously in some countries these differences will be greater than others. Thus, the existence of readily identifiable *and* meaningful regional systems of innovation will depend on how far a nation is said to have a homogenous regional structure relating to innovation. There are three dimensions which help to reinforce the importance of regional systems of innovation. They relate to:

1 the regional governance structure, both in relation to its administrative set-up and in terms of legal, constitutional and institutional arrangements;
2 the long-term evolution and development of regional industry specialisation; and
3 additional core/periphery differences in industrial structure and innovative performance.

Regional governance of innovation

The impact of the structure of the state, both directly in terms of the organisation of government administration and in relation to different legal, constitutional and educational arrangements (including the ability to levy taxes and taxation levels) are important here (Charles and Howells, 1992, pp. 92–6). Different taxation (Schmandt, 1990, p. 33) and legal differences can influence the whole institutional dynamics of business and financial services that support and advise local and regional industry. The field of industrial property, building and planning controls is just one small example where local planning regulation, building incentives, environmental legislation and tax incentives for real estate and industrial investment have meant a whole set of specialist professional, legal and financial advisers operating and being sustained at a regional level. The division of power between central states and regions is also important here (Bianchi, 1993, p. 26; Hassink, 1996, p. 181). For many industrial nations with strong regional governments – such as Germany with its Länder and Spain – the regional configuration of government together with its interaction at an institutional level have meant mutually reinforcing patterns of regional innovation regimes. This can be seen in education in Germany where, for example, the funding of universities is the responsibility of the Länder. Elsewhere, non-university higher education institutes (polytechnics, technical institutes and so on) in most European countries tend towards a high degree of regional orientation (see also Paget, 1990). More directly, in both Germany and Spain regional governments have separate Ministries of Technology which oversee and administer specific innovation programmes for their respective regions in conjunction with their national governments.

Over the long term the pattern and nature of regional government can influence the evolution of more general institutional arrangements in, and between, regions (Schmandt, 1990, p. 16). This is important as the issue of government and state involvement goes well beyond the formal description of differences in policy structures and mechanisms. It goes more fundamentally towards the notion of the state and its institutional framework (and indeed supra-national governance structures; Hirst and Thompson, 1994, p. 299). The state is an ensemble of institutions that has a degree of autonomy to advance its interests in the face of other groups of society (Dearlove, 1989, p. 528), it introduces more specifically the notion of the state as an *ensemble of institutions*. Thus the state, in both national and regional settings, represents itself through different combinations of institutions and over time the nature of this ensemble will change. Moreover the notion of governance structures goes beyond the structure of the state and includes public–private intermediaries and the private sector itself (Howells and Neary, 1995, p. 18). Indeed the different regional volume, nature and mix of these agencies and other organisations that act as intermediaries between the state at both national and regional levels may be one of the most significant factors in the development of distinct regional systems of innovation.

Regional specialisation and evolution

As has already been noted, many regions have tended to develop and evolve specific regional industry specialisations. These can often be traced back to medieval periods (for example, Toledo steel in Spain), through to the nineteenth century with the Lancashire cotton industry and through to the more recent examples of the 'Third Italy' (Brusco, 1982; Becattini, 1991). Some regions exhibit little or no prominent industry or sector specialisation, whilst those regions which have been associated with such specialisation can find that it disappears with the decline in the industry more generally, most evident in textiles, shipbuilding, iron and steel and mining industries. Indeed, this was a concern identified by Marshall back in the

1890s, when he noted: 'A district which is dependent chiefly on one industry is liable to extreme depression, in case of a falling off in the demand for its produce, or a failure in the supply of the raw material which it uses. This evil again is in a great measure avoided by those large towns, or industrial districts in which several distinct industries are strongly developed. If one of them fails for a time, the others are likely to support it in many ways, chiefly indirect . . .' (Marshall, 1932, p. 154).

What is important here is not just the impact of sectoral patterns of technical and industrial specialisation (see below) influencing the innovation trajectories of such industries, but also its influence on the development of the regional innovation infrastructure. This includes more direct technical, maintenance and testing services, but also specialist legal (intellectual propriety rights) advisers as well as banking and financial services (evident with the evolution of regional banks in the UK, such as the British Linen Bank and the Midland Bank).

Core/periphery differences

However, where there are no strong regional-based governance structures and where regional industry specialisation does not appear to be strong, there can still be significant differences on a regional basis in the absolute and relative rates of innovation. Indeed in some of the most centralised industrial economies, such as France and the UK, in terms of government administration strong core–periphery hierarchical differences are apparent in terms of power, decision-making and innovative performance. Thus, these nations are the ones most liable to create strong core–periphery differences in their spatial set-up and create centralisation of governmental and economic power, via location of headquarters, and in consequence of decision-making. Core regions of nation states display high concentrations of top-level government and administrative functions, corporate headquarters and key decision-making activities (Tornqvist, 1968; Thorngren, 1970) and, more particularly here, research and development functions (Malecki, 1980; Howells 1984) and high technology industries (Thompson, 1988).

By contrast peripheral, often depressed regions, supported by inward investment, have all too often become branch-plant economies (Firn, 1975), with little or no control or stake in their futures, low new firm formation and low levels of innovative activity and technological sophistication. The book *Le Desert Française* written by Garnier in 1947 described the impact of such centralising tendencies on French provincial economic and social life and this can equally be extended to that of so many present-day regions in terms of technical and industrial activity. Even though there is a high degree of nation-wide uniformity in governmental, political, legal, institutional and fiscal regimes, which would suggest less applicability for the presence of regional systems of innovation, there are still fundamental and pronounced differences in regional knowledge and information intensity (Pred, 1975) and institutional support and innovation performance.

The above provides further support for the issue of whether regional systems of innovation do exist and the nature and extent of their variation from each other. Some regions do indeed have a large degree of political and economic autonomy and specialisation which enable them to have qualities as distinctive as certain national systems of innovation. Such regions may contain many, if not all, of the same components and involve the same interactions as national systems of innovation. However, should these regional systems of innovation be considered as just aspiring 'proto' national systems of innovation? If regional systems of innovation are to be a useful and relevant concept it must reveal some new and different level of knowledge regarding the 'systems of innovation' debate and indicate why a regional, or sub-regional, perspective provides a valuable insight in to our understanding of the dynamics of technological innovation. The regional systems of innovation can therefore be more usefully seen as a subset of a wider 'systems nest' relating to knowledge and innovation.

This discussion has direct parallels with David and Foray's (1995) framework of analysis, a knowledge system, building upon Tassey's (1991) earlier concept of technology infrastructure (or 'infratechnologies', p. 356; see also Smith, 1995). The concept highlights the interdependence and interactions among the sub-processes in the overall system governing the production, distribution and utilisation of economically relevant knowledge. What David and Foray (1995, pp. 17–18) seek to emphasise here is that neither the idea of learning as central to the activities of individual economic agents and organisation, nor the pertinence of the systems approach to analysing the determinants of innovation and adaptive capability, imply that the national economy should be the relevant unit of analysis. To postulate that it is national systems that are the most meaningful entities for study would seem to imply an additional claim, namely that there exists a higher degree of systemic integrity for those processes in which participation is delimited on grounds of national affiliation, or where control is asserted by national governments. They go on to make the case for a national perspective, noting that national governments do indeed make policies and impose rules and regulations which influence the behaviour of individuals and organisations within their national territories. However, David and Foray (1995, pp. 18–9) conclude this discussion by noting that they still have some hesitancy talking about national systems thereby tending to de-emphasise if not totally obscure from view the significance of other, sub-national and supranational systems whose workings may be no less critical in shaping technological opportunities and the way the latter are exploited.

Regional innovation systems should be seen as part of this multi-layer approach and indeed there is also a rich and long-established vein of work focusing on firm and institutional interaction, knowledge and information sharing, technical externalities and innovative activity in a local and regional context (see below). Taking an individual firm (or enterprise or establishment), it will be presented with a number of different geographical levels within the innovation system. The highest macro level covers the global context of innovation relating to competitive change and increasing international regulation of various aspects of the technical environment. This covers what Lundvall ed. (1992) and Nelson ed. (1993) both admit as relevant transnational aspects of innovation systems which may be super-seding the national sphere (see also Chesnais, 1992). Below this is obviously the national level and under the national system are regional and even more localised, sub-regional systems of innovation. Lastly, alongside these geo-graphical layers, are overlapping sectoral layers or sectoral systems of innovation which cross-cut transnational, national and regional systems of innovation.

As one moves down the geographical scale the institutional and corpo-rate context becomes more specific, but at the same there will be more shared or fixed components that systems at the same level share. Thus as the patent regulatory system becomes harmonised at the international level (Howells and Neary, 1995, p. 165), national systems of innovation will increasingly share components of the overall innovation system. Similarly, at the next level, regions within the same country will have similarities with their counterparts in terms of a number of government and institutional compo-nents. These will include government departments and agencies, the legal system and practices and the educational system; their overarching innova-tion task environment or framework will therefore display many similarities. If one were to suggest a sub-regional or local system of innovation, even more components of the governmental, institutional and corporate fabric would be held constant. However it would equally be misleading to suppose that within those national boundaries the educational infrastructures, for example, would be homogenous everywhere (David and Foray, 1995, p. 19) and that by implication there would be significant inter-regional variations in these mainly national government sponsored activities.

However, the presence or absence and commonality of components between innovation systems is only one, mainly mechanistic, element in terms of such a systems approach. There are two other fundamental elements that are important in such a systems model and are particularly pertinent when considering regional innovation systems. They relate to:

firstly, even though innovation systems at the same level (for example, regions) may share common components in the form of similar, shared regulatory and educational environments, how these are *delivered* at a regional level are likely to be subtly different; and,

secondly, how firms and organisations *respond* to the separate components and their delivery is also likely to vary.

These other two elements are also important here. Even within similar institutional and governmental structures, how they are administered, organised and delivered regionally – i.e., the way they operate 'on the ground' as complete systems – can be critical. This is perhaps most apparent in terms of the institutional context which in much NSI literature is seen as a constant throughout a national territory. However, Amin and Thrift (1992) have shown that variations in effective institutional capacity or 'thickness' at the local level can be critically important in influencing the performance of local industry. Here again the effectiveness of such institutional capacity is not simply related to the quantity and variety of relevant institutions, but the effectiveness and degree of coordination amongst them.

Another example here related to knowledge infrastructure *articulation* is that educational provision varies significantly on a local and regional basis (Marshall, 1990, p. 226). More particularly, government expenditure on research and technology – for example, the concentration of government-funded research establishments or government finance and aid going towards innovation and technology – has also been highly uneven in its regional pattern (Malecki, 1979). However, even with equal distribution of innovation provision and support by government and non-governmental institutions the ability of private firms and establishments to respond to such stimuli also varies. Less favoured regions have been shown to have a much lower level of entrepreneurial activity in terms of new firm formation rates (Keeble, 1990), less autonomy in terms of investment decisions (because a high level of externally owned branch plants; Firn, 1975; Britton, 1976; Phelps, 1993) and lower innovative activity (Oakey, Thwaites and Nash, 1980; Thwaites, 1982). As a reflection of this firms in less-favoured regions have had a much lower take-up of national technology programmes.

Regional systems of innovation: a bottom-up perspective

So far the analysis has largely concentrated on a 'top–down' view of regional innovation systems by examining whether many of the conditions and elements of national systems of innovation still hold when moving down to the next level of geographical aggregation. Thus the identification of shared and distinct *components*, the way that they are *delivered* and how firms and organisations *respond* to such stimuli only represents one, largely top–down enquiry into the nature of innovation systems, particularly with regard to the regional level. However, a 'bottom–up' perspective is also valid in the analysis of regional systems of innovation. Specific innovation systems should also display their own *internal* set of interactions between players and institutional sets within the system and also impart wider qualities of operating as an identifiable system. This section will first briefly outline studies that have touched upon the notion of geographical innovation systems, before seeking to analyse in more detail the fundamental core of regional or sub-regional innovation systems.

Overview: regional systems of innovation and intangibles

There has been an important long-term interest in the *internal* dynamics of regional systems. It has been argued that regions do display significantly different structures of innovation system components, but it is at the level of the internal dynamics of the interaction of firms and organisations and their links back to the wider institutional structure within the regional system of innovation that is so important and make regions valuable for study in their own right. Regional systems of innovation represent crucial arenas for localised learning and tacit know-how sharing. The peculiarities of the institutional fabric are still crucial and vary significantly between regions, but it is at the regional level that informal links between key personal are formed and maintained and where the primary decision space of firms is based. Economic geographers, particularly belonging to the behavioural school, have studied this in relation to knowledge and information flows at the individual and firm level, in the geographical extent of personal and company knowledge and information scanning space and more generally in how this influences firms decision-making processes (Hägerstrand, 1966; Tornqvist, 1968; Taylor, 1975). It has also been recognised in a more specific body of literature relating to communication patterns within the R&D function, which show highly localised patterns of personal contact (Allen, 1977). Moreover although local face-to-face contacts remain important in knowledge sharing and tacit learning directly, studies have shown that distance decay patterns shown in terms of information scanning and knowledge acquisition is also important in shaping the subsequent diffusion of innovations (Hägerstrand, 1952; 1967; 1975; Malecki, 1977).

It is worth examining some of the background to those studies that have focused on the innovative environment at a regional level before examining in more detail some of the questions that past research raised in relation to study of regional systems of innovation. Economic geographers and regional economists have long recognised the importance of localisation, agglomeration and the regional economy in the wider dynamics of innovation and industrial growth and economic development. This has spawned a plethora of models and concepts that include some aspects of the innovation process in a local context, these include industrial neighbourhoods or districts (see Marshall, 1961); agglomeration economies (see Weber, 1909; Florence, 1948; Isard, 1956; Townroe and Roberts, 1980); innovation agglomerations; product life cycles, filter-down theory and profit cycles (see Hund, 1959; Lichtenburg, 1960; Vernon, 1960; Thompson, 1965; Howells, 1983; Markusen, 1985); the new industrial districts and rise of flexible specialisation (see Brusco, 1982; Amin and Robins, 1990; Becattini, 1991; Sunley, 1992; Harrison, 1992); innovation milieux (Aydalot, 1986; Aydalot and Keeble eds., 1988); and technology districts (Storper, 1992). Although many seek to trace the beginnings of such concepts to a single source, Alfred Marshall, and what has become known as Marshallian districts, in fact there have been a multiple set of similar, yet different sources and antecedents that have fed off each; these include, amongst others, the laws of industrial growth (Burns, 1934), growth pole (Perroux, 1955; Thomas, 1975) and long wave (Marshall, 1987) theories.

Obviously the contribution of Alfred Marshall back in the 1890s has undoubtedly been highly significant and created much of the initial interest into the concentration of specialised industries in particular localities (Marshall, 1932, p. 151). Commentators have tended to stress his neo-classical contribution to the factors involved in agglomeration economies, although his focus on the intangible and tacit benefits of industrial localisation are perhaps more significant here, with the focus on the contributions of both body and *mind* (Marshall, 1961, p. 139). This is evident in a number of Marshall's writings throughout the late nineteenth and early twentieth centuries. Thus in 1892 Marshall wrote:

When an industry has once thus chosen a locality for itself, it is likely to stay there long: so great are the advantages which people following the same skilled trade get from near neighbourhood to one another. The mysteries of the trade become no mysteries; but are as it were in the air, and children learn many of them unconsciously. Good work is rightly appreciated; inventions and improvements in machinery, in processes and the general organization of the business have their merits promptly discussed; if one man starts a new idea it is taken up by others and combined with the suggestions of their own, and thus becomes the source of further new ideas. And presently subsidiary trades grow up in the neighbourhood, supplying it with implements and materials, organizing its traffic, and in many ways conducing to the economy of its material. (Marshall, 1932, pp. 152–3; original 1892)

The direct economic benefits of locating within an industrial district (Marshall 1932, 154), should not be overplayed, in particular since he himself stressed (as noted earlier) that there could be significant disadvantages by locating in such districts (see also Sunley, 1992) and that there were significant benefits of production on a large scale (p. 156) that could outweigh production in smaller factories in a localised industry.

There is insufficient space here to outline in detail all the concepts and models listed above. Much of the early work focused on the direct economic benefits (the various economies) of geographical concentrations of industries, usually on a normative basis. Although technology was seen as an important factor ascribed to the benefits of locating in an agglomeration or district it has been subsumed under wider processes and factors associated with the success of such localities. Thus the recent debate about the emergence of new industrial districts has been part of a much wider discussion about the stated emergence and growth of flexible specialisation within advanced industrial economies (see, for example, Amin and Robins, 1990; Sunley, 1992; Harrison, 1992). There is insufficient space to review the debate concerning these models and concepts and readers are referred elsewhere for discussion, but much of the debate about the localisation of industry has therefore not been about technology per se. Certainly the discussion has recognised the importance of technology in some way, but it has remained largely an ephemeral component in the whole debate. In many respects research in this field has not gone much further than Marshall's own initial diagnosis concerning the 'mysteries' of knowledge and learning capabilities of such localities by saying it is 'in the air' (Marshall, 1932, p. 152).

This is however not to deny that there has been much work on the geography of technological innovation, in particular on seeking to accurately chart its locational pattern (the where) and to uncover at least some of the components (the how) associated with such patterns. Many of the details of the how have not been uncovered yet, whilst the more fundamental problem of why has been largely neglected. This should not be surprising given the empirical problems of measurement and data collection at the micro spatial scale (Alderman and Wood, 1994). Reflecting the study of innovation more widely, indicators that have been used to reflect the harder, quantitative sort of data associated with embodied technologies and technological inputs. This problem is heightened though in the context of the localisation of technological change, because many of the benefits assumed as deriving from agglomeration and districts have been seen to have derived from largely intangible knowledge and technology generation and linkage. Moreover those studies which have attempted more qualitative, case study research on the more intangible elements have been castigated by many observers. Taylor (1995) sees very little as having been added in terms of conceptualisation, or the discovery of new processes at work, since the early studies of industrial agglomeration in the inter-war and post-war years in Britain and elsewhere. Appold (1995, p. 28) reviewing the more general work on industrial districts has commented that the research has focused only on the allegedly successful districts and the mere existence of clustering of firms was assumed to be for the reason of the benefits of agglomeration (see also Amin and Robins, 1990). The debate goes on but little progress has been made in concentrating on the importance of localised knowledge generation, learning and technology transfer, the 'in the air' issue.

Core elements in the micro-foundations of localised systems of innovation: innovation arenas

Seeking to develop this bottom–up analysis, attention is now turned to the issue of the dynamics, elements and processes associated with a sub-national system of innovation. More specifically, it seeks to examine how small (in geographical or other terms) does a system have to become before it is no longer considered as credible or viable? What is the irreducible minimum of a system of innovation, below which it cannot be considered to exist or operate? This enquiry has parallels with Lundvall's (1988) examination of the 'micro-foundations' of user–producer interactions within national systems of innovation, although the context here is within a geographical framework. What are the basic minima of a system of innovation? What is the smallest spatial scale at which a system of innovation can be said to operate? However, the notion of a system of innovation is difficult to dissect. As Lundvall ed. (1992, p. 13) has noted elsewhere in this context 'a definition of the system of innovation must, to a certain degree, be kept open and flexible regarding which should be included and which processes should be studied'. More particularly, McKelvey (1994, p. 121) warns in her review of national systems literature that even at that level of analysis, innovation systems are not entirely reducible to individual components. The notion of *gestalt* seems to hang heavy in all systems studies. Certainly traditional systems theory itself provides little help in defining how small a system can get. A system may be defined as a structured set of object and/or attributes, which in turn consists of components or variables (i.e., phenomena which are free to assume variable magnitudes) that exhibit discernible relationships with one another and operate together as a complex whole, according to some observed pattern (see, for example, Hall and Fagen, 1956; Boulding, 1956; Ashby, 1958; Ackoff, 1960; Von Bertalanffy, 1962). On such a basis, this could involve a small set of firms and organisations involved in an innovation or series of innovations if a true dynamic relationship were said to occur. In terms of this issue of a 'complex whole', even a small number of organisations involved in innovation can lead to quite complex patterns of interaction. However, the smaller numerically and geographically the system of innovation becomes, the more 'open' it becomes leading to the possibility that the individual firms and organisations are going to have an increasing proportion of their relationships outside the system and therefore its coherence as a 'whole' becomes more suspect.

This analysis, at this micro level, rather than seeking to identify the core (static) elements of an innovation system instead attempts to identify the key (dynamic) processes that are fundamental to the operation (and conceptual viability) of a micro-innovation system. It moreover does this from the perspective of the firm, by examining what localised processes should be present for a viable micro-innovation system to exist, and create what might be termed an 'innovation arena'. Five such processes are identified here, they are:

1 localised communication patterns relating to the innovation process, both at (i) an individual level, and (ii) firm or group level;
2 localised search and scanning procedures relating to innovation and technology;
3 localised invention and learning patterns;
4 localised knowledge sharing;
5 localised innovation performance.

Each of theses issues will be briefly outlined in turn.

Localised patterns of knowledge communication

Work by Allen and others (Allen, 1970; 1977; Walsh and Baker, 1971) has stressed the importance of geographical distance both on micro (on the same site or within 1 kilometre) and macro scales in affecting the likelihood of knowledge and information links between individuals and organisations. This indeed echoes Lundvall's (1988, pp. 354–5) acknowledgement of the importance of space in shaping information flows between users–producers. Studies indicate to a lesser or greater extent a typical distance decay function in communication: the rate of contact falls roughly with the square of the separating distance. Even when researchers are in the same project team (intra-group communication), contact fell just as rapidly, though at a given distance it was greater than that between members of different teams (Allen and Fusfield, 1975). Undoubtedly advances being made in information and communication technologies (ICTs) are allowing researchers, technicians and engineers, in a small, but growing number of major multinational companies to communicate successfully between sites across the globe (Howells, 1995). Nonetheless the key issue here remains the importance of face-to-face contact in research and technical communication and the essential tacit nature of much that is being communicated (Howells, 1996), making geographical nearness, at least at present, a crucial factor in innovation. Indeed Von Hippel (1988, pp. 1–2) terms this pattern of close, informal knowledge flows that are difficult to recreate over wider spans as 'locational stickiness', which is in turn associated with cost of communicating and transferring knowledge over space (Hu, 1995).

Localised innovation search and scanning patterns

Geographical proximity has a fundamental influence on how a firm searches for a collaborative partner in terms of research or in identifying a new, more technically sophisticated component or piece of equipment. This is particularly true of smaller firms which have spatially much smaller scanning fields than larger, multi-site companies, in particular multinational companies (Taylor, 1975). The ability of smaller firms, therefore, to be aware of, and identify, collaborative partners or technology sources will owe much due to more geographically restricted scanning fields. Hence the total number of potential contacts will also tend to be smaller (MacPherson, 1991). However, by locating in more 'information rich' and contact-intensive innovation agglomerations or districts, smaller firms can improve their chances of making more effective technical linkages.

Localised invention and learning patterns

Studies have long indicated that inventive activity has revealed highly localised and concentrated distribution patterns (Jefferson, 1929). This is based on the unique user–producer interactions that have occurred in agglomerations and supported by skilled labour and investment capital (Feller, 1973). This localised pattern of invention is mirrored more generally in terms of innovation, centred around problem-solving and technological convergence. Innovation is often undertaken to resolve specific technical problems experienced in producing goods and these advances in manufacturing technology often occur as a response to particular problems arising in existing centres of concentration (Pred, 1966, p. 91). More recently studies have also stressed the highly localised nature of many forms of learning experience both in terms of what may be called psychological distance and technological proximity, but also geographical distance as well (Arcangeli, 1993). 'Learning by doing' first highlighted by Arrow (1962) and learning by using (Rosenberg, 1963) have been increasingly acknowledged as key components in successful innovation and are linked by direct and continuous physical proximity to the production process. The rise of the 'learning economy' (Lundvall and Johnson, 1994) where know-how sharing (rather than knowing how to do things in isolation, p. 25) has become more important in the innovation process, thereby heightening the importance of spatial proximity and the local relationships in technological and industrial performance (Camagni ed., 1991). It has also become part of a more conscious process by firms of shared learning experiences (Alder, 1990).

Localised knowledge sharing

Inventive activity also involves technological convergence (Rosenberg, 1963), the solution of technical problems common in many industries or the extension to other industries which share a common technology (Feller, 1975, p. 89). If technological convergence is therefore dependent upon the potential inventors' exposure to solutions to related problems outside his/her own industry, or more accurately, upon multiple exposure to solutions, possibilities of interaction are more likely in existing agglomerations or innovative milieux (Pred, 1966, p. 96). A key element here is the localised nature of tacit knowledge acquisition and transfer (Howells, 1996). This is centred around complex and loosely structured personal contact and discussions (Pavitt, 1991, p. 47). Although many parts of the innovation process can be codified and easily transferred over long distances, many elements of technological innovation remain tacit in form and indeed these may be the elements that have the most impact on corporate performance for the very reason that they are so difficult to learn off-site and to transfer to a different location.

Localised patterns of innovation performance

Localisation and agglomeration can also reduce the risks and uncertainty of innovation and increase its likelihood of success. Dislocation of risk and information, whereby decisionmakers are dislocated from the information to manage and reduce these risks, can form significant barriers to innovation (More, 1985, p. 206). Technologies tend to go through a shake-down process in their early stages and go through a period of high levels of uncertainty associated with the technical and economic performance of a new product or technique (Gertler, 1995, p. 3). It is the reduction in uncertainty following use by early risk-takers that helps build and sustain a 'bandwagon effect' in innovation diffusion (Mansfield, 1961) and obviously a concentration of early adopters provides the local or regional economy an advantage in technological innovation more generally. High concentrations of information and knowledge flows produce lower perceived and actual risks and uncertainty associated with innovation. This in turn is often supported by high levels of trust and reciprocity (Hansen, 1992, p. 103) and enables local and regional economies to improve their chances of success leading to improved innovative performance through the creation of such 'commensualistic environments' (Ring, 1992).

What has been outlined here have been the key processes that provide the fundamental conditions for the existence of a micro system of innovation operating at a localised level. It should be stressed here that such localised systems of innovation are not everywhere. Indeed there are many sub-regions (and indeed regions) which lack these concentration and localisation benefits, because of low density, peripherality, lack of dynamic, innovative firms and institutions and being simply knowledge and information poor. Moreover, because of inflexibility associated with institutional structures local economies can suffer from 'lock-in' arising from their inability to change their technological trajectory (Asheim, 1995, p. 6). Such a situation indeed both epitomises and lays bare the foundation of so much that is associated with the 'regional problem.' Trying to untangle and reverse these complex and multi-faceted problems remains extremely hard and helps to explain why cumulative causation remains such an enduring facet of regional policy. This is why commentators find examples of regional success in terms of innovation so unhelpful in a policy sense (Wiig and Wood, 1995, p. 3).

Globalisation: the death of regional systems of innovation?

Globalisation has often been hailed as bringing an end to cohesive and creative regions under the assumption that somehow every locality will merge into a homogenous mass, with increasingly open economies, cheap transport and virtually instantaneous communication between any part of the world. However, in terms of the major advances being made in telecommunications, only a limited number of major multinational companies are using ICTs to allow researchers, technicians and engineers to communicate between different sites across the globe and the more widespread use of ICTs in multi-site R&D is still some way off (Howells, 1995). The key issue here remains the importance of face-to-face contact in research and technical communication and the essential tacit nature of much that is being communicated.

However aside from whether there has been much, if any, globalisation of research and technology in recent years, many researchers believe that if it does occur it is more likely to further support and encourage regional specialisation in terms of sectors, functions and technologies rather than erode them (Howells, 1997, pp. 23–4). The use of expressions such as global-localisation (Cooke *et al.*, 1992), glocalisation and global technology districts (Storper, 1992) highlight the view that the process of globalisation will heighten the importance of place and specialisation. On this basis, different systems of innovation will increasingly trade on their particular strengths and specialisms within a wider global regime (Niosi and Bellon, 1994). This links in with Porter's (1990, p. 75) view of the competitive process where the four determinants of industry competitiveness (firm strategy, factor conditions, demand conditions and supporting industries) as a system operate most strongly at the national *and* local level.

However, although specialisation will occur, some observers note that there will also be a process of geographical integration as more and more places are drawn into what has become known as global networks. Thus the functional status of individual localities within these global networks is seen as becoming more complex, though less hierarchical than previously (Amin, 1993, p. 291). How all these complex processes will be worked through depends on the complicated interaction of Porter's determinants of industry competitiveness, but places and regions are likely to remain important in the new geographical workplace.

Conclusions

This chapter has sought to establish the case for regional systems of innovation. As stated in the introduction, this is not to suggest that RSIs should supplant NSIs but rather provide an additional layer to such a systems approach to innovation. The analysis, from a top–down perspective, also sought to suggest that on one level regional systems of innovation have much directly in common with national systems in terms of their mutual components and nature of interactions, although on a smaller geographical scale. Regions do display distinctive systems compared to each other not only in the nature of the institutional arrangements, industry and technology specialisation, but also in the overall level of innovativeness and the distinctiveness of the corporate organisation of firms within the region.

However, regional systems are more than just 'proto' national innovation systems, instead they should be seen more as layers within a knowledge system outlined by David and Foray. Moreover geographical distance, accessibility, agglomeration and the presence of externalities provide a powerful influence on knowledge flows, learning and innovation and this interaction is often played out within a more micro-geographical arena. To this end, this analysis has sought to outline the key processes that might be associated with the presence and dynamic operation of a more localised system of innovation.

Equally regional and sub-regional systems of innovation should not just be viewed as one layer down from national systems. They are increasingly being framed within an international arena. Some have seen this as a threat to the existence, or foreclosure, of regional (and indeed national) innovation systems. However, it is likely that the impact of globalisation will not entail a direct erosion of regional systems of innovation, indeed it is likely to deepen regional differentiation in terms of innovation and economic growth. Competition between regions will be heightened as they become more open economies and innovation systems. The importance of geography and distance will remain, although its impact will evolve under further rounds of internationalisation, changes in the production system and via changes in technology itself.

Note

Thanks go to all those who commented on an earlier version of this text presented at the Rome conference, especially Daniele Archibugi, Bengt-Åke Lundvall and Keith Pavitt, and to contributions made by my colleagues at CRIC working on the Innovation Systems and Innovation Policy project Birgitte Andersen, Stan Metcalfe and Bruce Tether. The research has been funded by the Innovation Programme, DG XIII of the European Commission and by the UK Economic and Social Research Council through CRIC.

References

Ackoff, R. L. 1960. Systems, organization, and interdisciplinary research, *General Systems Yearbook*, 5: 1–8.

Alder, P. 1990. Shared learning, *Management Science*, 36: 938–57.

Alderman, N. and Wood, M. 1994. Surveys of regional innovation? A feasibility study for Europe, *EIMS Publication* 9, Innovation Programme, DGXIII, Commission of the European Communities, Luxembourg.

Allen, T. J. 1970. Communication networks in R&D laboratories, *R&D Management*, 1: 14–21.

1977. *Managing the Flow of Technology*, Cambridge, MA, MIT Press.

Allen, T. J. and Fusfield, A. R. 1975. Research laboratory architecture and the structuring of communications, *R&D Management*, 5: 153–164.

Amin, A. 1993. The globalization of the economy: an erosion of regional networks?, in Grabher (ed.).

Amin, A. and Robins, K. 1990. The re-emergence of regional economies? The mythical geography of flexible accumulation, *Environment and Planning*, D 8: 7–34.

Amin, A. and Thrift, N. 1992. Neo-Marshallian nodes in global networks, *International Journal of Urban and Regional Research*, 16: 571–87.

Appold, S. J. 1995. Agglomeration, interorganizational networks and competitive performance in the US metalworking sector, *Economic Geography*, 71: 49–54.

Arcangeli, F. 1993. Local and global features of the learning process, in Humbert (ed.).

Archibugi, D. and Michie, J. (eds.) 1997. *Technology, Globalisation and Economic Performance*, Cambridge, Cambridge University Press.

Archibugi, D. and Pianta, M. 1992. *The Technological Specialization of Advanced Countries*, Dordrecht, Kluwer.

Arrow, K. 1962. The economic implications of learning by doing, *Review of Economic Studies*, 29: 155–73.

Ashby, W. R. 1958. General system theory as a new discipline, *General Systems Yearbook*, 3: 1–6.

Asheim, B. 1995. Industrial districts as 'learning regions': a condition for prosperity?, *STEP Report* 95.3, N-0155 Oslo, STEP Group.

Aydalot, P. (ed.) 1986. *Milieux Innovateurs en Europe*, Paris, Gremi.

Aydalot, P. and Keeble, D. (eds.) 1988. *High Technology Industry and Innovative Environments: The European Experience*, London, Routledge.

Becattini, G. 1991. The industrial district as creative milieu, in Benko and Dunford (eds.).

Benko, G. and Dunford, M. (eds.) 1991. *Industrial Change and Regional Development: The Transformation of New Industrial Spaces*, London, Belhaven.

Bianchi, P. 1993. Industrial districts and industrial policy: the new European perspective, *Journal of Industry Studies*, 1: 16–29.

Boulding, K. 1956. General systems theory – The skeleton of science, *General Systems Yearbook*, 1: 11–17.

Britton, J. 1976. The influence of corporate organisation and ownership on the linkages of industrial plants: a Canadian enquiry, *Economic Geography*, 52: 311–24.

Brown, L. A. 1981. *Innovation Diffusion: A New Perspective*, New York, Methuen.

Brusco, S. 1982. The Emilian model: productive decentralization and social integration, *Cambridge Journal of Economics*, 6: 167–84.

Burns, A. F. 1934. *Production Trends in the United States since 1870*, New York, National Bureau of Economic Research.

Camagni, R. 1991. Local milieu, uncertainty and innovation networks: towards a new dynamic theory of economic space, in Camagni (ed.).

Camagni, R. (ed.) 1991. *Innovation Networks: Spatial Perspectives*, London, Belhaven Press.

Carlsson, B. and Jacobsson, S. 1994. Technological systems and industrial dynamics – implications for firms and governments, Paper presented at the International J. A. Schumpeter Conference, Münster, Germany, 17–20 August 1994.

Carlsson, B. and Stankiewicz, R. 1991. On the nature, function and composition of technological systems, *Journal of Evolutionary Economics*, 1: 93–118.

Carlton, D. L. and Coclanis, P. A. 1995. The uninventive South? a quantitative look at region and American inventiveness, *Technology and Culture*, 36: 302–326.

Charles, D. and Howells, J. 1992. *Technology Transfer in Europe: Public and Private Networks*, London, Belhaven.

Chesnais, F. 1992. National systems of innovation, foreign direct investment and the operations of multinational enterprises, in Lundvall (ed.).

Collins, L. and Walker, D. F. (eds.) 1975. *Locational Dynamics of Manufacturing Industry*, London, Wiley.

Conti, S. E., Malecki, J. and Oinas, P. (eds.) 1995. *The Industrial Enterprise and its Environment: Spatial Perspectives*, Aldershot, Avebury.

Cooke, P., Mouleart, F., Swyngedouw, E., Weinstein, O. and Wells, P. 1992. *Towards Global Localisation*, London, UCL Press.

David, P. A. and Foray, D. 1995. Accessing and expanding the science and technology knowledge base, *STI Review*, 16: 13–68.

1996. Information distribution and the growth of economically valuable knowledge: a rationale for technological infrastructure policies, in Teubal, Foray, Justman and Zuscovitch (eds.).

Dearlove, J. 1989. Bringing the constitution back in: political science and the state, *Political Studies*, 37: 521–32.

Dosi, G., Freeman, C., Nelson, R., Silverberg, G. and Soete, L. (eds.) 1988. *Technical Change and Economic Theory*, London, Pinter.

Feller, I. 1973. Determinants of the composition of urban inventions, *Economic Geography*, 49: 47–57.

1975. Invention, diffusion and industrial location, in Collins and Walker (eds.).

Firn, J. R. 1975. External control and regional development: the case of Scotland, *Environment and Planning*, A7: 393–414.

Florence, P. S. 1948. *Investment Location and Size of Plant*, London, National Institute of Economic and Social Research.

Freeman, C. 1987. *Technology Policy and Economic Performance: Lessons from Japan*, London Pinter.

1988. Japan: a new national system of innovation?, in Dosi, Freeman, Nelson, Silverberg and Soete (eds.).

1995. The national system of innovation in historical perspective, *Cambridge Journal of Economics*, 19: 5–24. Reprinted in Archibugi and Michie (eds.) 1997.

Gertler, M. 1995. Being there: proximity, organization and culture in the development and adoption of advanced manufacturing technologies, *Economic Geography*, 71: 1–26.

Gilfillan, S. C. 1930. Inventiveness by nation: a note on statistical treatment, *Geographical Review*, 20: 301–4.

Grabher, G. (ed.) 1993. *The Embedded Firm: On the Socioeconomics of Industrial Networks*, London, Routledge.

Hägerstrand, T. 1952. The propagation of innovation waves, *Lund Studies in Geography*, Series B, 4: 3–19.

1966. Aspects of the spatial structure of social communication and the diffusion of information, *Papers and Proceedings, Regional Science Association*, 16: 27–42.

1967. *Innovation Diffusion as a Spatial Process*, Chicago, University of Chicago Press.

Hall, A. D. and Fagen, R. E. 1956. Definition of system, *General Systems Yearbook*, 1: 18–28.

Hall, M. 1959. Introduction, in Hall, M. (ed.) *Made in New York*, Cambridge, MA, Harvard University Press.

Hall, M. (ed.) 1959. *Made in New York*, Cambridge, MA, Harvard University Press.

Hansen, N. 1992. Competition, trust and reciprocity in the development of innovative regional milieux, *Papers in Regional Science*, 71: 95–105.

Harrison, B. 1992. Industrial districts: old wine in new bottles? *Regional Studies*, 26: 469–483.

Hassink, R. 1996. Technology transfer agencies and regional economic development, *European Planning Studies*, 4: 167–84.

Hirst, P. and Thompson, G. 1994. Globalization, foreign direct investment and international governance, *Organization*, 1: 277–303.

Hodgson, G. and Screpanti, E. (eds.) 1994. *Rethinking Economics – Markets, Technology and Market Evolution*, Aldershot, Edward Elgar.

Howells, J. 1983. Filter-down theory: location and technology in the UK pharmaceutical industry, *Environment and Planning*, A 15: 147–64.

1984. The location of research and development: some observations and evidence from Britain, *Regional Studies*, 18: 13–29.

1995. Going global: the use of ICT networks in research and development, *Research Policy*, 25: 169–84.

1996. Tacit knowledge, innovation and technology transfer, *Technology Analysis & Strategic Management*, 8: 91–106.

1997. The globalisation of research and technological innovation: a new agenda?, in Howells and Michie (eds.).

Howells, J. and Michie, J. (eds.) 1977. *Technology, Innovation and Competitiveness*, Cheltenham, Edward Elgar.

Howells, J. and Neary, I. 1995. *Intervention and Technological Innovation: Government and the Pharmaceutical Industry in the UK*, Basingstoke, Macmillan.

Hu, Y.-S. 1995. The international transferability of the firm's advantage, *California Management Review*, 37: 73–88.

Humbert, M. (ed.) 1993. *The Impact of Globalisation on Europe's Firms and Industries*, Pinter, London.

Hund, J. M. 1959. Electronics, in Hall (ed.).

Isard, W. 1956. *Location and the Space Economy*, Cambridge, MA, MIT Press.

Jaffe, A. B. Trajtenberg, M. and Henderson, R. 1993. Geographic localization of knowledge spillovers as evidenced by patent citations, *Quarterly Journal of Economics*, 108: 577–98.

Jefferson, M. 1929. The geographical distribution of inventiveness, *Geographical Review*, 19: 649–61.

Jevons, F. and Saupin, M. 1991. Capturing regional benefits from science and technology: the question of regional appropriability, *Prometheus*, 9: 265–73.

Keeble, D. 1990. Small firms, new firms and uneven regional development in the United Kingdom, *Area*, 22: 234–45.

Kenney, M. and Florida, R. 1994. The organization and geography of Japanese R&D: results from a survey of Japanese electronics and biotechnology firms, *Research Policy*, 23: 305–23.

Kitschelt, H. 1991. Industrial governance structures, innovation strategies, and the case of Japan: sectoral or cross-national comparative analysis?, *International Organization*, 45: 453–93.

Lichtenburg, R. M. 1960. *One-Tenth of a Nation*, Cambridge, MA, Harvard University Press.

Link, A. N. and Tassey, G. 1993. The technology infrastructure of firms: investments in infratechnology, *IEEE Transactions on Engineering Management*, 40: 312–15.

Lundvall, B.-Å. 1988. Innovation as an interactive process – from user–producer interaction to National Systems of Innovation, in Dosi, Freeman, Nelson, Silverberg and Soete (eds.).

1992. Introduction, in Lundvall (ed.).

Lundvall, B.-Å. (ed.) 1992. *National Systems of Innovation: Towards a Theory of Innovation and Interactive Learning*, London, Pinter.

Lundvall, B.-Å. and Johnson, B. 1994. The learning economy, *Journal of Industry Studies*, 1: 23–42.

MacPherson, A. 1991. Interfirm information linkages in an economically disadvantaged region: an empirical perspective from metropolitan Buffalo, *Environment and Planning*, A23, 591–606.

Malecki, E. J. 1977. Firms and innovation diffusion, *Environment and Planning*, A9: 1291–1305.

1979. Locational trends in R&D by large US corporations, 1965–1977, *Economic Geography*, 55: 309–23.

1980. Corporate organization of R and D and the location of technological activities, *Regional Studies*, 14: 219–34.

1985. Industrial location and corporate organization in high technology industries, *Economic Geography*, 61: 345–69.

Mansfield, E. 1961. Technical change and the rate of imitation, *Econometrica*, 29: 741–66.

Markusen, A. 1985. *Profit Cycles, Oligopoly, and Regional Development*, Cambridge, MA, MIT Press.

Marshall, A. 1932. *Elements of Economics, Volume 1: Elements of Economics of Industry*, London, Macmillan 3rd Edition, (first published 1892).

1961. *Principles of Economics*, London, 9th edition, Macmillan (first published 1890).

Marshall, M. 1987. *Long Waves of Regional Development*, London, Macmillan.

Marshall, R. 1990. The impact of elementary and secondary education on state economic development, in Schmandt and Wilson (eds.).

McDermott, P. J. 1976. Ownership, organization and regional dependence in the Scottish electronics industry, *Regional Studies*, 10: 319–35.

McKelvey, M. 1994. How do national systems of innovation differ? A critical analysis of Porter, Freeman, Lundvall and Nelson, in Hodgson and Screpanti (eds.).

Metcalfe, J. S. 1995. Technology systems and technology policy in an evolutionary framework, *Cambridge Journal of Economics*, 19: 25–46. Reprinted in Archibugi and Michie (eds.) 1997.

More, R. A. 1985. Barriers to innovation: intraorganizational dislocations, *Journal of Product Innovation Management*, 3: 205–8.

Nelson, R. R. (ed.) 1993. *National Innovation Systems: A Comparative Analysis*, New York, Oxford University Press.

Nelson, R. R. and Rosenberg, N. 1993. Technical innovation and national systems, in Nelson (ed.).

Niosi, J. and Bellon, B. 1994. The global interdependence of national innovation systems: evidence, limits and implications, *Technology in Society*, 16: 173–197.

Nye, M. J. 1986. *Science in the Provinces: Scientific Communities and Provincial Leadership in France, 1860–1930*, Berkeley, University of California Press.

Oakey, R. P., Thwaites, A. T. and Nash, P. A. 1980. The regional distribution of innovative manufacturing establishments in Britain, *Regional Studies*, 14: 235–53.

Paget, K. M. 1990. State government-university cooperation, in Schmandt and Wilson (eds.).

Pavitt, K. 1991. Key characteristics of the large innovating firm, *British Journal of Management*, 2: 41–50.

Perroux, F. 1955. Note sur la notion de pôle de croissance, *Economie Appliquée*, Jan–June, 307–20.

Phelps, N. A. 1993. Branch plants and the evolving spatial division of labour: a study of material linkage in the Northern region of England, *Regional Studies*, 27: 87–102.

Porter, M. E. 1990. *The Competitive Advantage of Nations*, London, Macmillan.

Porter, R. and Teich, M. (eds.) 1992. *The Scientific Revolution in a National Context*, Cambridge, Cambridge University Press.

Pred, A. R. 1966. *The Spatial Dynamics of US Industrial Growth, 1800–1914*, Cambridge, MA, MIT Press.

1975. Diffusion, organizational, spatial structure and city system development, *Economic Geography*, 51: 252–68.

Ring, P. S. 1992. Cooperating on tacit know-how assets, Paper presented at the First Annual Meeting of the International Federation of Scholarly Association of Management, Tokyo, September 1992.

Rosenberg, N. 1963. Technical change in the machine tool industry, 1840–1910, *Journal of Economic History*, 23: 414–43.

Schmandt, J. 1990. Regional rôles in the governance of the scientific state, in Schmandt and Wilson (eds.).

Schmandt, J. and Wilson, R. (eds.) 1990. *Growth Policy in the Age of High Technology: The Role of Regions and States*, London, Unwin Hyman.

Smith, K. 1995. Interactions in knowledge systems: foundations, policy implications and empirical methods, *STI Review*, 16: 69–102.

Storper, M. 1992. The limits of globalisation: technology districts and international trade, *Economic Geography*, 68: 60–92.

Sunley, P. 1992. Marshallian industrial districts: the case of the Lancashire cotton industry in the inter-war years, *Transactions of the Institute of British Geographers*, N.S. 17: 306–20.

Tassey, G. 1991. The functions of technological infrastructure in a competitive economy, *Research Policy*, 20: 345–61.

Taylor, M. J. 1975. Organisational growth, spatial interaction and location decision-making, *Regional Studies*, 9: 213–23.

1995. The business enterprise, power and patterns of geographical industrialisation, in Conti, Malecki and Oinas (eds.).

Teubal, M., Foray, D., Justman, M. and Zuscovitch, E. 1996. An introduction to technological infrastructure and technological infrastructure policy, in Teubal, Foray, Justman and Zuscovitch (eds.).

Teubal, M., Foray, D., Justman, M. and Zuscovitch, E. (eds.) 1996. *Technological Infrastructure Policy: An International Perspective*, Dordrecht, Kluwer.

Thomas, M. D. 1975. Growth pole theory, technological change and regional economic growth, *Papers of the Regional Science Association*, 34: 3 25.

Thompson, C. 1988. High-technology development and recession: the local experience in the United States, 1980–1982, *Economic Development Quarterly*, 2: 153–67.

Thompson, W. R. 1965. *A Preface to Urban Economics*, Baltimore, MD, John Hopkins University Press.

Thorngren, B. 1970. How do contact systems affect regional development?, *Environment and Planning*, A 2: 409–27.

Thwaites, A. T. 1982. Some evidence of regional variations in the introduction and diffusion of industrial products and processes within the British manufacturing industry, *Regional Studies*, 16: 371–81.

Tornqvist, G. 1968. Flows of information and the location of economic activities, *Lund Studies in Geography, Series B*, 30: 1–137.

Townroe, P. M. and Roberts, N. J. 1980. *Local-External Economics for the British Manufacturing Industry*, Farnborough, Gower.

Tulder, van R. and Ruigrok, W. 1993. Regionalisation, globalisation, or glocalisation: the case of the world car industry, in Humbert (ed.).

Ullman, E. L. 1958. Regional development and the geography of concentration, *Papers and Proceedings, Regional Science Association*, 4: 179–98.

Vernon, R. 1960. *Metropolis 1985*, Cambridge, MA, Harvard University Press.

Von Bertalanffy, L. 1962. General system theory – a critical review, *General Systems Yearbook*, 7: 1–20.

Von Hippel, E. 1988. *The Sources of Innovation*, New York, Oxford University Press.

Walsh, V. M. and Baker, A. G. 1971. Project management and communication patterns in industrial research, *R&D Management*, 2: 103–9.

Weber, A. 1909. *Theory of the Location of Industries*, Chicago, University of Chicago Press.

Wiig, H. and Wood, M. 1995. What comprises a regional innovation system? An empirical study *STEP Report* 95.1, STEP Group, N-0155 Oslo, Norway.

Wood, P. 1992. The scientific revolution in Scotland, in Porter and Teich (eds.).

6 Global corporations and national systems of innovation: who dominates whom?

KEITH PAVITT AND PARIMAL PATEL

1 Introduction

We shall show that the activities generating the skills and know-how that give firms competitive advantage are less internationalised than all other dimensions of corporate activity. Even very large corporations in most cases perform most of their R&D at home. As a consequence, companies' innovative activities are significantly influenced by their home country's national system of innovation: the quality of basic research, workforce skills, systems of corporate governance, the degree of competitive rivalry, and local inducement mechanisms, such as abundant raw materials, the price of labour and energy, and persistent patterns of private investment or public procurement.

We do not foresee any fundamental changes in future. The efficiency gains from the geographical concentration of innovative activities will remain, even if firms increasingly seek out unique skills in foreign countries. The State will continue to provide infrastructure, incentives and institutions that strongly influence the rate and direction of innovative activities in locally based corporations. There are no mechanisms to ensure that national systems of innovation converge in either their characteristics or their performance. Nor are there any signs of the emergence of a European system of innovation: the dominant system is likely to remain the German one.

Other authors have come to similar conclusions, most notably Porter (1990), based mainly on in-depth case studies, and Hu (1992) based on an analysis of the nature and the behaviour of multinational firms.[1] Our research is based on systematic information on the world's largest firms that were technologically active in patenting in the USA in the 1980s. It consists of 587 firms, of which 249 were US owned, 17 from Canada, 143 from Japan and 178 from Europe (Patel and Pavitt, 1991). The key data that we have

Table 6.1. *Nationalities of the top 20 firms in US patenting in eleven broad technological fields, 1985–90*

Broad technological field	Japan	United States	West Europe	Correlation of shares of the top 20 in 1985–90 with their shares in 1969–74
Industrial chemicals	1	11	8	0.66*
Fine chemicals	1	12	7	0.54
Defence related technologies	0	14	6	0.37
Electrical machinery	6	10	4	0.68*
Telecommunications	6	10	4	0.70*
Motor vehicles	11	5	4	0.15
Raw materials-based technologies	1	16	3	0.45
Materials	4	13	3	0.41
Electronic capital goods	8	9	3	0.51
Non-electrical machinery	9	8	3	0.41
Electronic consumer goods	14	4	2	0.27

Note:
* = significant at the 5% level.

for each firm are its sales, principal sector of activity, country of origin, and the US patents granted to it since 1969, including those granted to divisions and subsidiaries with names different from the parent company. For each company patent, we have the following information:

(i) The technical field. We have developed and used different levels of dis-aggregation. Here we use 11 broad fields (see table 6.1), based on the US patent classification.
(ii) The country of residence of the inventor. This is not necessarily the country from which their patent application was filed, and is a more accurate reflection of the country in which the technological activity was performed.
(iii) The country of the parent company.
(iv) The main product line of the company. See table 6.2 for the 17 sectors.

The advantages and drawbacks of patenting statistics as an indicator of technological activities have been discussed extensively elsewhere.[2] For the purposes of our analysis, the main drawbacks are that US patenting does

Table 6.2. *The source of large firms' patenting in the USA, according to their principal product group, 1985–90*

Product group	Abroad %age	Of which			
		USA	Europe	Japan	Other
Drink and Tobacco (18)	30.8	17.5	11.1	0.4	1.8
Food (48)	25.0	14.8	8.5	0.0	1.7
Building materials (28)	20.6	9.1	9.8	0.1	1.6
Other transport (5)	19.7	2.0	6.8	0.0	10.9
Pharmaceuticals (25)	16.7	5.5	8.3	1.1	1.7
Mining and petroleum (47)	15.0	9.7	3.5	0.1	1.6
Chemicals (72)	14.4	8.0	5.1	0.3	1.0
Machinery (68)	13.7	3.5	9.1	0.1	1.1
Metals (57)	12.8	5.4	5.7	0.1	1.6
Electrical (58)	10.2	2.6	6.8	0.3	0.4
Computers (17)	8.9	0.1	6.6	1.1	1.1
Paper and wood (34)	8.1	2.4	4.9	0.1	0.7
Rubber and plastics (10)	6.1	0.9	2.4	0.4	2.4
Textiles, etc. (18)	4.7	1.4	1.8	0.8	0.6
Motor vehicles (43)	4.4	0.9	3.2	0.1	0.2
Instruments (20)	4.4	0.4	2.8	0.5	0.8
Aircraft (19)	2.9	0.3	1.8	0.0	0.7
All firms (587)	11.0	4.1	5.6	0.3	0.9

Note:
Number of firms between brackets.
Source: Patel, P. (1995).

not fully reflect improvements in software technology, since the practice in the USA of protecting software technology through patents is of recent origin. On the other hand, our patenting database offers greater coverage, comparability and detail than any other available measure of technological activities. It also yields results that are consistent with those derived from other measures (like R&D activities), when the two can be compared.

2 The continuing domestication of large firms' innovative activities

2.1 The non-globalisation of large firms' innovative activities

Our analysis confirms the conclusions of Porter (1990) that the rate and direction of technological activities in large firms are strongly domesticated. Table 6.3 shows that our large firms continue to perform a high pro-

Table 6.3. *The source of large firms' patenting in the USA, according to their country of origin, 1985–90*

Firm nationality	% age share from		Abroad of which			
	Home	Abroad	USA	Europe	Japan	Other
Japan	98.9	1.1	0.8	0.3	–	0.0
USA	92.2	7.8	–	6.0	0.5	1.3
Europe	82.0	18.0	16.7	–	0.4	1.0
Canada	66.8	33.2	25.2	7.3	0.3	0.5
Italy	88.1	11.9	5.4	6.2	0.0	0.3
France	86.6	13.4	5.1	7.5	0.3	0.5
Germany	84.7	15.3	10.3	3.8	0.4	0.7
Finland	81.7	18.3	1.9	11.4	0.0	4.9
Norway	68.1	31.9	12.6	19.3	0.0	0.0
Sweden	60.7	39.3	12.5	25.8	0.2	0.8
UK	54.9	45.1	35.4	6.7	0.2	2.7
Switzerland	53.0	47.0	19.7	26.1	0.6	0.5
Netherlands	42.1	57.9	26.2	30.5	0.5	0.6
Belgium	36.4	63.6	23.8	39.3	0.0	0.6
All firms (587)	89.0	11.0	4.1	5.6	0.3	0.9

Source: SPRU large firm database.

portion of their innovative activities in their home countries. According to Cantwell (1992), the share of large firms' innovative activities performed outside their home country is significantly related to the share of foreign production. About 25 per cent of our firms' production is performed abroad, compared to only 11 per cent of their innovative activities, which shows that their foreign production is in general much less innovation intensive than their domestic production. Surveys show that the purpose of most foreign innovative activities is to adapt products and processes to local factor endowments and consumer tastes (Casson ed., 1991).

Table 6.3 also shows that the main differences amongst countries and regions are as follows:

> Japanese firms have the least 'globalised' structure of innovative activities, and European firms the most, with one sixth of their innovative activities located in the USA.
> Within Europe, the degree of 'globalisation' of firms' innovative activities varies considerably, largely as a function of the (small) size of the home country. However, only Belgian and Dutch large firms perform more than half their innovative activities outside their home country, whilst

(West) German, French and Italian firms perform more than 80 per cent domestically.[3]

Elsewhere in Europe is the preferred location of foreign innovative activities for most large European firms. Germany is the overwhelming first choice, probably reflecting its position as both the largest market and the largest European location of innovative activities.

UK large firms do not fit into this pattern. Although a large country, they perform 45.1 per cent of their innovative activities abroad. Although a European country, they perform more than a third in the USA.

In addition, table 6.2 shows that, with the notable exception of pharmaceuticals, the proportion of innovative firms' activities performed domestically increases with the technology intensity of the industry and of the firm (Patel, 1995, 1996). This probably reflects the influence of the following factors:

1 at the industry level, the need to adapt 'traditional' products to local tastes (e.g., food and drink, building materials), and to locate innovative activities close to available raw materials (e.g., petroleum, food and drink, building materials);
2 at the industry level, the smaller need to adapt high-technology products (e.g., civil aircraft, automobiles) to local requirements;
3 at the industry and firm level, the concentration of innovative activities in the home country probably reflects (a) the positive external economies of links with the local science base and supply of skills, sources of finance, and local suppliers and customers; (b) the efficiency gains within firms from the close coordination of functional activities, and integration of tacit knowledge, necessary for the launching of major innovations (Rothwell, 1977; Patel and Pavitt, 1991).

Finally, foreign large firms generally establish technological activities in host countries in fields reflecting the parent firm's (and often home country's) strengths, rather than the particular technological strengths of the host country. This is the case for firms from Japan, FR Germany, The Netherlands, Switzerland and Sweden, although the pattern is inconclusive for firms from France and the USA (Patel and Pavitt, 1991). From the side of the host country, the technological activities of foreign large firms are most strongly established in fields of relative national weakness in Canada, France, FR Germany and the USA. Only in Belgium are the fields of overall national and of foreign firms' technological strengths closely correlated, reflecting the unusually strong position of foreign firms there (Patel and Pavitt, 1991).

2.2 The dominance of national systems of innovation

In addition, we have found that country effects dominate over company effects in explaining large firms' technological performance. Cross-country comparisons show that domestically controlled large firms' technology intensities (US patents/sales) – and their rates of growth of technological activities – correlated significantly with those of other national firms, but not with their own foreign technological activities[4] (Patel and Pavitt, 1991). In addition, table 6.1 shows that, in general, the global technological competitiveness of large firms in major technological fields is the same as that of their home country.[5] US firms are relatively strongest in defence and raw materials technologies, Japanese firms in consumer electronics and motor vehicles, and European firms in chemicals and defence-related technologies. However, the relative European strength in non-electrical machinery is not apparent, given the predominance of small firms. The last column shows that European firms have been relatively more successful in technological fields where the positions of the leading firms have not changed radically over the past 20 years.[6] Within Europe, the leading firms again reflect the strengths of their home country: Germany in chemicals, motor vehicles and defence-related technologies; France in defence-related technologies and telecommunications, UK in defence-related technologies and chemicals, and The Netherlands in electronics (Patel and Pavitt, 1994a).

We should be aware that R&D statistics overestimate the relative importance of large firms in national systems of innovation. In the late 1980s (1986–90) our large firms' share of total US patenting was about 45 per cent (Patel and Pavitt, 1991). Although difficult to compare directly, this is much smaller than their share of R&D activities, which in most countries is heavily concentrated in firms with more than 10,000 employees. This is because US patenting also reflects technological activities performed outside R&D departments – in particular, the largely machinery-related technological activities of small firms.

Table 6.4 shows that, in Europe, the overall share of large firms in total innovative activities is higher than in the USA, but well below that in Japan. Within Europe, the shares of large firms vary considerably amongst countries, from above 60 per cent in the Netherlands to below 30 per cent in Italy, Norway and Finland. These international differences in the relative importance of large firms are not reflected in international differences in technological performance, as measured by the share of business-funded R&D activities in GDP (Patel and Pavitt, 1991). Rather, they reflect differing sectoral patterns of national technological advantage, with high

Table 6.4. *Large firms in national technological activities, 1985–90*

| Country | Large firms | | Other firms and institutions | Total |
	National	Foreign		
Japan (143)	64.9	0.7	34.4	100.0
Europe* (178)	41.2	10.9	47.9	100.0
United States (249)	37.0	2.6	60.5	100.0
Canada (17)	7.6	13.5	78.9	100.0
Netherlands (9)	53.5	8.1	38.4	100.0
Germany (43)	43.0	9.9	47.1	100.0
Switzerland (10)	37.6	5.8	56.6	100.0
France (26)	31.5	9.3	59.2	100.0
UK (56)	28.8	17.7	53.5	100.0
Finland (7)	20.7	0.2	79.1	100.0
Sweden (13)	20.5	11.5	68.0	100.0
Italy (7)	19.0	9.0	71.9	100.0
Norway (3)	13.9	9.2	76.9	100.0
Belgium (4)	7.1	35.8	57.1	100.0

Notes:
( ) = number of firms based in the country.
* Europe is the aggregate of all the European countries in this table.

shares of large firms reflecting national advantage in industries where technological activities are concentrated in large firms – chemicals, vehicles, electronics – and low shares of large firms reflecting national advantage in sectors where they are not – non-electrical machinery.

Table 6.4 also shows that foreign large firms are relatively much more important sources of innovative activities in Europe than in either Japan or the USA. Within Europe, foreign large firms vary from less than 1 per cent of the total in Finland to more than 10 per cent in Sweden and the UK, and more than a third in Belgium. Cross-country comparisons show no statistically significant relationship between strong national technological performance (as measured by industry-funded R&D as a percentage of GDP), and the share of either national or foreign large firms in national technological activities (Patel and Pavitt, 1991).

3 National systems of innovation

So far, we have shown that the level and pattern of large firms' innovative activities are strongly influenced by their home countries' systems of innovation, and that managements of high-tech firms probably have legitimate reasons of efficiency for concentrating their innovative activities in their home country. We shall now examine in more detail some of the key features of what are now called 'national systems of innovation' (Lundvall ed., 1992; Nelson ed., 1993; Patel and Pavitt, 1994b, Freeman, 1995), some of which also appear in the 'competitive diamond' developed by Porter (1990). We shall concentrate on factors that are not company specific, whilst recognising that the discretionary choices and actions of managers and workers do matter.

3.1 Public support for basic research

In the past, public policy for basic research has been strongly supported by economic analysis. Governments provide by far the largest proportion of the funding for such research in the OECD countries. The well-known justification for such subsidies was provided by Nelson (1959) and Arrow (1962): the economically useful output of basic research is codified information, which has the property of a 'public good' in being costly to produce, and virtually costless to transfer, use and re-use. It is therefore economically efficient to make the results of basic research freely available to all potential users. But this reduces the incentive of private agents to fund it, since they cannot appropriate the economic benefits of its results: hence the need for public subsidy for basic research, the results of which are made public.

This formulation was very influential in the 1960s and 1970s, but began to fray at the edges in the 1980s. In an increasingly open and interdependent world, it has been argued that the very 'public good' characteristics that justify public subsidy to basic research also make its results available for use in any country, thereby creating a 'free-rider' problem.[7] In this context, Japanese firms in particular have been accused of dipping into the world's stock of freely available scientific knowledge, without adding much to it themselves.

But the main problem has been the difficulty of measuring the national economics benefits (or 'spillovers') of national investments in basic research. Table 6.5 shows that countries with excellent records in basic research (e.g., USA and UK) have performed less well technologically and economically than countries with less impressive records in basic research (e.g., FR Germany and Japan, where business funded R&D is a larger share of output). This should be perplexing – even discouraging – to the new growth theorists who give central importance to policies to stimulate technological spillovers, and where public support to basic research should therefore be one of the main policy instruments to promote technical change.

Table 6.5. *National performance in basic research (mean citations per paper) and in technology (business-funded R&D as percentage of GDP)*

Country	Mean citations per scientific paper, 1981–90	Business financed R & D as percentage of GDP in 1985
Switzerland	7.33	2.16
Sweden	6.72	1.71
USA	6.65	1.44
Denmark	6.22	0.61
Netherlands	6.01	0.99
United Kingdom	5.62	0.96
FR Germany	5.47	1.65
Belgium	5.39	1.20
Canada	5.31	0.56
France	5.05	0.92
Finland	4.97	0.85
Norway	4.85	0.80
Japan	4.42	1.84
Italy	4.26	0.49
Ireland	3.94	0.35
Spain	3.17	0.26
Portugal	<2.19	0.11

Source: Science Watch, 1991, and OECD.

Yet the experiences of FR Germany and Japan, especially when compared to the opposite experience of the UK, suggest that the causal linkages run the other way: not from basic research to technical change, but from technical change to basic research. In all three countries, trends in relative performance in basic research since World War Two have lagged relative performance in technical change (Patel and Pavitt, 1994b).[8] This is not an original observation. More than one hundred years ago, de Tocqeville and then Marx saw that the technological dynamism of early capitalism would stimulate demand for basic research knowledge, as well as resources, techniques and data for its execution.[9]

At a more detailed level, it has also proved difficult to find convincing and comprehensive evidence of the direct technological benefit of the information provided by basic research. The reason is that the benefits that business practitioners identify from public support for basic research are much broader than the 'information', discoveries' and 'ideas' that tend to be stressed by economists, sociologists and academic scientists. Practitioners attach smaller importance to these contributions than to the provision of

Table 6.6. *Qualifications of the workforce in five European countries*

Level of qualification Year	Britain 1988	N'lands 1989	Germany 1987	France 1988	Switz'l 1991
University degrees	10	8	11	7	11
Higher technician diplomas	7	19	7	7	9
Craft/lower tech. dips.	20	38	56	33	57
No vocational qualifications	63	35	26	53	23
Total	100	100	100	100	100

Source: Prais (1993).

trained researchers, improved research techniques and instrumentation, background (i.e., tacit) knowledge, and membership of professional networks.[10] In general terms, basic research and related training improve corporate (and other) capacities to solve complex problems.[11] Most of the contributions are person-embodied and institution-embodied tacit knowledge, rather than information-based codified knowledge. This explains why the benefits of basic research turn out to be localised, rather than available indifferently to the whole world (Hicks *et al.*, 1996; Jaffe, 1989; Narin, 1992). For corporations, scientific publications are signals to academic researchers about fields of corporate interest in their (the academic researchers') tacit knowledge (Hicks, 1995). And Japan has certainly not been a 'free rider' on the world's basic research, since nearly all the R&D practitioners in their corporations were trained with Japanese resources in Japanese universities.[12]

3.2 Workforce skills

Another factor in national systems of innovation is the skill profile of the workforce. Table 6.6 shows that within Western Europe there are considerable differences in the level of training of the non-university trained workforce. These broad statistical differences are confirmed by more detailed comparisons of educational attainment in specific subjects, and their economic importance is confirmed by marked international differences in productivity and product quality (Prais, 1993). There is also partial evidence that the USA resembles the UK, with a largely unqualified workforce, whilst Japan and the East Asian tigers resemble Germany and Switzerland (Newton *et al.*, 1992).

These international differences in the technological competencies are reflected in fields of national technological strength and weakness. US and

UK strengths in pharmaceuticals and software reflect the concentration of their human capital endowments in clever graduates, whilst German and Japanese strengths in automobiles, machinery and production engineering reflect the additional endowment of skilled production workers and technicians.

3.3 Business-funded R&D

Empirical studies have shown that technological activities financed by business firms largely determine the capacity of firms and countries both to exploit the benefits of local basic research, and to imitate technological applications originally developed elsewhere (Gibbons and Johnston, 1974). Thus, although the output of R&D activities have some characteristics of a 'public good', they are certainly not a 'free good', since their application often requires further investments in technological application (to transform the results of basic research into innovations), or reverse engineering (to imitate a product already developed elsewhere). This helps explain why international differences in economic performance are partially explained by differences in proxy measures of investments in technological application, such as R&D expenditures, patenting and skill levels.

Table 6.7 shows no signs of convergence amongst the OECD countries in the proportion of business funded R&D spent on R&D activities. Japan, Germany and some of its neighbours had already caught up with the US level by the early to mid 1970s. At least until 1989, they were forging ahead, so that the 1980s saw marked divergence (i.e., increases in the standard deviation of the distribution), which could – unless the changed trends in the early 1990s are an inflexion rather than a perturbation – have disquieting implications for future international patterns of economic growth.[13]

3.4 National systems of finance and management

In spite of their major implications for both science and economic policies, relatively little attention has been paid to explaining these international differences. The conventional explanations are in terms of either macroeconomic conditions – Japan has an advantage over the USA in investment and R&D because of differences in the cost of capital (see Bernheim and Shoven, 1992); or in terms of market failure – given lack of labour mobility, Japanese firms have greater incentives to invest in workforce training (Teece ed., 1987).

But while these factors have some importance, they may not be the whole story. Some of the international differences have been long and persistent,

Table 6.7. *Trends in business-funded R&D as percentage of GDP*

	1967	1969	1971	1975	1977	1979	1981	1983	1985	1987	1989	1991	1993
Japan	0.83	1.00	1.09	1.12	1.11	1.19	1.38	1.59	1.81	1.82	2.05	2.13	1.90
Sweden	0.71	0.69	0.80	0.96	1.07	1.11	1.24	1.45	1.71	1.73	1.65	1.69	1.86
Switzerland	1.78	1.78	1.67	1.67	1.71	1.74	1.68	1.67	1.79	1.92	2.05	1.79	1.79
USA	0.99	1.03	0.97	0.98	0.98	1.05	1.17	1.31	1.42	1.37	1.41	1.60	1.57
FR Germany	0.94	1.03	1.13	1.11	1.12	1.32	1.40	1.48	1.65	1.80	1.78	1.58	1.45
Finland	0.30	0.32	0.44	0.44	0.49	0.53	0.62	0.73	0.90	0.99	1.09	1.10	1.20
France	0.60	0.64	0.67	0.68	0.69	0.75	0.79	0.88	0.92	0.92	0.98	0.98	1.05
UK	1.00	0.92	0.81	0.80	0.80	0.82	0.91	0.86	0.95	1.02	1.04	0.99	1.04
Belgium	0.66	0.64	0.71	0.84	0.91	0.95	0.96	1.02	1.09	1.16	1.03	1.01	1.01
Denmark	0.34	0.39	0.41	0.41	0.41	0.42	0.46	0.53	0.60	0.66	0.71	0.86	0.87
Netherlands	1.12	1.04	1.02	0.97	0.87	0.86	0.83	0.89	0.97	1.11	1.06	0.91	0.86
Norway	0.35	0.39	0.41	0.49	0.49	0.50	0.50	0.61	0.80	0.88	0.81	0.77	0.80
Italy	0.33	0.38	0.44	0.43	0.37	0.40	0.43	0.42	0.49	0.49	0.56	0.61	0.63
Canada	0.40	0.39	0.38	0.33	0.32	0.39	0.49	0.46	0.57	0.57	0.55	0.58	0.58
Ireland	0.19	0.23	0.30	0.23	0.22	0.23	0.24	0.25	0.33	0.39	0.43	0.56	0.56
Spain	0.08	0.08	0.11	0.18	0.18	0.18	0.18	0.22	0.25	0.29	0.34	0.38	0.37
Portugal	0.04	0.06	0.09	0.05	0.04	0.09	0.10	0.11	0.11	0.11	0.12	0.12	0.12
Standard Deviation													
All countries	0.46	0.46	0.43	0.43	0.45	0.47	0.48	0.52	0.57	0.58	0.60	0.57	0.55
Excl. US	0.47	0.46	0.43	0.44	0.45	0.47	0.49	0.52	0.57	0.59	0.61	0.57	0.55

Source: OECD.

Table 6.8. *Own R&D expenditures by world's 200 largest R&D spenders (1994)*

Country ( ) = No. of firms	R&D as % of:			Profits/ sales (%)	Cost of funds/ profits (%)
	Sales	Profits	Costs of funds		
Sweden (7)	9.2	73.4	194.3	12.5	37.8
Switzerland (7)	6.9	69.0	140.4	10.0	49.1
Netherlands (3)	5.6	103.8	201.0	5.4	51.6
Japan (60)	5.5	204.0	185.6	2.7	109.9
Germany (16)	4.9	149.0	202.9	3.2	73.4
France (18)	4.6	256.5	111.9	1.8	229.2
USA (67)	4.2	43.8	96.6	9.6	45.3
UK (12)	2.6	23.7	52.3	11.0	45.3
Italy (4)	2.3	n/a	34.0	n/a	n/a
TOTAL (200)	4.7	72.1	119.1	6.5	4.1

Notes:
Profits = 'Profit before Tax' as disclosed in the accounts.
Cost of funds = (equity and preference dividends appropriated against current year profits) + (interest servicing costs on debt) + (other financing contracts such as finance leases).
Source: Company Reporting Limited (1995).

and none more so (and nor more studied) than the differences between the UK and Germany, which date back to at least the beginning of this century, and which have persisted through the varied economic conditions associated with imperialism, labour corporatism and Thatcherite liberalism in the UK, and imperialism, republicanism (including the great inflation of 1924), nazism and federalism in Germany. The differences in performance can be traced to persistent differences in institutions (Keck, 1993; Walker, 1993), their incentive structures, and their associated competencies (i.e., tacit skills and routines) that change only slowly (if at all) in response to international differences in economic incentives.

One of the most persistent differences has been in the proportion of corporate resources spent on R&D and related activities.[14] New light is now being thrown on this subject by improved international data on corporate R&D performance. Table 6.8 shows that, in spite of relatively high profit rates and low 'cost of funds' as a share of profits, the major UK and US firms spend relatively low proportions of their sales on R&D. Similarly, despite higher 'cost of funds' as a share of profits, German and Japanese firms spend higher shares of profits and sales on R&D than UK and US firms. As far as this (recently developed) data allow us to judge, these differences are consistent across sector and stable across time.[15]

And they cannot be explained away very easily. In a matched sample of firms of similar size in the UK and Germany, Mayer (1994) and his colleagues found that, in the period 1982–8, the proportion of earnings paid out as dividends were two to three times as high as in the UK firms. Tax differences could not explain the difference: indeed, retentions are particularly heavily discouraged in Germany. Nor could differences in inflation or in investment requirements. Mayer attributes the differences to the structures of ownership and control. Ownership in the UK is dispersed, and control exerted through corporate take-overs. In Germany, ownership is concentrated in large corporate groupings, including the banks, and systems of control involve suppliers, purchasers, banks and employees, as well as shareholders. On this basis, he concludes that the UK system has two drawbacks:

'(F)irst . . . the separation of ownership and control . . . makes equity finance expensive, which . . . causes the level of dividends in the UK to be high and inflexible in relation to that in countries where investors are more closely involved. Second the interests of other stakeholders are not included. This discourages their participation in corporate investment.

UK-style corporate ownership is therefore likely to be least well suited to co-operative activities that involve several different stakeholders, e.g. product development, the development of new markets, and specialised products that require skilled labour forces.[16] (p.191).

Similar (and independently derived) analyses have emerged in the USA, especially from a number of analysts of corporate behaviour at Harvard Business School (Abernathy and Hayes, 1980; Chandler, 1992). In addition to deficiencies in the financial system, they stress the importance of command and control systems installed by corporate managers. They point to the growing power of business school graduates, who are well trained to apply financial and organisational techniques, but have no knowledge of technology. They maximise their own advantage by installing decentralised systems of development, production and marketing, with resource allocations and monitoring determined centrally by short-term financial criteria. These systems are intrinsically incapable of exploiting all the benefits of investments in technological activities, given their short-term performance horizons, their neglect of the intangible benefits in opening new options, and their inability to exploit opportunities that cut across established divisional boundaries. Managers with this type of competence therefore tend to underinvest in technological activities.

3.5 Competitive rivalry

We have found amongst our large firms no increasing or decreasing returns to scale in R&D or patenting activities: in other words, firms' R&D or patenting increases more or less linearly with their sales or employment. There is, therefore, no justification for either mergers or deconcentration in order to increase the volume of innovative activities (Patel and Pavitt, 1992). Fields of relative technological strength in each of the three main regions (Japan, USA, Europe) are associated with a relatively large number of firms, thereby confirming another of Porter's (1990) conclusions stressing the importance of rivalry in domestic markets. Only for Europe is the above-average size of firm associated with technological fields of international competitive advantage. But even this is not a sufficient justification for public policies to increase company size, which (like a relatively large number of firms) may be as much the result of innovative dynamism as its cause.

3.6 Inducement mechanisms and sectoral technological advantage

So far, we have compared trends in aggregate technological performance. Table 6.9 shows trends in the three main regions' technological strengths and weaknesses, in the same broad technological fields as in table 6.1. For each country-region and technological field, we have calculated an index of 'revealed technology advantage' (RTA) for 1963–8 and 1985–90.[17] They reveal markedly different patterns and trends amongst the three main, technology-producing regions of the world – USA, Europe and Japan. The USA has seen rapid decline in motor vehicles and consumer electronics; growing relative strength in technologies related to weapons, raw materials and telecommunications; and an improving position in chemicals. In Japan, almost the opposite has happened: growing relative strength in electronic consumer and capital goods and motor vehicles, together with rapid relative decline in chemicals, and continued weakness in raw materials and weapons. In Western Europe, the pattern is different again, and very close to that of its dominant country – FR Germany: continuing strength in chemicals, growing strength in weapons, continued though declining strength in motor vehicles, and weakness in electronics.

In an earlier paper (Patel and Pavitt, 1994a), we have examined the similarities and differences amongst 18 OECD countries' technological specialisations in greater and more systematic detail.[18] We used correlation analysis to measure both the stability over time of each country's sectoral strengths and weaknesses in technology, and the degree to which they are similar to those of other countries. We found that, with a few exceptions

Table 6.9. *Sectoral patterns of revealed technological advantage, 1963–8 to 1985–90*

Country/region Period	USA		Japan		Europe*	
	1963–8	1985–90	1963–8	1985–90	1963–8	1985–90
Fine chemicals	0.89	0.97	2.95	0.72	1.34	1.33
Industrial chemicals	0.93	0.98	1.62	0.92	1.29	1.19
Materials	1.04	0.95	1.02	1.42	0.86	0.83
Non-electrical machinery	1.01	0.99	0.77	0.85	0.99	1.13
Motor vehicles	0.89	0.55	0.83	2.21	1.48	1.02
Electrical machinery	1.00	1.01	1.17	1.08	1.00	0.92
Electronic capital goods	1.02	0.97	1.47	1.65	0.92	0.61
Telecommunications	1.03	1.04	1.06	0.97	0.91	0.94
Electronic consumer goods	0.94	0.65	1.99	2.50	1.26	0.59
Raw materials-based technologies	1.08	1.28	0.44	0.37	0.61	0.83
Defence-related technologies	0.99	1.15	0.36	0.09	1.14	1.40

Notes:
* Europe = European Countries in table 6.3 + Austria, Denmark, Ireland, Portugal and Spain.

(Australia, Ireland, Italy, Portugal and the UK), OECD countries have a statistically significant degree of stability in their technological strengths and weaknesses between the 1960s and the 1980s: ten at the 1 per cent level, and a further four at the 5 per cent level, thereby confirming the path-dependent nature of national patterns of accumulation of technological knowledge. We also found very different strengths and weaknesses in Japan, the USA and Western Europe: each is negatively correlated with the other two, and significantly so in two cases out of three (the USA with the other two regions). More generally, countries tend to differ markedly in their patterns of technological specialisation.[19] Less than one fifth are positively and significantly correlated at the 5 per cent level. Amongst these we find FR Germany similar to Switzerland (chemicals and machinery), and Canada similar to Australia, Finland and Norway (raw material-based technologies). Japan has a unique pattern of specialisation, with no significant positive correlations with other countries, but plenty of negative ones.

These international differences in the sectoral patterns of technological accumulation emerge from the localised nature of technological accumulation, and the consequent importance of the local inducement mechanisms that guide and constrain firms along cumulative technological trajectories. We know from earlier debates about the relative importance of 'technology push' and 'demand pull' that these inducement mechanisms are numerous, and that their relative importance varies amongst sectors. It is nonetheless possible to distinguish three mechanisms:

Factor endowments: examples include the stimulus of scarce labour for labour-saving innovations in the USA; and the different technological trajectories followed by the automobile industries of the USA, and of Europe and East Asia, as a consequence of very different fuel prices.

Directions of persistent investment: especially those with strong inter-sectoral linkages: examples include the extraction and processing of natural resources (N. America, Australia and Scandinavia), defence (USA, France, UK), public infrastructure (France) and automobiles (Japan, Germany, Italy).

The cumulative mastery of core technologies and their underlying knowledge bases: examples include Germany in chemicals and machinery, Sweden in machinery, Switzerland in fine chemicals, Netherlands in electronics; Japan in electronics and automobiles; the USA in chemicals and electronics; the UK in chemicals.

The relative significance of these mechanisms change over time. In the early stages, the directions of technical change in a country or region are strongly influenced by local market inducement mechanisms related to scarce (or abundant) factors of production and local investment opportunities. At higher levels of development, the local accumulation of specific technological skills itself becomes a focusing device for technical change. At this stage, firms become less dependent on the home country for creating the appropriate market signals, and more so for its provision of high quality skills and knowledge bases that local firms can exploit on world markets.

4 Conclusions and speculations

Our analysis shows that the technological competitiveness of firms inevitably depends on national systems of innovation, and national systems of innovation inevitably depend on government policy. The level of business-funded R&D is influenced by national policies (e.g, competition, macroeconomics), and also by the behaviour of national institutions (e.g., agencies funding basic research, banks and stock markets, systems of corporate governance).[20] Comparative (or competitive) advantage in high technology markets is not God-given, but made through learning activities reflecting the conscious and interdependent decisions of business firms, national governments and a range of national institutions. As a result, all playing fields are inevitably bumpy, and there would be less technical and economic progress if they were made completely flat.

Nor do we see this state of affairs changing in future. We shall now argue that, based on past experience, private firms' innovative activities will not become globalised, State functions and activities will continue to be essential, national systems of innovation will not converge, and European systems of innovation will be slow to emerge.

4.1 The (continuing) non-globalisation of corporate innovative activities

We do not foresee an even spread of corporate R&D and related technological activities across the world, in spite of the following changes. First, as a result of their increasing technology-based competitiveness, leading Japanese companies (soon to be followed by those from Korea and Taiwan) will increase their foreign production, in part in order to forestall protectionist pressure. As a consequence, Japanese firms' R&D outside Japan will increase, in order to support local production, monitor important foreign sources of science and technology, and respond to pressure from foreign governments. Japan (and later its neighbours) will thus become more like other OECD countries of equivalent importance (USA, Germany), with up to 10 per cent of its corporate R&D outside Japan, compared to about 1 per cent today. Again like companies from these other countries, most of this foreign R&D will be concentrated in relatively few countries.

Second, advances in information technology will increase the possibilities for coordination, monitoring and exchange in routine and codified activities across national boundaries. It may also accentuate the shift towards the international sourcing of routine software production. However, developments in information technology are unlikely to eliminate the need for geographical proximity in the development and launching of major innovations, given the continuing importance of fast decisions to cope with uncertainty, and of the integration of tacit knowledge from different functions – particularly R&D, production and marketing.

Third, large firms may designate certain foreign countries as the world centre in specific product groups and technologies, if there are durable local advantages; but – as the history of the US automobile industry shows – this can create difficulties if such specialisation becomes a barrier to subsequent transfer or integration of technological competencies across national boundaries. In certain cases, large corporations may also shift their headquarters and nationality, if the technology-related advantages of the home base decline enough; but this is merely the movement from dependence on one national system of innovation to another.

Finally, in spite of the increasing talk of 'techno-globalism', there is no strong evidence that most of our firms are consciously re-structuring and internationalisng their innovative activities. Between the early and the late 1980s, large firms did on the whole increase the proportion of their innovative activities performed outside their home country. The increase was biggest for European firms, was concentrated mainly in the USA, and more than half came from mergers and acquisitions. The foreign shares of Japanese and US firms increased much less, and mainly as a result of internal re-deployment, rather than mergers and acquisitions. Within Europe, the trends varied greatly amongst countries. The increases were highest for UK and Swedish[21] firms, where most of the expansion of activity was in the USA, as a consequence of mergers and acquisitions. Firms from all other European countries except Germany and The Netherlands, increased their international technological activities more in Europe than the USA. The increases in foreign shares in German, French and Italian firms were relatively small (Patel, 1995). After these increases, about 60 per cent of our large firms still had no foreign technological activity at the end of the 1980s, about a quarter were active in one or two foreign countries, and only about 15 per cent in more than two (Patel, 1996) – clearly not a process that can reasonably be described as 'globalisation'.

However, since the late 1980s, the shares of European firms' technological activities in the medical and (to a lesser extent electronics) fields in the USA has increased considerably, mainly through local acquisitions, the purpose of which has been to obtain access to the latest advances. It remains to be seen how successful these firms will be in achieving the necessary degree of integration of the (often tacit and person-embodied) skills and know-how in these acquisitions, with the geographically distant remainder of their technological activities.

4.2 The 'Stateless corporation'?

Even Adam Smith's 'night-watchman' state had irreplaceable functions and these will not disappear with the advent of the global corporation. In relation to innovation, there will be continuing need for a state-established framework to monitor and enforce competition, to eliminate negative externalities like pollution and accidents; there will also be the need to provide essential public goods like education, training and basic research. In addition, we are persuaded by the arguments of Hu (1992), that so-called multinational or global corporations are – in terms of their ownership structures and management hierarchies – mostly nationally based corporations, producing and selling in many countries. Understanding and explaining their behaviour requires specific knowledge of their home country, of the host country and of the product markets in which they are active. We would also stress the importance of the technologies in which they are active. For example, we would expect pharmaceutical firms to have very different policies to automobile firms for the international location of R&D, given the importance of linkages to high quality academic research and to national regulatory agencies in the former, and the importance of integration amongst R&D, design, production and marketing in the latter. In particular, we would expect R&D to be much less closely coupled to production in pharmaceuticals than in automobiles.

4.3 Convergence of national systems of innovation?

Nor do we expect national systems of innovation to converge in terms of their capacities to generate a given rate and direction of innovative activities. First, technological (and related managerial) competencies – including imitative ones – take a long time to learn, and are specific to particular fields and to particular inducement mechanisms.[22] As we have seen in section 4.6, sectoral patterns of technological strength (and weakness) persist over periods of at least 20 to 30 years.

Second, the location and rate of international diffusion and imitation of best practice depend (amongst other things) on the cost and quality of the local labour force. With the growing internationalisation of production, firms depend less on any specific labour market and are therefore less likely to commit resources in investment in local human capital. In other words, firms can adjust to local skill (or unskilled) endowments rather than attempt to change them. National policies to develop human capital (including policies to encourage local firms to do so) therefore become of central importance.

Third, education and training systems change only slowly, and are subject to demands in addition to those of economic utility. In addition there may be self-reinforcing tendencies intrinsic in national systems of education, management and finance. For example:

> the British and US structure of human capital, with well-qualified graduates and a poorly educated workforce, allows comparative advantage in sectors requiring this mix of competencies, like software, pharmaceuticals and financial services. The dynamic success of these sectors in international markets reinforces demand for the same mix of competencies. In Germany, Japan and their neighbouring countries, the dynamics will, on the contrary, reinforce demands in sectors using a skilled workforce;

decentralised corporate management systems based on financial controls breed managers in the same mould, whose competencies and systems of command and control are not adequate for the funding of continuous and complex technical change. Firms managed by these systems therefore tend to move out (or are forced out) of sectors requiring such technical change;[23]

the British financial system develops and rewards short-term trading competencies by buying and selling corporate shares on the basis of expectations about yields, whilst the German system develops longer-term investment competencies in dealing with shares on the basis of expected growth. These competencies emerge from different systems of training and experience, and are largely tacit. It is therefore difficult, costly and time-consuming to change from one to the other. And there may be no incentive to do so, when satisfactory rates of return can be found in both activities.

Needless to say, these trends will be reinforced by explicit or implicit policy models which advocate 'sticking to existing comparative advantage', or 'reinforcing existing competencies'.

4.4   A European system of innovation?

Finally, we see few signs of the emergence of a strong European system of innovation. Certainly, responsibility for some of the incentives, pressures and inducement mechanisms set out earlier have been, or are being, transferred from the national to the European level: in particular, competition, trade, regulatory aspects of energy and the environment, and a variety of (sometimes dubious) programmes to fund R&D and related activities in firms (Sharp and Pavitt, 1993). But others are likely to remain stubbornly national: education and training, corporate governance, natural resources, consumers' tastes and defence procurement. Nor are there strong signs of the Europeanisation of scientific and technological activities, more strictly defined. The European Union's share of the total European R&D budget remains very small. R&D networks still tend to be mainly national (Narin, 1992; Hicks *et al.*, 1996), and (with the exception of The Netherlands) business R&D is still mainly performed in the home country.

But as with monetary matters, so with technology. The closest thing to a European system of innovation is likely to be the German system of innovation. Germany alone accounts for more than 40 per cent of all Europe's technological activities (Patel and Pavitt, 1994a). Large firms from other European countries (except the UK) choose Germany as their favourite European location for performing R&D activities. And modified German systems of innovation exist in The Netherlands, Switzerland, Scandinavia and (eventually) the candidate countries of Central Europe, with their emphases on workforce skills, engineers as managers, relational systems of corporate governance, and high levels of both scientific and technological activities (Keck, 1993). We have set out above our reasons for doubting the spread of this (or any other) system to the rest of Europe. But for reasons of European cohesion, economic dynamism and well-being, we would happily be proved wrong.

Notes

This chapter is based on research at the Centre for Science, Technology and Energy and Environment Policy (STEEP), funded by the Economic and Social Research Council (ESRC) within the Science Policy Research Unit, University of Sussex.

1　His main conclusion is also the title of his paper: 'Global corporations are national firms with international operations'.

2　See, for example, Basberg, 1987; Griliches, 1990; Pavitt, 1988; Archibugi and Pianta, 1992.

3　High R&D spending firms with more than 50 per cent of their technological activities performed outside their home countries include AKZO, Nestle, Philips, Racal, ITT, Electrolux, SKF, Solvay, GKN, Wellcome, Roche, Sandoz.

4　An important exception to this general rule was the pharmaceutical industry.

5　See section 3.6 below for countries' relative technological strengths and weaknesses

6　Or, put another way, European firms have not been challenged by Japanese firms in chemicals with the same vigour and success as in electronics.

7　The analyses of Nelson and Arrow implicitly assumed a closed economy. Harry Johnson (1975) later raised the international 'free-rider' problem, and then avoided it by concluding that basic research was a cultural good with no economic utility.

8　By 1990, FR Germany had overtaken the UK in citations per paper, and Japan had amongst the highest rates of increase in papers and citations.

9　See de Tocqueville, 1840; and Rosenberg, 1976.

10　See, in particular, the studies of Brooks, 1995; Faulkner and Senker, 1995; Gibbons and Johnston, 1974; Klevorick *et al.*, 1995; Mansfield, 1995; Rosenberg and Nelson, 1994.

11　According to one eminent engineer, this is done as follows: 'we construct and operate . . . systems based on prior experiences, and we innovate in them by open loop feedback. That is, we look at the system and ask ourselves "How can we do it better?" We then make some change, and see if our expectation of "better" is fulfilled. . . . This cyclic, open loop feedback process has also been called "learning-by-doing", "learning by using", "trial and error", and even "muddling through". Development processes can be quite rational or largely intuitive, but by whatever name, and however rational or intuitive, it is an important research process . . . providing means of improving systems which lie beyond our ability to operate or innovate via analysis or computation' (Kline, 1995, p. 63).

12 But what about the large Dutch companies that perform about half their R&D outside The Netherlands, presumably employing researchers trained mainly with non-Dutch tax-payers' money? See table 6.3.

13 Some analysts have concluded that the OECD countries' levels of productivity stopped converging in the late 1970s. See Soete and Verspragen, 1993.

14 See table 6.7 above. Anglo-German differences can be traced back much further. See Patel and Pavitt, 1989.

15 Preliminary regression analysis based on 165 of these firms, confirms that each firm's R&D intensity (R&D/sales) is influenced significantly by its principal product and its profitability (profits/sales), but not by the share of sales taken by Cost of Funds (CoF/sales).

16 In addition, the UK financial system is likely to be relatively more effective in the arms-length evaluation of corporate R&D investments that are focused on visible, discrete projects that can be evaluated individually – for example, aircraft, oil fields and pharmaceuticals. It will be less effective when corporate R&D consists of a continuous stream of projects and products, with strong learning linkages amongst them – for example, civilian electronics.

17 RTA is defined as a country's or region's (or firm's) share of all US patenting in a technological field, divided by its share of all US patenting in all fields. An RTA of more than one therefore shows a country's or region's relative strength in a technology, and less than one its relative weakness. These measures correspond broadly to the measures of comparative advantage used in trade analyses.

18 For this analysis we use a more detailed breakdown, dividing technologies into 34 fields.

19 Archibugi and Pianta (1992) also show that OECD countries' degree of technological specialisation is increasing over time.

20 See, for example, Chandler (1992) on the US firms and Lawrence (1980) on German managers.

21 According to Häkanson (1992), some Swedish firms' R&D was located elsewhere in Europe as part of a political campaign to join the European Union.

22 See, for example, US strength in chemical engineering, the initial development of which was strongly influenced by the opportunities for (and problems of) exploiting local petroleum resources. See Landau and Rosenberg, 1992.

23 See, for example, Geenen's ITT in the USA, and Weinstock's General Electric Company in the UK (*Economist*, 1995; Chandler, 1992).

References

Abernathy, W. and Hayes, R. 1980. Managing our way to economic decline, *Harvard Business Review*, July/August: 67–77.

Archibugi, D. and Michie, J. (eds.) 1997. *Technology, Globalisation and Economic Performance*, Cambridge, Cambridge University Press.

1998. *Trade, Growth, and Technical Change*, Cambridge, Cambridge University Press.

Archibugi, D. and Pianta, M. 1992. *The Technological Specialisation of Advanced Countries*, Dordrecht, Kluwer Academic Publishers.

Arrow, K. 1962. Economic welfare and the allocation of resources for invention, in Nelson (ed.).

Basberg, B. 1987. Patents and the measurement of technological change: a survey of the literature, *Research Policy*, 16: 131–43.

Bernheim, D. and Shoven, J. 1992. Comparing the cost of capital in the United States and Japan, in Rosenberg *et al.* (eds.).

Brooks, H. 1994. The relationship between science and technology, *Research Policy*, 23: 477–86.

Cantwell, J. 1992. The internationalisation of technological activity and its implications of competitiveness, in Granstrand *et al.* (eds.).

Casson, M. (ed.) 1991. *Global Research Strategy and International Competitiveness*, Oxford, Blackwell.

Chandler, A. 1992. Corporate strategy, structure and control methods in the United States in the 20th century, *Industrial and Corporate Change*, 1: 263–84.

Company Reporting Ltd. 1995. *The 1995 UK R&D Scoreboard*, Edinburgh, Scotland.

de Tocqueville, A. 1840. *Democracy in America*, New York, Vintage Classic edn. 1980.

Dimsdale, N. and Prevezer, M. (eds.) 1994. *Capital Markets and Corporate Performance*, Oxford, Clarendon Press.

Economist (The) 1995. The death of the geenen machine, 17 June: 86–92.

Faulkner, W. and Senker, J. 1995. *Knowledge Frontiers*, Oxford, Clarendon Press.

Freeman, C. 1995. The 'national system of innovation' in historical perspective, *Cambridge Journal of Economics*, 19: 5–24. Reprinted in Archibugi and Michie (eds.) 1997.

Freeman, C., Clark, J. and Soete, L. 1982. *Unemployment and Technical Innovation*, London, Pinter.

Gibbons, M. and Johnston, R. 1974. The roles of science in technological innovation, *Research Policy*, 3: 220–42.

Granstrand, O., Häkanson, L. and Sjolander, S. (eds.) 1992. *Technology Management and International Business*, Chichester, Wiley.

Griliches, Z. 1990. Patent statistics as economic indicators, *Journal of Economic Literature*, 28: 1661–707.

Häkanson, L. 1992. Locational determinants of foreign R&D in Swedish multinationals, in Granstrand *et al.* (eds.).

Hicks, D. 1995. Published papers, tacit competencies and corporate management of the public/private character of knowledge, *Industrial and Corporate Change*, 4: 401–24.

Hicks, D., Izard, P. and Martin, M. 1996. A morphology of Japanese and European corporate networks, *Research Policy*, 23: 359–78.

Hu, Y. S. 1992. Global or transnational corporations are national firms with international operations, *Californian Management Review*, 34: 107–26.

Jaffe, A. 1989. Real effects of academic research, *American Economic Review*, 79: 957–70.

Johnson, H. 1975. *Technology and Economic Interdependence*, London, Macmillan.

Keck, O. 1993. The national system for technical innovation in Germany, in Nelson (ed.).

Klevorick, A., Levin, R., Nelson, R. and Winter, S. 1995. On the sources and significance of inter-industry differences in technological opportunities, *Research Policy*, 24: 185–205.

Kline, S. 1995. *Conceptual Foundations for Multi-Disciplinary Thinking*, Stanford, Stanford University Press.

Landau, R. and Rosenberg, N. 1992. Successful commercialisation in the chemical process industries, in Rosenberg *et al.* (eds.).

Lawrence, R. Z. 1980. *Managers and Management in W. Germany*, London, Croom Helm.

Lundvall, B.-Å. (ed.) 1992. *National Systems of Innovation: Towards a Theory of Innovation and Interactive Learning*, London, Pinter.

Mansfield, E. 1995. Academic research underlying industrial innovations: sources, characteristics and financing, *Review of Economics and Statistics*, 77: 55–62.

Mayer, C. 1994. Stock markets, financial institutions, and corporate performance, in Dimsdale and Prevezer (eds.).

Narin, F. 1992. *National Technology has Strong Roots in National Science*, Haddon Heights, N J, CHI's Research Inc.

Nelson, R. 1959. The simple economics of basic scientific research, *Journal of Political Economy*, 67: 297–306.

Nelson, R. (ed.) 1962. *The Rate and Direction of Inventive Activity*, Princeton, N J, Princeton University Press.

1993. *National Innovation Systems: A Comparative Analysis*, New York, Oxford University Press.

Newton, K., de Broucker, P., McDougal, G., McMullen, K., Schweitzer, T., and Siedule, T. 1992. *Education and Training in Canada*, Ottawa, Canada Communication Group.

OECD various years. *Main Science and Technology Indicators*, Paris, OECD.

Olivastro, D. 1995. *Personal Communication. Based on Data from US Patent Office*, Haddon Heights, N J, CHI Research Inc.

Patel, P. 1995. The localised production of global technology, *Cambridge Journal of Economics*, 19: 141–53. Reprinted in Archibugi and Michie (eds.) 1997.

1996. Are large firms internationalizing the generation of technology? Some new evidence, *IEEE Transactions on Engineering Management*, 43: 41–7.

Patel, P. and Pavitt, K. 1989. A comparison of technological activities in FR Germany and the UK, *National Westminster Bank Quarterly Review*, May: 27–42.

1991. Large firms in the production of the world's technology: an important case of non-globalisation, *Journal of International Business Studies*, 22: 1–21. Reprinted in Granstrand *et al.* (eds.) 1992.

1992. The innovative performance of the world's largest firms: some new evidence, *Economics of Innovation and New Technology*, 2: 77–95.

1994a. Uneven (and divergent) technological accumulation among advanced countries, *Industrial and Corporate Change*, 3: 759–87. Reprinted in Archibugi and Michie (eds.) 1998.

1994b. National innovation systems: why they are important, and how they might be measured and compared, *Economics of Innovation and New Technology*, 3: 77–95.

1997. Technological competencies in the world's largest firms: complex and path-dependent, but not much variety, *Research Policy*, 26: 141–56.

Pavitt, K. 1988. Uses and abuses of patent statistics, in van Raan (ed.).

Porter, M. 1990. *The Competitive Advantage of Nations*, London, Macmillan.

Prais, S. 1993. Economic performance and education: the nature of Britain's deficiencies, London, National Institute of Economic and Social Research, Discussion Paper No. 52.

Rosenberg, N. 1976. Karl Marx on the economic role of science, *Perspectives on Technology*, Cambridge, Cambridge University Press.

Rosenberg, N., Landau, R. and Mowery, D. (eds.) 1992. *Technology and the Wealth of Nations*, Stanford, C A, Stanford University Press.

Rosenberg, N. and Nelson, R. 1994. American universities and technical advance in industry, *Research Policy*, 23: 323–48.

Rothwell, R. 1977. The characteristics of successful innovators and technically progressive firms, *R&D Management*, 7: 191–206.

Science Watch, 1991. World standings in science, 1981–90, January–February: 2: 2.

Sharp, M. and Pavitt, K. 1993. Technology policy in the 1990s: old trends and new realities, *Journal of Common Market Studies*, 31: 129–51.

Soete, L. and Verspagen, B. 1993. Technology and growth: the complex dynamics of catching up, falling behind, and taking over, in Szirmai, van Ark and Pilat (eds.).

Szirmai, A., van Ark, B. and Pilat, D. (eds.) 1993. *Explaining Economic Growth*, Amsterdam, Elsevier.

Teece, D. (ed.) 1987. *The Competitive Challenge: Strategies for Industrial Innovation and Renewal*, Cambridge, MA, Ballinger.

van Raan, A. (ed.) 1988. *Handbook of Quantitative Studies of Science and Technology*, Amsterdam, North-Holland.

Walker, W. 1993. National innovation systems: Britain, in Nelson (ed.).

7 Globalisation and financial diversity: The making of venture capital markets in France, Germany and UK

MICHAEL F. KLUTH AND JØRN
B. ANDERSEN

1 Introduction

Globalisation is widely equated with institutional convergence (Kluth and Andersen, 1996, 1997). Finance is quoted as the first and foremost example of how key economic institutions are conforming to common modes of operation and design across the OECD. This chapter will advance the opposite perspective. Taking various national schemes aimed at promoting the allocation of capital to innovative SMEs as the point of departure, we intend to demonstrate that financial institutions are indeed subject to national trajectories of development even when attempting to cater for new market and/or policy demands.

Europe's lack of ability to create new jobs during the economic upturns of the mid1980s and 1990s has largely been attributed to an inflexible industry structure featuring paramount shortage of new market entrants particularly in the high-technology segment. European financial institutions have been pointed out as a key source of industry structure rigidity. In response a venture capital system, modelled along American lines, has been suggested as the optimal way to ensure capital and managerial skills for European high-technology entrepreneurs and SMEs. Consequently a number of European-level initiatives has been launched, such as 'Euroventures' in the 1980s and 'EASDAQ' in the 1990s, to bring about a functioning venture capital market.

While the venture capital approach has been dominant in political and academic debate, national approaches to eliminate the lack of capital and managerial skills for high-technology entrepreneurs and SMEs have been extremely diverse and display a stronger allegiance to existing institutional set-ups than to the original model operating in the US.

This chapter will investigate various national approaches to the channelling of capital and managerial skills to high-technology entrepreneurs and SMEs. France, Germany and the UK will be subject to scrutiny.

2 The political economy of national innovation systems

Societal complexity, as reflected in the fairly crude description of markets and the State, has in particular been appreciated by the national systems of innovation (NSI) approach. Christopher Freeman's study on Japanese technology policy introduced the concept NSI in modern evolutionary economics (Freeman, 1987).

NSI denotes the structural and institutional factors affecting the manner in which technological and organisational knowledge is created, implemented, applied and diffused into the economy. Production structures and institutions vary between countries and are subject only to gradual changes. The process of change itself will follow national trajectories as institutions are socially embedded. The character of change consequently is evolutionary in the sense that it is a mechanism of mutual adaptation rather than actors engaged in power struggles which constitute the basic dynamics.

NSI both contains tangible and intangible elements. A company's innovative capacity is thus in part determined by its access to the right sources of knowledge, managerial skills and finance. But in addition institutional features in line with what David Soskice has labelled the National Framework of Incentives and Constraints (NFICs) are of vital importance (Soskice, 1991). Soskice advocates that NFICs create distinctive national product markets and innovation strategies for firms. Or to use the words of Dosi and Orsenigo:

[S]ocial rules, inherited norms and attitudes, the laws of organisation of the linkages between and within various groups of economic agents do matter in determining the set of admissible strategies and behaviours, and of observed innovative performances. The specification of the institutional rules constraining individual behaviour becomes therefore a crucial task in the analysis of the patterns of technical change, which accounts for the observed differences across countries within the same technologies. (Dosi and Orsenigo, 1988)

Technology policies in most OECD countries have recently given far greater emphasis to the role of institutions performing bridging, financing and educational functions. The provision of techno-economic framework conditions that enable companies to be at the forefront technology wise, and hence remain competitive in increasingly fierce global markets, is a core component of industrial policy. In light of this growing emphasis, it appears difficult for proponents of the NSI approach to maintain the evolutionary image of institutional development as government policy is increasingly geared towards designing or redesigning institutional properties of national techno-economic framework conditions. Politics is thus a vital – although hitherto ignored – element of national innovation systems.

As argued elsewhere (Kluth and Andersen, 1996; 1997), adaptation strategies in face of pressures for globalisation follow distinct national trajectories. When analysing the workings of markets in countries like France, Germany and the UK, political economists have pointed to the historical specificities of national institutional configurations (e.g., Shonfield, 1965; Katzenstein, 1978; Zysman, 1983).

John Zysman's study of financial systems remains the key institutional political economy contribution to the body of research in the field (Zysman, 1983). He identifies three roads to political-economic management in industrial countries: (1) a State-led path with developmental objectives in which the distribution of costs and gains is imposed by political manipulation of the market; (2) a negotiated path with a corporatist tone in which there are explicit bargains among elites representing segments of society; and (3) a company-led approach with the government acting principally as a regulator and umpire leaving political settlements to the market while providing compensation to uncomplaisant losers. These systems of overall political economic design both determine and are determined by the role and functioning of domestic financial regimes.

National banking systems have been subject to immense pressure due to the deregulation process and the prominence of the free capital movement discourse. The effects of this on individual financial systems have varied as national institutional features have influenced the character of the adaptation process. As will be demonstrated later, German banking consequently does not resemble American or British banking as an outcome of globalisation even though the dominant discourse associated with the globalisation of banking is biased towards British and American styled systems.

Trajectories of institutional development can by and large be attributed to institutional rigidity which in turn is caused by social embeddedness. But institutions may be subject to changes and in any case are to be considered as frameworks for actions for economic and political actors rather than the sole source of development.

Institutions are historically rooted and culturally embedded, consequently their impact on national economic operations extend beyond macro-level economic policy. Institutions can be altered but the direction of change cannot be fully determined in advance and generally institutional properties exhibit a vast element of rigidity.

3 Venture capital: global credit versus national innovation

Advanced economies depend heavily on capital. Since the nineteenth century, banks have been crucial to all industrialised countries for the financing of production. Credit is the lifeblood of a developed economy. Banks lend to entrepreneurs and governments at home and increasingly abroad. Growing interdependence of national financial markets – often denoted globalisation – have prompted several scholars to argue that States no longer have the tools at their disposal to manage their domestic economies so as to accelerate growth and foster structural adaptation. It is the argument of this chapter that the notion of States' diminishing ability to influence credit formation for the financing of economic development is correct only in the sense that it applies to those parts of the national economies which are full-fledged international in scope and able to borrow at the international market. Hence the population of SMEs and entrepreneurs – which in most OECD countries have received increased attention in relation to industrial policies up through the 1980s and 1990s – still rely on financial mechanisms within the realm of national regulatory control. These enterprises are believed to hold the potential for restructuring the West´s mature economies and are seen as major generators of growth in employment (see, e.g., Birch, 1987).

By looking at the financing of enterprises which still depend on national credit institutions, it is possible to discern financial structures which vary from country to country due to historical traditions. Patterns of variation in the manner these domestically oriented financial institutions operate individually and collectively (i.e., the division of labour as regards financing different segments of the firm base) reveal that the globalisation of technology and economic activity does not necessarily lead to convergence.

Venture capital is a key source of long-term funds to SMEs with high growth potential – often referred to as new technology based firms (NTBF). Fast growing companies backed by venture capital produce many new well-paid and highly skilled jobs, and are an important source of applied technological innovation. Consequently venture capital is considered an important instrument assisting in spurring economic growth and industrial renewal by the OECD countries (OECD, 1996).

The operating principles of venture capital may crudely be explained as involving the following: entrepreneurs seeking venture capital present a business plan to venture capitalists. Such a plan provides a detailed account of the product, market, financial statements and projections of the company. This plan serves as a starting point for evaluating a company's potential. Venture capitalists estimate that they invest in only between 1 and 5 per cent of the opportunities presented to them.

Venture capitalists usually work closely with the entrepreneurs who have created the businesses. Banks, pension funds, insurance companies, States and non-financial companies (e.g., private persons, the so-called business angels) are major players. Venture capital financing is broadly defined as progressing through five stages from seed-investment, start-up, expansion, mezzanine and buy-out/buy-in (Prakker, 1988; Harrison and Mason eds., 1996). There is great variation as to at which stage different venture capital funds invest. Most funds specialise in one particular stage and define their strategy according to this. It follows that a particular investor seldom remains as a holder through all stages of a company's development.

It is thus estimated that the average period of investment by venture capitalists is five years in the US and only three to four years in the United Kingdom, whereas it is seven years in Germany. In addition German venture capital firms, which are frequently associated with banks, often continue to hold their shares after an initial public offering (IPO). Another variation from country to country is the length of time from the start-up of a company to initial public offering or acquisition by another operating company. In the US the average length of this process is five to seven years. At the other extreme we find Japan where the average period from start-up to going public is 29 years (OECD, 1996).

At the cross-national level, different patterns can be observed both with regards to the average period of investment by venture capitalists as in the preferred stage of investment. Similarly there are several different types of venture capital organisations that can be categorised according to their management structure, their ownership and the manner in which they raise funds. The OECD uses a three-point classification system as follows:

Independent funds. These are often privately held or publicly listed companies.

Captives. These are venture capital subsidiaries of industrial corporations or financial institutions.

Public sector. These are venture capital organisations which are principally funded from government sources (OECD, 1996).

Each kind can be found in most OECD countries. It is however clear that one type of organisation tends to dominate over the others according to the country in question.

Global venture capital is thus far from homogeneous. Investment is still predominantly domestic in character. Only 13.5 per cent of the total invested by EVCA (European Venture Capital Association) members in 1990 was invested outside the venture capitalist's home countries. This is hardly surprising, as venture fund management requires tacit skills and is ultimately a business learned by making investments within certain industries – often confined to a limited geographical area. Indeed, European venture capital is almost Channel capital: more than 80 per cent of the total pool rest in those four countries bordering the English channel, and heavily dominated by Britain in terms of funds raised. Industry structure differs from nation to nation. There are more firms in the US, but the average size of venture funds is larger in the UK and smaller in the rest of Europe.

About 85 per cent of the capital in the EVCA goes to management buy-outs, buy-ins, LBO and to restructuring and expansion. In a European context the term venture capital is a bit of a misnomer. Traditional concepts such as Merchant capital or business development capital more accurately reflects the investment strategies of Europe's venture funds. Leading industry tracker, *Venture Capital Journal*, thus cautioned readers in December 1989 that there is no accepted definition of venture capital even within a single country, let alone world-wide. It can be quite misleading if one regards European venture funds as classical US style venture capital. Confusion has partly arisen because the venture capital industry is an American invention. Venture capital has its origins in the US and was initially exported both physically and conceptually. Physically a number of American venture funds have established close linkages with new funds in other parts of the world and occasionally even assisted in setting them up. Some American funds have even invested in promising European, Asian and Israeli SMEs. Conceptually venture capital has been regarded by policy makers all over the world as an outstanding method of ensuring funds and managerial skills to particularly high technology entrepreneurs.

The relationship between finance and industry often appears problematic in times of rapid economic and technological change due to increased uncertainty about future market development. Arrow's demonstration that a market economy would tend to underinvest in research and development gives rise to the issue of State intervention. This problem of underinvestment can in essence be conferred back to the concepts of information and risk aversion.

As rapid market changes makes information hazy agents face problems of acquiring adequate information. This produces moral hazard in the sense that both industry and finance becomes more reluctant to make long-term contracts. The usual method of examining the market and making decisions, i.e., *ex ante* behaviour of the market, thus becomes not even approximately valid and may be fatal *ex post* to the decisions taken. This situation tends to be self-perpetuating as the market itself is not able to solve the problem due to asymmetric information among agents, caused by, for example, monopolisation within the market. On the contrary, the number of 'poor risk takers' increases, which again forces banks to claim a higher premium among those remaining firms that have the 'animal spirit', i.e., high risk-taking firms, to stay on the market (Williamson, 1983; Svensson and Ulvenblad, 1995).

Should States compensate for this informational market failure by, e.g., positioning itself as a body of administrative financial guidance like MITI in Japan? Should they try to restore the balance of the market by deregulating and decentralising it as has been done in the US and in England with the Big Bang and the Eurobond Market on a regional level? Or should States opt for a third strategy aiming at developing market institutions in the context of the existing set-up acting as information intermediaries thus reducing uncertainty?

In the following section we look into the ways that Germany, the United Kingdom and France have dealt with the problem of developing national systems ensuring capital, credit and managerial skills to high-technology start-ups and SMEs. Focus is on the broad strategic issues as outlined above. The story of venture capital in Europe will hopefully provide important insights as to how the properties of central institutions in national innovation systems are sought in political struggles.

3.1 Germany

In Germany large banks and insurance companies are the dominant private actors on the venture capital market. In 1994, banks accounted for 55 per cent and insurance companies 12 per cent of Germany's venture capital funds, known as Kapitalbeteiligungsgesellschaften.

Financing innovation increasingly becomes a strategic edge for banks as it means creating a clientele for future banking services. However, as the OECD stipulates, the capacity of a financial system to back innovation depends on its own capacity to adjust and innovate (OECD, 1994).

Traditionally banks apply methods for assessing companies solvency by quantitative means employing different kinds of processes like cash flow or track record analysis (comparison of consecutive annual reports). Today these methods, relying exclusively on financial reports, are considered unreliable in relation to NTBFs. Qualitative methods are currently gaining ground in relation to valuation of risks. Qualitative assessments reveal more information about the enterprise than financial figures. Importance is attached to management, customer base and organisation.

German banks especially have engaged in new modes of improving assessment capabilities in relation to innovative projects. At the national level Deutsche Bank has recently established a new venture capital subsidiary for innovative technology-based firms. Although Deutsche Bank possess vast internal human resources it has decided to employ external scientists and technologists from the Fraunhofer Society (FhG) to support the task of technological appraisal. This rather neatly sets the stage for the German version of venture capital. Large organisations, be they private or public, engage in long-term collaboration in order to address new problems.

The German federal system is characterised by a complex division of labour between the Federal and Länder governments. One of the areas in which Länders have their own responsibilities is technology policy. Hence, it is instructive to look at the approaches employed to ensure finance and managerial skills to NTBFs at the Länder level.

Bavaria is a good case in point. Bavaria has undergone rapid economic development during the last 40 years. Only 15–20 years ago Bavaria was considered an agricultural economy with little industry. Today Bavaria hosts several of Germany's high-tech companies and can be said to have jumped from agriculture to a high-tech information-based society, and thus skipped the traditional period of industrial development. As such one could expect that the problem of financing technology-based firms would be a particular problem in Bavaria, as they have limited tradition and time to develop models for dealing with the special aspects of financing innovation and high-tech projects. This seems, however, not to be the case.

The Bavarian response to bridging the so-called 'equity-gap' for high-tech start-ups has notably been through the technology service organisation called Ostbayerisches Technologie Transfer Institut (OTTI) which is a network of technology transfer institutes. It is a non-profit organisation established in 1977. The foundation was laid at a time when the Federal Ministry for Research and Development gave money to the establishment of technology transfer organisations all over Germany. The concept behind OTTI was formulated by Regensburg's chamber of commerce for trade and industry in concert with a number of other local actors. In 1989 OTTI counted 548 members consisting of 447 companies, several private persons, 45 different financial institutions and officials from the Länder government, all represented in the steering committee.

In 1989 OTTI took, in close cooperation with 31 local banks and Sparekassen, the initiative to set-up a venture capital fund called ReFIT Gmbh and Co. KG. The establishment of ReFIT was based on the experiences OTTI had built up through its involvement with technology advice in relation to R&D projects in Bavarian firms. Companies receive financial guidance at ReFIT as well as comprehensive advice on all kinds of technical problems. At ReFIT companies get: financial support at the expansion stage that requires large amounts of capital and access to people with practical experience in assisting and running start-ups or SMEs. The firm owner continues as firm director and there are no requirements as to collateral or other financial guarantees. Lastly, while ReFIT gets a share of firm profits, ReFIT also gives financial assistance in cases of loss. Finally, ReFIT is in principle open to all persons wishing to start up technology-based firms and existing companies which are R&D oriented in addition to smaller enterprises at an early stage of development counting less than ten employees (Clement, 1994).

Other regional venture capital funds such as Innotec GmbH and Bayern Kapital Risikobeteiligungsgesellscaft, also cooperate with local Sparkassen, banks, chambers of commerce, the Bavarian Ministry of Economic Affairs, and local RTOs like OTTI. The issue of risk assessment is approached by knitting a close meshed network of locally based technologists, consultants, technology parks, technology transfer agencies, public liaison officers, etc., which are consulted *ad hoc* or with short notice in an informal manner. However, as these networks suffer from the limited range of expertise to be found locally, they are trying to link up with supraregional – and eventually international – networks of external experts for technology appraisal. In response FhG has set up a regional one-stop shop service that is currently being tested (Interview in Munich, 1996).

Similar models for financing can be found in other parts of Germany. For instance a networking model around technology transfer organisations, banks, local chambers of commerce and the Länder government also operates in Baden-Württemberg, where the technology transfer organisation Steinbeis-Stiftung utilises its vast know-how on technology projects in close cooperation with local representatives of the financial community, etc.

Although Bavaria and Baden-Württemberg do not amount to all of Germany, they bear witness to the operations of the country's venture capital industry. Looking at the adjusted percentage in the grand total of R&D in Germany, it appears that more than half of total public R&D expenditures are made by Federal government. Of the remaining (i.e., regional) more than half are performed by the three Länder Bavaria, Baden-Württemberg and Nordrhein-Westfalen (MERIT, 1993, appendix). Given that venture capital tend to cluster and concentrate in areas dominated by above-average national level of R&D performance and innovative start-ups, it seems likely that the bulk of the institutional ramifications of venture capital operations in Germany can be deduced from these three Länders. In other words, Bavaria and Baden-Württemberg may be seen as the equivalent to California, New York or Massachusetts in the U.S where almost two-thirds of that country's venture capital pool is concentrated (OECD, 1996).

It is estimated that only half a dozen classic US style venture capital firms exist in Germany and the venture capital industry is dominated by former bank credit managers (Bygrave and Timmons, 1992). Despite the recent expansion of the German venture market it is still relatively small compared to the overall size of the economy with cumulative investment equivalent to about 0.2 per cent of GDP compared with over 1 per cent in the UK – it in addition remains entirely focused on German investment opportunities. A number of factors hamper the development of German venture capital. Firstly, traditional lenders have tended to regard venture capital as a competitive threat. Secondly, firms show reluctance to provide outside investors with information concerning firms' objectives and financial standing. This attitude persists and is aligned to the belief among German firms that their *raison d'être* is to generate cash surpluses in order to remain in business, rather than maximising profit for distribution among shareholders. In sum particularly Mittelstand firms harbour considerable aversion to external equity investors (Abbott and Hay, 1995).

Today the recipients of venture capital are largely Mittelstand firms which are politically and economically quite powerful in Germany. Perhaps as a consequence of Mittelstand reservations, two major methods for capital investment are employed: a direct investment in equity, or an investment using a stille beteiligung – or silent partnership. The two methods are often combined. While equity investment is basically the same as in the UK, the silent partnership is unique to Germany. An essential feature of silent partnership is that it allows venture capital funds to make large investments in firms without becoming active majority shareholders.

Accordingly evidence suggests that the German venture capital industry is developing in a manner which is both more flexible and more closely attuned to the needs of its customers than elsewhere in Europe. In addition, the dominant role played by the bank-owned venture capital groups, supported by the Länder banks, is leading to quicker integration of the industry into the financial infrastructure of the country (Abbott and Hay, 1995).

The main problems of this model *vis-à-vis* SME financing is the issue of cost! Intimate relations between banks and industry are fairly time consuming and hence expensive to operate. A minimum of scale economies needs to be applied by banks subject to resource scarcity in terms of manpower. By joining up with multiple regional actors such as Research and Technology Organisations (RTOs), Chambers of Commerce and other financial institutions banks partially escape the costs of extending the intimate bank–industry relations from the corporate to the SME level.

Venture capital in Germany is thus used as a device to strengthen basic features of the political economy rather than changing it. The so-called 'Mittelstand' constituting German SMEs in manufacturing have traditionally been tied to the corporate sector through intimate supplier networks conducive for strong user–producer linkages. Yet many Mittelstand firms have had to operate in a fairly volatile business environment as users of their products may abandon them since they rarely enjoy mutual ownership links as is the case in the corporate sector.

3.2 The United Kingdom

The dominant organisational design of UK venture capital is that of independent funds. An independent fund may be the offspring of corporations, insurance companies, pension funds or wealthy individuals.

In the UK context mechanisms bridging entrepreneurs with the venture capitalist are widely considered a prerequisite for a well-functioning venture capital market. The way that entrepreneurs gain access to the venture capitalist is through an intermediary, such as a banker or acquaintances providing introductions to venture capitalists. Entrepreneurs relying on intermediaries have better chances of finding funding. Professional intermediaries who are familiar with investors criteria also serve a valuable role to the venture capitalist as a first filer of deals. The system of networking through intermediaries is aided by and results from the geographical clustering of entrepreneurial firms and their venture capitalists. In some instances public agencies may act as intermediaries, most notably by establishing networks which match individual investors with entrepreneurs. The way that venture capitalists maintain their visibility with the intermediaries who present them with deals is often through an informal network of contacts. Seen through these lenses UK venture capital is really not about capital but about having the right addresses, in the sense that without a well-established networking mechanism to convey the right information there will be limited basis for a venture capital market.

Hence in contrast to Germany informal private investors commonly referred to as business angels play a greater role in the British venture capital market. We will consequently focus upon this kind of investor in order to capture the institutional setting of British venture capital. Different studies of informal investors reveal that the typical profile of the business angel is that they are almost exclusively male and mostly middle aged. They are highly educated and generally in business or engineering disciplines. The vast majority are experienced in business: many are themselves successful entrepreneurs; others are high-income business professionals, e.g., accountants, consultants, lawyers and senior executives in large companies often with a golden handshake (Harrison and Mason, 1996). Most business angels are experienced investors and prefer to act independently. Confident in their own ability to make good decisions they rely more on instincts than formal research. The task of matching entrepreneurs with investors – bridging – is handled by informal networks of trusted friends and business associates. Personal networks thus serve as the main information channels through which business angels identify investment opportunities. Accountants are the most frequent referral source of information on investment opportunities, and studies suggest that the informal venture capital market in the UK is at least twice as important to the SME sector as formal venture capital (Hermer *et al.*, 1995).

Activity in the informal venture capital market is somewhat invisible. Business angels are not listed in any directories, there are no public records for their investments and many have a passion for anonymity. Nevertheless, studies in the UK indicate that a majority of informal investors are dissatisfied with their referral sources and believe that there is a need for improved channels of communication. The fragmented nature of informal venture capital markets has been described as a giant game of hide-and-seek with everyone blindfolded (Gaston, 1989). One of the British ways to overcome the sources of information asymmetry between entrepreneurs and informal investors is by the establishment of business angel networks (BANs). Examples of BANs seem first and foremost to be found in Canada, the US and the UK. While BANs are found on both sides of the Atlantic, at least one important difference can be observed with regards to their mode of operation. Business angels in the US thus often invest as a part of a syndicate in which there is typically a key individual – an archangel – who brings the syndicate together by referring the deal to friends, business associates or relatives. This type of networking or syndicated investments is rarely encountered in the UK (Harrison and Mason ed., 1996).

There are two types of BANs in the UK, those operating locally and those operating nationally. In the UK, most BANs are operated by Training and Enterprise Councils and Business Links. Yet, more than one-third of the UK's BANs operate nationally, the majority of which are private sector operations. Two newer such examples are the established networks of NatWest Angels Network, operated by the National Westminster Bank plc, and VentureNet, which is a subsidiary of Enterprise Support Group, a private sector business consultancy firm. BANs typically operate through the publication of investment bulletins containing descriptions of companies seeking capital which are circulated among investors registered with the network.

Evaluations of BANs in the UK are mixed as to their rate of success. Some suggest a growing success of this type of organisation of informal venture capital. Other studies point to the fact that BANs have had limited success in terms of attracting investors, achieving awareness amongst active and potential investors, entrepreneurs, etc.

Two aspects seem important in this respect. First, BANs require long-term funding for marketing in order to accumulate a critical mass of investors and entrepreneurs and to establish credibility. Second, the geographical context is important as BANs are most successful in, or close to, major population centres and regions with significant captive venture capital fund activity and high concentrations of 'high-tech' firms – as around Cambridge and Oxford Universities, where notably Cambridge Science Park constitutes such an area.

Networking between BANs, particularly between local and national ones, seem to be a viable solution to the problem of accumulating a critical mass of investors and entrepreneurs, thereby improving the probability of successful matches.

A major problem for the BAN approach is that evidence suggests that they cannot be operated on a full cost-recovery scale. The main source of revenue for BANs is the subscription fees levied on firms and investors. However, subscribers are not likely to be willing to pay more than £200–£300, thus the amount of revenue that can be generated from subscription fees is limited and insufficient to cover the full operating costs of the service. Thus, BANs have had to rely on government funding, or, in its absence, sponsorship from the corporate sector and their host organisations (Universities and Chambers of Commerce). The UK government has partly chosen to support some BANs as a way to develop a networking component into the British venture capital market. The financial commitment required to support BANs is minuscule compared with the costs of alternative strategies for closing the equity gap. The key to developing BANs is to achieve high visibility and credibility in the local/regional business community, e.g., by conference arrangements of all kinds for professional and civic organisations, developing networks with organisations that can be a source of high-quality referrals and maximising public relations opportunities that will lead to articles in newspapers and magazines and coverage on TV and Radio.

Institutional capital is naturally also, as indicated above, engaged in the UK venture capital industry. National Westminster Bank has developed a complex scheme called New Technologies Appraisal Service. Nat West's Service uses external technology or marketing experts which provide advice and guidance both for bankers and managers of affected enterprises. NatWest regards the establishing of an external network of experts as a cheap and fast way for appraising innovative businesses while minimising risks. Although this strategy resembles that of major German banks it is notable that the UK bank first and foremost justifies the move on grounds of cost efficiency (Hermer *et al.*, 1995). Another trend separating the behaviour of UK institutional actors from their German counterparts follows the focus on individuals as implied in the BAN approach. While German venture capital participants emphasise technological viability, personal qualities are of importance in the UK. As part of a risk assessment programme the Yorkshire Enterprise Ltd has thus suggested psychometric testing and personality profiling techniques.

The British BAN model as outlined above places banks, SMEs and public agencies in distinct political economy segments from which they venture forth to meet as autonomous bargaining partners. As such it introduces a strong network component, the character of which is a function of institutional properties, such as, for example: trust relations, societal perception (group versus individual), and notions of public authority.

In sum the British approach for introducing venture capital relies on market dynamics allowing for State intervention only in relation to perceived market failures. While a number of successful funds operate in the high-tech corridors connecting Oxford, Cambridge and London, a national twist has been added to the original American formula in that some of the virtues of Merchant Banking, involving specialised engagements in high risk sectors not encompassing a technological dimension, are replicated under the flashy 'Venture Capital' heading.

3.3 France

The present surge of venture capitalism in Europe is the second attempt to develop such an industry. Previous efforts were made in the early 1960s by the then General Doriot. The success of ARD in the US led to the establishment of the European Enterprises Development Company S.A (EED), with offices in Luxembourg and Paris. Its array of investors included: Aktiebolaget (Sweden), Banco Español, Banque Nationale pour le Commerce de Paris, Continental International Finance Corporation (Chicago), Credit Lyonnais, Dresdner Bank A.G., Lehman Brothers, Morgan Guarantee International Finance Corporation, Rotterdamsche Bank N.V., Société Générale (Paris), M.M. Worms and Cie (Paris) (Bygrave and Timmons, 1992).

Nowadays the French approach to problems of financing innovation among SMEs is more along the traditional lines of French industrial politics. Beyond high-profile national champions, French State efforts to palliate for an insufficiently supportive banking sector extend to SMEs. The report on SMEs of the Industrial Commission of the Xth Plan could, in the words of Jonah D. Levy, just as easily have been titled problems of SME financing. Reading more like a banking analysis than an industrial analysis, it focuses almost exclusively upon the various handicaps that French SMEs suffer in their quest for investment capital (Levy, 1994). The planning document puts forward a lot of proposals ranging from reform of inheritance and transmission taxes to the stimulation of venture capital and unsecured stock markets targeted at SMEs. Additionally, each of the four prime ministers during the second Mitterand term has put forward some kind of plan to boost the financial position of French SMEs.

On top of these general measures on behalf of SMEs, a variety of State programmes emerged to channel capital to SMEs at critical moments in their development. One such programme is the SOFARIS which is the French company for venture capital insurance. SOFARIS is a financial institution (government controlled corporation) which was set up in 1982 with the support of the government, the financial and banking community and existing agencies offering some sort of venture capital insurance in order to unite and manage most of the guarantee funds existing at that time.

The mission of SOFARIS is to manage the government financed guarantee funds used to assume some of the risk connected with granting loans and owner's equity contributions to SMEs. SOFARIS manages about ten funds which try to meet the overall needs of SMEs and focus particularly on three important stages in the life of enterprises: start-up, development and transfer. Over the past ten years SOFARIS has guaranteed more than FF 40 billion where 63 per cent went to development stages in SMEs. The basic principles of SOFARIS is that the application for a loan is submitted by the lending bank. The decision to grant the loan is made by the bank, subject to approval by the regional office of the SOFARIS for amounts up to FF 2 million. Above this amount, the decision is made by the regional officer of the SOFARIS, and in the case of very large proposals, by the SOFARIS' directorate general (OECD, 1995, p. 28). SOFARIS is thus essentially a hierarchically ordered organisation resembling traditional French State agencies.

The French State has clearly been the driving force in identifying the problems of capital allocation to innovative SMEs and consequently attempted to devise a solution through the instruments traditionally employed in national economic management. Once again the central planning institutions of the Republic, embedded in the offices and grand corps of finance and the première, 'crowd out' the policy arena thus leaving all other potential actors passive in anticipation of central initiatives.

4 European venture capital: the politics of institutional adaptation

Institutional import is a tricky business as it has been recognised by policy and business communities alike in the world's most well-established political economies. Venture capital has its roots in an institutional setting in which a Product Market Rationale has enjoyed relative supremacy. As in the case of the Merchant Banks of London, which developed in response to the needs of special financial services of UKs international traders, the founding and growth of UK venture capital has been in response to a need for special financial services in the technologically most innovative regions of the country. Essentially venture capital is in itself an institutional adaptation as it introduces some of the micro-level virtues of the money market rationale into political economies dominated by the product market rationale. Close finance–industry relations based on a mutual sense of purpose (engineers wanting to make money) stretching over a fairly long time span was what was needed by firms (SMEs) engaged in industries with high R&D spending and market volatility.

Transferring such a system naturally proved easier to countries already exhibiting a strong product market rationale as is the case in the UK. The UK have led the European surge in raising and establishing venture capital funds since the 1980s. And the maturation of the industry in Europe by the end of the 1980s was most evident in the UK. France mimicked the UK pattern in about three years with little success and two or three years later Germany followed with banks dominating the scene.

However there are pervasive differences in the way business is conducted in various European countries. The highly selective, educational systems and cultures of France and the decentralised and negotiated patterns of economic management in Germany have produced networks of relationships at the top of the financial business and government institutions that are unparalleled in the UK. Institutional infrastructures drawing on economic, administrative and political culture thus assist in replicating core features of economic regimes even when erecting entirely new business systems.

In conclusion even the most global of industries – finance – essentially subdued national preferences on institution design when responding to new demands spurred by 'international' developments. The dynamics of national institutional development are essentially political. Although informed by institutionalised norms and ideals coming out of social (economic) practice, the rigidity of national configurations should not be overestimated. National systems consequently exhibit varying levels of stability. France thus seems prone to radical change while Britain and Germany display a more harmonic development.

References

Abbot, S. and Hay, M. 1995. *Investing for the Future, New Firm Funding in Germany, Japan, the UK and the USA*, London, Pitman Publishing.
Archibugi, D. and Michie, J. 1995. The globalisation of technology: a new taxonomy, *Cambridge Journal of Economics*, 19: 121–40. Reprinted in Archibugi and Michie (eds.).
Archibugi, D. and Michie, J. (eds.) 1997. *Technology, Globalisation and Economic Performance*, Cambridge, Cambridge University Press.
Ash, A. and Hausner, J. (eds.) 1997. *Beyond Market and Hierarchy – Interactive Governance and Social Complexity*, Cheltenham, Edward Elgar.

Birch, D. 1987. *Job Creation in America*, New York, Free Press.

Blake, J. 1994. Venture capital fund structures in Europe, venture capital – Special Paper, EVCA, Zaventem.

Borrus, M. 1993. The architecture of the supply-base, BRIE Working Paper, Berkeley.

Bygrave, W. D. and Timmons, J. A. 1992. *Venture Capital at the Crossroads*, Boston, Harvard Business School Press.

Carsten, J. and Torfing, J. 1995. *Nyere statsteories: status og perspektiver*, Aalborg, Aalborg Universitetsforlag.

Chesnais, F. 1993. The French national system of innovation, in Nelson (ed.).

Clement, K. 1994. *Regional Policy and Technology Transfer: A Cross National Perspective*, Glasgow, European Research Centre.

Department of Trade and Industry (UK) 1994. *Business Link – Prospectus for One stop shops for business*, London.

Dosi, G. and Orsenigo, L. 1988. Industrial structure and technical change, in Heertje (ed.).

Dosi, G. *et al.* (eds.) 1988. *Technical Change and Economic Theory*, London, Frances Pinter.

Dyrberg, T. and Torfin, J. 1995. Politik og institutioner, in Carsten and Torfing (eds.)

Edquist, C. and Johnson, B. 1997. Institutions and organisations in systems of innovation, in Edquist (ed.).

Edquist, C. (ed.) 1997. *Systems of Innovation: Technologies, Institutions and Organisations*, London, Pinter.

Ergas, H. 1986. Does technology policy matter?, CEPS Paper 29 (Centre for European Policy Studies), Brussels.

Freeman, C. 1987. *Technology Policy and Economic Performance: Lessons from Japan*, London, Pinter.

   1996. History, co-evolution and economic growth, Unpublished paper, MERIT/SPRU.

Gaston, R. J. 1989. *Finding Private Venture Capital for Your Firm*, New York, John Wiley & Sons.

Gren, B. (ed.) 1995. *Risky Business – An Anthology of Findings and Reflections from the Risk Research Project in Sweden 1991–1994*, Stockholm, Akademitryck-AB Edsbruk.

Harrison, R. and Mason, C. (eds.) 1996. *Informal Venture Capital – Evaluating the Impact of Business Introduction Services*, London, Prentice Hall.

Heertje, A. (ed.) 1988. *Innovation, Technology and Finance*, Oxford, Blackwell.

Hermer, J., Kulicke, M., Harrison, R. and Bannock, G. 1995. Innovation Financing: Private Investors, Banks and Technology Appraisal, Draft Background Paper for European Innovation Monitoring System (EIMS) – Innovation Policy Workshop, Luxembourg.

Howells, J. and Michie, J. (eds.) 1997. *Technology, Innovation and Competitiveness*, Cheltenham, Edward Elgar.

Katzenstein, P. 1978. *Between Power and Plenty: Foreign Economic Policies of Advanced Industrial Countries*, Madison, WI, University of Wisconsin Press.

1985. *Small States in World Markets*, Ithaca, NY, Cornell University Press.

Kluth, M. F. and Andersen, J. B. 1996. The globalisation of European research and technology organisations, in Ash and Hausner (eds.) 1997.

1997. Pooling the technology base?, in Howells and Michie (eds.).

Levy, J. 1994. After étatisme: dilemmas of institutional reform in post-dirigiste France, final chapter in *Toqueville's Revenge: Dilemmas of institution building in Post-dirigiste France*, Political Science Department, University of California, Berkeley.

Lundvall, B.-Å. 1988. Innovation as an interactive process: user–producer relations, in Dosi *et al.* (eds.).

Meek, R. L. 1967. *Economics and Ideology and Other Essays*, London, Chapman & Hall.

MERIT 1993. *Technology Policy in Eight European Countries: A Comparison*, Maastricht.

Ministry of Business and Industry/Danish Agency for Development Trade and Industry 1995. *Teknologisk service*, Copenhagen.

Nelson R. (ed.) 1993. *National Innovation Systems. A Comparative Perspective*, Oxford, Oxford University Press.

OECD 1992. *TEP – The Technology Economy Programme – Technology and the Economy: The Key Relationships*, Paris.

1994. National systems for financing innovation, Draft Document of the TIP (Technology and Innovation Policy) Working Group, Paris.

1995. *Best Practice Policies – for Small and Medium Sized Enterprises*, Paris.

1996. *Financial Market Trends*, 63.

Prakker, F. 1988. The financing of technical innovation, in Heertje (ed.).

Reinert, E. 1994. Competitiveness and its predecessors – A 500 year cross national perspective, Paper presented at the Nordic Innovation Network Conference, Copenhagen.

Shonfield, A. 1965. *Modern Capitalism*, London, Pickering & Chatto Ltd.

Skocpol, T. 1979. *States and Social Revolutions*, Cambridge, Cambridge University Press.

Soskice, D. 1991. The institutional infrastructure for international competitiveness: A comparative analysis of the UK and Germany, Unpublished Paper (Berlin).

Streeck, W. 1992. *Social Institutions and Economic Performance*, London, Sage Publications.

Svensson, K. and Ulvenblad, P. O. 1995. Management of bank loans to small firms in a market with asymmetric information. An integrated concept, in Gren (ed.).

Sweeney, G. 1985. *Innovation Policies: An International Perspective*, London, St. Martin Press.

Tönnies, F. 1972. *Gemeinschaft und Gesellschaft: Grundbegriffe der reinen Soziologie*, Darmstadt, Wissenschaftliche Buchgesellschaft.

Walker, W. 1993. National innovation systems. Britain, in Nelson (ed.).

Weegloop, P. 1996. Innovation, firm strategy and government policy: why and how should they be linked, Ph.D.-afhandlinger, Rosklide.

Williamson, O. E. 1983. *Markets and Hierarchies*, New York, Free Press.
Zysman, J. 1983. *Governments, Markets and Growth*, Ithaca, Cornell University Press.
1993. Trade, technology and national competition, restricted paper presented at the first meeting of the working group on Innovation and Technology Policy, OECD, Paris.

8 Patterns of national specialisation in the global competitive environment

PAOLO GUERRIERI

1 Introduction

National environments differ in their capability of stimulating, facilitating or preventing innovative activities of firms, and historically national economies and their institutional set-up have had a considerable influence on the firms' competitive success. A vast recent literature by formulating the concept of the 'national system of innovation' has confirmed that the structural characteristics of a national economy, such as its specific production structure, its technical infrastructure and other institutional factors, can strongly influence firms' innovative performances (Freeman and Soete, 1997; Lundvall ed., 1992; Nelson ed., 1993; Edquist ed., 1997). It has been shown that differences in national systems are particularly important between the United States, Japan and the EU, and between the European countries themselves.

The concept of national specificities determining national performance, however, has been recently challenged on the grounds that the current wave of globalisation and sophistication of financial markets are aligning national economies. The growing role of transnational corporations (TNCs) in the current global competitive phase, as many point out, is changing the face of the world economy in the direction of standardisation and convergence of national structures and performances. A few even predict that the nation state will soon be obsolete and that national diversities, that were very important in the past, are likely to disappear in the near future. The limiting case would be of a fully transnational economy without any residual disparities across countries (Ohmae, 1990).

This chapter assesses the issue of the linkage between globalisation and national specificities by looking at the dynamics of world trade and trade specialisation of major economies. It is divided into four sections. As pointed out, there is no doubt that a major trend toward globalisation of

139

economic activity is under way: the more advanced countries have become more interdependent through the internationalisation of production, the spread of multinational corporations and the booming of capital mobility. This has had a major impact on the dynamics of the world trading relations. The first part assesses these radical changes in the world trading environment. The second important issue is related to the impact of the globalisation of economic activity on trade specialisation and performances at the national level. In the past the firms and sectors integrated within the world trade displayed in general very different national specialisation patterns to cope with the challenge of structural competitiveness at world level (Archibugi and Pianta, 1992; Guerrieri and Tylecote, 1997). By using an original database and a conceptual framework where inter-industry differences are very important in shaping national specificities, the second and third sections try to assess the extent to which these differences in trade specialisation between the EU, Japan and the United States, and between European countries themselves, are still important and play a significant role during the current globalisation phase. In the final section, the chapter's main findings are summarised and some overall implications are drawn.

2 The world trading environment in the global phase

Over the past decade, globalisation has exerted a significant influence on the evolution of world trading relations, with relevant implications for international competition at country and firm level. In this respect, three facts could be stressed: (i) the simultaneous rise in foreign direct investment and trade; (ii) the changing structure of world trade; (iii) the increasing regionalisation of trade flows.

At the level of the world market, a first important trend is the extraordinary rise in capital mobility, and especially of foreign direct investment. Cross-over foreign direct investments (FDI) between Europe and the US, between Japan and the US, and, to a lesser degree, between Japan and Europe, has increased sharply. But also FDI related to developing economies has increased substantially. In the second half of the 1980s overall FDI grew at an average annual rate of more than 24 per cent, compared with 14.3 per cent for exports of goods and non-factor services, and 10.8 for GDP at factor cost. During the first half of the current decade the annual growth rate of FDI has been smaller (12,7 per cent), but it has still remained significantly above those of world exports (3,8 per cent) and GDP (4,3 per cent) (UNCTAD, 1996).

The surge of FDI as an important device for organising production and distribution has been accompanied by new linkages with trade flows. Foreign direct investment and trade in goods and services are becoming

Table 8.1. *Weights of the sectoral groups in total exports**

	1970	1979	1991	1995	Change in the share 1995 to 1970
Food items	9.8	8.0	5.2	4.6	−5.3
Fuels	6.5	14.8	6.8	4.7	−1.7
Other raw materials	2.9	1.8	1.0	0.9	−2.0
Food industries	7.2	6.2	5.7	5.5	−1.7
Resource intensive	10.1	9.2	7.2	6.6	−3.5
Agricultural P. and raw					
materials	*36.5*	*40.0*	*25.8*	*22.2*	*−14.2*
Traditional	14.9	14.5	16.9	16.8	1.9
Scale-intensive	24.7	23.0	25.2	25.0	0.3
Specialised suppliers	10.9	9.2	10.4	10.5	−0.4
Science-based	9.5	10.9	18.9	21.5	12.1
Manufactures	*60.0*	*57.6*	*71.4*	*73.8*	*13.9*
Others	*3.6*	*2.4*	*2.8*	*3.7*	*0.1*

Note:
*Average value in each sub-period (in percentage).
Source: SIE, World Trade Data Base (see Guerrier: and Milana, 1988, pp. 192 and 206, note 6).

increasingly interrelated and to a certain extent they complement each other. On the other hand, the rise of FDI and TNCs has meant that a large share of world trade is accounted for by the exchange of goods and services within a single firm and/or a corporate network based in different countries. Thus a significant proportion of world trade is conducted on the basis of corporate strategies that may or may not conform to the rules of the market.

Another evident sign of the globalisation of economic activity has been the change in the structure of the world trade, together with the overall increase in the share of trade in world output, that has continued and accelerated in all major groupings of economies. The weight of manufactured products has increased over the past decade to cover more than 73 per cent of world trade, and conversely there has been a fall in the share of agricultural products and raw materials (table 8.1). For the world as a whole the increase of nearly 14 percentage points in the share of manufactured products in total world exports between 1985 and 1995 has been compensated for by a corresponding drop in the share of primary products.

The growth of trade and manufactured exports is the result of several factors, such as recent liberalisation trends and the opening up of new areas for investment in many countries and regions, as in the case of the NICs in Asia. A sign of that is the slight increase, in the more recent period, of the share of *traditional* labour-intensive industries (such as garments, furniture, shoes, etc.) in the world trade of manufactures.

The dramatic acceleration of technological progress has also played an important role, through: (i) the drastic decrease of the costs of information and communication; (ii) the increasing range of product and process innovations requiring new specialisations and exchange of goods and services; (iii) the increasingly high cost of R&D and fixed costs, that encourages the search for new foreign markets.

Among the manufactured exports, the shares of *scale-intensive* and *specialised suppliers* have stayed about the same, while that of *science-based* exports has increased more than twice, from 9.5 percentage points by 1970 to more than 21 percentage points by 1995.

Thus, there has been an evident shift towards industrial sectors characterised by higher technological content, since *science-based* goods are related in that they embody either directly, or indirectly, through the intermediate goods used in their production, relatively intensive research and development inputs (Scherer, 1992). Other common features are equally important in shaping the competitive advantage of firms in the production and trade of high-technology goods (OECD, 1992; Scherer, 1982): (i) the cumulative effect of innovative advantage, characterised by steep learning curves and significant dynamic economies of scale; (ii) the capability of generating positive external economies, in terms of hard-to-appropriate spillovers from one activity to another; (iii) strategic oligopolistic environments, in which small numbers of large interdependent companies compete through trade and transnational investment.

In industries with these characteristics, the relative advantage of one country *vis-à-vis* others stems not only from differences in national factor endowments, but as theory suggests and empirical evidence confirms, is also largely a function of differential technological knowledge and capability, which are created and reproduced through time. This has several implications for the competitiveness of countries and firms as shown in the next section.

Finally the rise in regional integration is another fundamental trend that has accompanied the globalisation of economic activity and has significantly influenced world trading relations. Three regional groupings have emerged: (i) Europe, with the development of the Single European Market and the European Economic Space; (ii) North America, with the admission of Mexico into a North American Free Trade Area; (iii) and Asia, including Japan and the NICs of different generations.

As is well known, there are no objective criteria to evaluate the economic role of regional groupings. Despite the increasing attention devoted in

Table 8.2. *Shares of intra-regional trade of the three regional groupings (percentage)*

	IMPORT			EXPORT		
	1970	1985	1995	1970	1985	1995
EUROPE*						
Towards						
NAFTA	12.3	9.1	9.1	9.6	11.3	7.8
ASIA	3.6	6.7	10.4	3.5	4.5	8.1
EUROPE	**64.6**	**65.8**	**69.6**	**70.3**	**68.0**	**70.2**
ASIA*						
Towards						
NAFTA	28.3	21.6	19.1	32.1	37.3	25.2
ASIA	**30.0**	**40.2**	**51.5**	**32.0**	**32.8**	**48.8**
EUROPE	14.5	11.9	15.5	17.0	14.0	16.0
NAFTA*						
Towards						
NAFTA	**42.1**	**34.0**	**37.8**	**36.8**	**44.5**	**46.2**
ASIA	17.4	30.9	33.2	14.0	17.2	22.7
EUROPE	24.9	21.5	17.8	28.8	20.3	18.0

Notes:
* Declaring area.
ASIA: Japan, NICs in ASIA (Hong Kong, Singapore, Korea, Taiwan), Malaysia, Philippines, Thailand, Indonesia, China.
Source: SIE World Trade Data Base.

recent periods to this trend (see Oman, 1995 for a survey), we are very far from a consensus on the nature and impact of these regional evolutions. Table 8.2 provides indicators related to intra-regional trade of the three major regions at different years in order to assess the pattern of regional integration especially in the past decade. Obviously, this exercise does not pretend to provide any ultimate evidence, but only a rough indication on the size and direction of current regional trends.

As expected, Europe boasts the highest level of intra-regional trade, reflecting its advanced stage of integration. The completion of the internal market and the recent widening to the EFTA countries has further consolidated intra-regional trade and investment in the EU. The case of NAFTA is different: (i) the level of intra-regional trade is much smaller than that in Europe; (ii) external markets, in Asia and Europe, continue to play a very important role for NAFTA's member countries. Finally, regional trends in East Asia provide a third different pattern. Regional economic integration has been under way since the second half of the 1980s mostly as a result of firm strategies and the restructuring of Japan and NICs economies' (Urata, 1993). Moreover, in the case of Asia data uncover a rapidly increasing regional orientation of trade in recent years.

To sum up, although data display great differences between the structure and dynamics of the three regions, they confirm a consolidation of intra-regional trade in the more recent period. On the other hand, the evolution of the three regional groupings tends to reinforce a regional dynamics of competition in the new global environment rather than strengthening protectionist trends in classical terms.

3 Trade specialisation of the United States, Japan and the European Union

As pointed out, the idea is that globalisation, international competition, and regional integration naturally operate to produce convergence across nations in the structures of production and of the economy at large in the most advanced countries. Variations may be found from country to country, because of different historical roots, but such differences fade over time, giving way to common economic structures.

In terms of trade relations, this implies a significant trend towards convergence of trade specialisation of major national economies in the new global competitive environment. This section and the next assess whether this trend exists and its nature.

To evaluate specialisation patterns of the EU, Japan and the United States, our analysis uses a long-term approach (1970–95) trying to depict overall stylised facts with regard to major changes in industrial trade specialisation and innovation capabilities. In this respect, to analyse the relationship between technological capability and international trade specialisation of all major economies, following work by Pavitt (1984), a taxonomy of industrial sectors is used with reference to different features of technology (Guerrieri, 1993, 1997). It identifies six type of industries: *primary resource-intensive, supplier-dominated or traditional sectors, science based, scale-intensive, specialised suppliers* plus the group of *food industries* that is considered separately. Each type represents a different style of technological learning.

In the natural resource-intensive group the availability of abundant raw materials strongly influences production localisation choice and countries' comparative advantage (e.g., *petroleum, refineries, non-ferrous metal basic industries, pulp and paper*); the group of 'supplier-dominated' (traditional) sectors encompasses the more traditional consumer and non-consumer goods industries such as *textiles, clothing, furniture, leather and shoes, ceramics, the simplest metal products.* Both sectors are net purchasers of process innovations and innovative intermediate inputs from other suppliers of productive equipment and materials since technical change mostly comes from suppliers of machinery and other production equipment. So, in both sectors technology is easily accessible, and international technology transfers are relatively easy, and factor endowments have a major influence on the generation of comparative advantages. Furthermore, firms' competitiveness is notably sensitive to price factors, although in a few traditional sectors it is also influenced by 'non-price factors' such as product design and quality.

Scale-intensive sectors, such as *automobiles,* certain *consumer electronics* and *consumer durables*, and the *rubber* and *steel* industries, include typical oligopolistic large firm industries, with high capital intensity, wide economies of scale and learning, high technical or managerial complexity and significant in-house technological accumulation through design and production engineering operating experience. Process and product technologies therefore develop incrementally.

Specialised-suppliers, which include most producers of machinery, components and software in mechanical engineering and control instrumentation (such as the *machinery for specialised industries*) are characterised by high diversification of supply, high 'economies of scope', relatively medium to small companies and a notable capacity for product innovation that enters most sectors of scale-intensive and supplier-dominated groups as capital inputs (Rosenberg, 1976; 1982; Von Hippel, 1988).

Finally, the so-called 'science-based' sectors include industries such as *fine chemicals, electronic components, telecommunications* and *aerospace,* which are all characterised by innovative activities directly linked to high R&D expenditures and academic research; a large number of other sectors heavily rely on them as capital or intermediate inputs, and their product innovations generate broad spillover effects on the whole economic system (OECD, 1992).

In these three categories of products (*science-based, scale-intensive, specialised suppliers*) comparative and absolute advantages are dominated by technological activities, as shown by many studies (Soete, 1987; Fagerberg, 1988; Dosi, Pavitt and Soete, 1990; Amendola, Guerrieri, Padoan, 1992; Lall, 1995).

The industrial taxonomy is completed by grouping all the other non-industrial products into three broad economic categories (*agricultural product* and *raw materials, fuels, other raw materials*) for a total of nine product groups (see appendix).

One should point out that the above taxonomy is related to the findings of the theoretical and empirical literature on technological change over the past 15 years (Freeman and Soete, 1997). Technological capabilities and innovative activities are widely recognised as key factors driving the international trade performance and competitiveness of single countries. According to recent innovation theory, innovative activity is a cumulative process which is both country and firm specific, since it is differentiated in both its technical characteristics and its market application. Processes of technological change tend to assume varying sectoral features, in terms of differences in technological opportunities, sources and appropriability conditions. In this respect, the linkages between various industrial sectors assume great importance, i.e., in terms of innovation user–producer relationships. Technological change also affects these structural linkages and, through them, affects the competitiveness of each sector, and hence of the industrial system as a whole. On the other hand, uncertainty, bounded rationality and localised learning dominate microeconomic behaviour and the dynamic world of technological change.

This taxonomy is applied to an original trade database (SIE – World Trade) based on the United Nations and OECD statistical sources (450 product classes, 98 sectors and 25 commodity groups) for more than 80 countries (OECDs, NICs, ex-CMEA and LDCs), which allows us to analyse the changing pattern of world trade at a rather disaggregated level.

In order to individuate the countries' specialisation patterns and their changes over time, we use the contribution to trade balance as an indicator of countries' trade specialisation or revealed comparative advantage. Unlike the more-used Balassa indicator for RCA which is based exclusively on exports, this indicator also takes imports into consideration as a measure of a country's specialisation.

The formula is the following:

$$CTBj = \left[\frac{(Xij - Mij)}{(Xi + Mi)/2} - \frac{(Xi - Mi)}{(Xi + Mi)/2} * \frac{(Xij + Mij)}{(Xi + Mi)} \right] * 100$$

with Xij = exports of product j of country i; Mij = imports of product j of country i; Xi = total exports of country i and Mi = total imports of country i.

In practice, values greater than 0 (less than 0) of the CTB indicator identify those sectors which give a contribution to the overall trade balance which is higher (lower) than their percentage share in the country's total trade, thus revealing sectors of specialisation (despecialisation) in a country (CEPII, 1983; Guerrieri, 1993).

At a glance, the pattern of specialisation of the EU countries as a whole mostly reflects a relative stable pattern over time (table 8.3). European industry maintained highly stable comparative advantages in many chemical and mechanical sectors belonging to *specialised-supplier* and *scale-intensive* groups. In particular EU specialisation increased in basic metals and mechanical engineering, such as machine-tools and machinery for specialised industries; the latter, it must be recalled, continue to represent vital investment goods for many manufacturing industries (Patel and Pavitt, 1994). One should note, however, that in *scale-intensive* (chemical, auto, electric and electronic consumer goods, etc.) and *specialised-supplier* sectors (mechanical engineering) market shares of the EU were very high in the past but have been significantly decreasing during the last one and half decades, especially in the first half of the 1990s (Guerrieri, 1997).

In contrast to these areas of relative strength, EU specialisation patterns reveal a declining trend in *traditional* sectors, and especially in the *science-based* industries, particularly in microelectronics and in 'information technology' hardware. This weakness should not be underestimated, as electronic products represent vital inputs in the current manufacturing restructuring of all major countries.

In *traditional* and *science-based* sectors the EU has also suffered the heaviest losses on both domestic and world markets (Guerrieri, 1997). In *traditional* products (textile, apparel, leather, footwear, furniture, etc.) there was a dramatic decrease in the EU market shares mostly to the advantage of the NICs in Asia and, more recently, China; a loss that should be considered to a large extent unavoidable given the upsurge in these labour-intensive sectors of a large group of new industrialising countries over the past decade.

On the other hand, in *science-based* sectors the EU competitive position, relatively strong in the past, experienced a net deterioration in the period considered here. The EU countries suffered dramatic decrease in their world market shares during the first half of the 1980s and especially in the first part of the current decade (Guerrieri, 1997; Guerrieri and Milana, 1995). These negative trends affected all EU major countries, including Germany, that confirms its specific weakness in this area (Guerrieri and Milana, 1995).

Foodstuffs and the food industry constitute a special case as they increased their positive contribution to the EU trade balance, thanks mainly to the strong protectionist attitude of European agricultural policy (CAP). Especially in the food industry, the competitive position of the EU was very strong in the past and improved substantially in the period considered here through a huge increase in market shares (Guerrieri, 1997).

The relative stability of the EU specialisation patterns strongly contrasts with the dynamic changes characterising the Japanese specialisation-competitive position in the same period (table 8.3). In the early 1970s, the *scale-*

Table 8.3. *Patterns of trade specialisation*: United States, Japan and the EU*

	1970–3	1980–3	1992–5	Change in the share 1995 to 1970
UNITED STATES				
Agricultural products	10.3	10.8	3.9	−6.4
Fuels	−3.0	−19.6	−6.4	−3.3
Other raw materials	−1.4	−0.2	0.1	1.4
Resource-intensive ind.	−5.8	−4.0	−0.5	5.2
Food ind.	−3.2	0.7	2.0	5.3
Traditional ind.	−9.6	−5.8	−9.5	0.1
Scale-intensive ind.	−6.5	−3.1	−3.9	2.5
Specialised supplier ind.	9.8	7.6	3.6	−6.1
Science-based ind.	11.5	12.9	9.5	−2.1
Others	−2.2	0.8	1.2	3.3
JAPAN				
Agricultural products	−24.8	−14.4	−12.5	12.3
Fuels	−19.1	−44.9	−16.3	2.8
Other raw materials	−11.8	−5.3	−2.9	8.8
Resource-intensive ind.	−7.6	−7.5	−5.1	2.4
Food ind.	−4.1	−3.4	−7.6	−3.6
Traditional ind.	9.7	3.9	−9.8	−19.5
Scale-intensive ind.	46.3	47.7	24.7	−21.6
Specialised supplier ind.	5.9	11.9	12.4	6.5
Science-based ind.	4.9	11.6	17.8	12.9
Others	0.5	0.3	−0.6	−1.1
EU (15)				
Agricultural products	−6.0	−3.4	−1.9	4.1
Fuels	−8.1	−14.3	−4.2	3.9
Other raw materials	−1.7	−1.2	−0.6	1.1
Resource-intensive ind.	−1.8	−0.8	−0.5	1.3
Food ind.	−1.0	1.1	0.8	1.8
Traditional ind.	3.1	2.3	−0.4	−3.5
Scale-intensive ind.	9.5	8.7	3.3	−6.2
Specialised supplier ind.	4.9	5.1	3.6	−1.3
Science-based ind.	1.4	1.8	−0.3	−1.7
Others	−0.3	0.7	0.2	0.5

Notes:
Indicator of comparative advantage (>0) or disavantage (<0). For the formula see text.
* Average value in each sub-period.
Source: SIE, World Trade Data Base.

intensive and *traditional* sectors represented the strong points (comparative advantages) of the Japanese specialization patterns. Since then, the latter has been characterised by a dynamic reallocation of productive resources, oriented towards a sharp strengthening of *special-supplier* and *science-based* sectors in the past decade. In contrast, scale-intensive sector contributions to the trade balance have been decreasing, and traditional sectors have greatly changed their role.

The difference in EU specialisation compared with that of the US is also very pronounced (table 8.3). US comparative advantages have been and are increasingly concentrated in R&D-intensity product groups (science-based), confirming the high-level scientific research capability and the large availability of 'primary' innovation of the US industry. The nature of the relation, however, between the strengthening of US specialisation in R&D-intensive products and the overall trade (industrial) US performance is far from being clear. One should also note the sharp decrease in the positive contribution to the US trade balance (ICTB) of the specialised-supplier sectors, such as mechanical engineering, although they were able to maintain positive comparative advantage by the mid 1990s.

The above evidence clearly shows the growing heterogeneity and differences in terms of performances and specialisations of the three major advanced economic poles (Europe, US and Japan). It also displays that the three areas continue to be characterised by significantly different patterns of trade composition and specialisation. Each major area has a very different sectoral pattern of technological and trade advantage (disadvantage), and these patterns show on average considerable stability over time and no sign of convergence across the three economic areas.

It follows that in the new global environment, whilst market forces are indeed very important, nations have continued to play a significant role in corporate strategies, including those of transnational corporations. In other words, the structural features of national economies such as production and management organisation, technical infrastructure and other institutional factors, have continued to exert a significant influence on firms' performances. Even more so that the new global competition has more and more blurred the distinction between international and domestic policies, determining both a diminished autonomy of national policies, as well as wider cross-border spillovers of domestic (innovation, competition and industrial) policies (Gourevitch and Guerrieri eds., 1993). The terms of 'structural competitiveness' and 'national system of innovations', as already pointed out, have been used to assess these national specificities (Porter, 1990; Nelson ed., 1993; OECD, 1992; Edquist ed., 1997). Not surprisingly they point out that differences in national technological capabilities endure. The deep changes in the competitive positions of major countries and areas during the past decade can be interpreted in this perspective.

4 Individual European countries' trade specialisation patterns

The EU overall trend is only an average pattern and masks the sharp differences that have characterised the trade specialisation patterns of individual EU countries.

Germany's relatively stable pattern of specialisation is based on a relatively wide range of industries including both *scale-intensive* industries (especially motor vehicles and transportation equipment, chemicals and related products) and *specialised-supplier* sectors (metalworking machinery, special and general industrial machinery – mechanical engineering generally) (table 8.4). In comparison with the other two more advanced economic poles, the US and Japan, German specialisation shows relatively poor performance in those *science-base* products of key importance for 'primary' innovation such as electronics (table 8.4). Furthermore, the *German* economy registered a significant deterioration in its overall competitive position in manufactured products, that has continued in the first half of the 1990s and has been concentrated especially in the extra-EU markets (Guerrieri, 1997).

The *United Kingdom,* on the other hand, had a distinctly negative trade performance, having registered the largest net losses in market shares over the period considered here, which have been spread across a wide range of industries (Guerrieri, 1997). This deterioration in competitiveness is only partially reflected in the unfavourable evolution of specialisation patterns for the same period, especially in *scale-intensive* and *specialised-supplier* sectors. Comparative advantage indicators maintained high positive values in science-based sectors, especially in chemical and pharmaceutical industries where also the British competitive position was and has remained very strong (table 8.4).

The *French economy*, unlike other European economies, is characterised by an overall low level of trade specialisation (table 8.4). Many significant qualitative and quantitative changes have been occurring in its comparative advantage structure in the period considered here. *Science-based* (high R&D-intensity) sectors have emerged as new strong points of French specialisation, with a transfer of resources to these new activities largely made through major public programs. But so far there has been limited diffusion of technological skill and capabilities outside their sector of origin. Thus, net losses have been experienced in most *specialised supplier* sectors and involved many sophisticated goods belonging to the machinery industries (Guerrieri, 1997).

Among the northern European countries, *Sweden* has been able to achieve significant specialisation in a small set of technologically inter-related industries, mostly producing capital and intermediate goods. The list includes a wide variety of *specialised-supplier* industries (in mechanical

Table 8.4. *Patterns of trade specialisation*: Germany, France and the United Kingdom*

	1970–3	1980–3	1992–5	Change in the share 1995 to 1970
GERMANY				
Agricultural products	−10.8	−6.8	−3.8	7.0
Fuels	−5.8	−14.7	−4.9	1.0
Other raw materials	−2.9	−1.7	−0.8	2.1
Resource-intensive ind.	−6.4	−5.9	−2.2	4.1
Food ind.	−5.7	−1.6	−1.6	4.1
Traditional ind.	−2.9	−2.5	−5.5	−2.6
Scale-intensive ind.	16.9	18.0	10.0	−6.9
Specialised supplier ind.	14.5	10.8	8.5	−6.0
Science-based ind.	5.3	3.6	0.7	−4.6
Others	−2.0	0.8	−0.3	1.7
FRANCE				
Agricultural products	−0.7	1.5	0.9	1.6
Fuels	−11.1	−21.6	−5.7	5.3
Other raw materials	−1.4	−0.8	−0.4	1.0
Resource-intensive ind.	−3.5	−2.0	−2.2	1.3
Food ind.	2.8	3.8	2.9	0.1
Traditional ind.	3.0	−0.2	−3.7	−6.7
Scale-intensive ind.	11.3	13.1	3.8	−7.5
Specialised supplier ind.	−0.2	2.7	−0.1	0.0
Science-based ind.	−0.3	3.1	2.7	3.0
Others	0.0	0.4	1.9	1.8
UNITED KINGDOM				
Agricultural products	−9.9	−4.1	−2.2	7.8
Fuels	−8.4	5.5	1.4	9.8
Other raw materials	−2.4	−1.6	−0.5	1.8
Resource-intensive ind.	−5.0	−2.7	−0.6	4.4
Food ind.	−7.8	−3.0	−1.0	6.8
Traditional ind.	2.3	−4.2	−4.5	−6.8
Scale-intensive ind.	14.3	0.8	1.2	−13.1
Specialised supplier ind.	8.6	4.4	1.9	−6.7
Science-based ind.	6.8	3.9	3.8	−2.9
Others	1.5	1.0	0.4	−1.1

Notes:
Indicator of comparative advantage (>0) or disadvantage (<0). For the formula see text.
* Average value in each sub-period.
Source: SIE, World Trade Data Base.

engineering areas), and many types of *scale-intensive* goods (such as ship-building), along with both a group of *natural resource-intensive* industries (like pulp and paper) (table 8.5). Yet the evolution of the Swedish trade and specialisation performance, especially in the most recent period, shows a relatively negative trend. Swedish industry has been continuously losing shares in world exports, which are spread across all the most sophisticated technological sectors and which seem to indicate ongoing difficulties in the restructuring and upgrading of trade and technological specialisation of the Swedish economy (table 8.5).

Italy distinguishes its position in the EU by its highly heterogeneous specialisation pattern with respect to the other major member countries. Italy has done well in the set of industries where it has traditionally been strong, especially in *traditional* goods ('other industrial products'), and has shown strengthening specialisation and competitiveness in a number of mechanical engineering areas, particularly *specialised-supplier* sectors, like special industrial machinery, and metal working machinery. This was the result of the process of extensive restructuring in Italian industry in the past decade, based largely on application and diffusion of mostly imported technology, which also allowed some so-called mature sectors to be revitalised. In contrast, Italy is generally losing position in sectors where it has been weak, as in many *science-based* goods (like electronics) and in *scale-intensive* goods (especially chemicals and related products), with negative implications for the future position of Italian industry in the world economy (table 8.5).

The specialisation pattern of *Spain,* unlike that of Italy and other southern member countries, has been characterised by significant changes which have modified its comparative advantage structure in the period considered here. *Traditional* industries, such as textiles, clothing, footwear and so on, have encountered increasing difficulties from the new Asian competition which drastically decreased their contribution to Spain's specialisation. The food industry, the other strong point of Spanish trade specialisation in the 1970s, has also suffered a decreasing trend in the last ten years, while *scale-intensive* and, to a much lesser extent, *resource-intensive* goods, have emerged and gradually consolidated over the past decade their capability of providing sound comparative advantages. Finally, the highly external dependence of Spain on *science-based* goods has been confirmed, especially in recent years (table 8.5).

To sum up, although the variance of trade specialisation is diminished in most EU countries, both inter-country and inter-industry differences appear to be very important in the EU in shaping national specificities in terms of national competitive advantage and disadvantage. Each major European country has a very different sectoral pattern of technological and trade advantage (disadvantage), and national patterns show on average

Table 8.5. *Patterns of trade specialisation*: Sweden, Italy and Spain*

	1970–3	1980–3	1992–5	Change in the share 1995 to 1970
SWEDEN				
Agricultural products	−2.8	−3.4	−3.3	−0.6
Fuels	−3.2	−13.0	−5.5	−2.3
Other raw materials	2.5	0.6	0.5	−2.0
Resource-intensive ind.	5.4	5.3	8.0	2.6
Food ind.	−3.7	−2.0	−3.2	0.5
Traditional ind.	−1.6	−0.1	−3.1	−1.5
Scale-intensive ind.	2.8	7.9	5.7	2.9
Specialised supplier ind.	1.3	4.8	2.8	1.5
Science-based ind.	−0.8	−0.4	−2.6	−1.8
Others	0.0	0.3	0.8	0.8
ITALY				
Agricultural products	−10.9	−6.3	−4.6	6.2
Fuels	−14.1	−25.6	−6.0	8.0
Other raw materials	−1.5	−1.0	−0.8	0.7
Resource-intensive ind.	−0.1	−1.5	−3.5	−3.4
Food ind.	−5.7	−2.7	−2.9	2.8
Traditional ind.	19.1	22.2	19.7	0.6
Scale-intensive ind.	6.3	4.5	−4.8	−11.1
Specialised supplier ind.	6.9	10.0	10.5	3.5
Science-based ind.	0.8	0.4	−4.3	−5.1
Others	−0.8	0.1	−3.2	−2.4
SPAIN				
Agricultural products	0.0	−2.5	1.1	1.0
Fuels	−12.2	−33.6	−7.8	4.5
Other raw materials	−1.9	−1.6	−0.6	1.3
Resource-intensive ind.	0.2	4.3	0.9	0.8
Food ind.	10.6	5.8	0.7	−9.8
Traditional ind.	16.4	15.2	2.6	−13.8
Scale-intensive ind.	3.5	16.0	9.4	5.9
Specialised supplier ind.	−6.8	1.1	−1.4	5.4
Science-based ind.	−8.5	−3.9	−5.3	3.2
Others	−1.2	−0.7	0.4	1.6

Notes:
Indicator of comparative advantage (>0) or disadvantage (<0). For the formula see text.
* Average value in each sub-period.
Source: SIE, World Trade Data Base.

considerable stability over time. There is also a persistent significant north–south difference in the specialisation patterns within the EU. Rich countries in the north of the Community rely on specialisation patterns characterised by relatively technologically advanced sectors, whereas in the countries in the south labour-intensive *traditional* sectors still constitute the key sources of their competitive advantages.

5 National specificities and global competition

The current wave of globalisation has revived debates about the effect of growing economic interdependence on national economic diversities and specificities. This chapter starts from this trend towards globalisation to show the radical change produced by the latter on the dynamics of world trading relations. In this respect, three facts have been stressed: the simultaneous rise in foreign direct investment and trade, the changing composition of world trade and the increasing regionalisation of trade flows.

As to the impact of the globalisation of economic activity on trade specialisation and performances at the national level, the evidence reported in this chapter shows that the prediction of the end of national specificities should be taken with great caution.

Certainly, the evidence here reported is indicative of complex trends in trade performance and specialisation which cannot be unequivocally interpreted, but two trends should be stressed.

The first pertains to the growing heterogeneity and differences in terms of performances and specialisations of the three major advanced economies (Europe, US and Japan). The three areas continue to be characterised by significantly different patterns of trade composition and specialization. Each major area has a very different sectoral pattern of technological and trade advantage (disadvantage), and these patterns show on average considerable stability over time. All that seems to confirm that domestic innovative activities are still a major determinant for specialisation and competitiveness, and that although technology may have become more internationally mobile, geographical proximity continues to play a very significant role for knowledge flows (Porter, 1990; Guerrieri and Tylecote, 1997; Sjoholm, 1996).

The second point is that this is true also within Europe, where although the variance of trade specialisation is diminished in most EU countries, both inter-country and inter-industry differences appear to be very important in shaping national specificities in terms of national competitive advantage and disadvantage. Each European country succeeds not in isolated sectors, but in clusters of sectors connected through vertical and horizontal relationships at technological and production levels. Furthermore, each major European country has a very different sectoral pattern of technological and trade advantage (disadvantage), and national patterns show on average considerable stability over time. There is also a persistent significant north–south difference in the specialisation patterns within the EU.

In all cases firms and sectors integrated within world trade seem to display in general very different national specialisation patterns to cope with the challenge of global competitiveness at the world level.

To sum up the evidence reported here, seems to confirm the contentions of those who have argued that while the trend towards globalisation might appear to reduce the importance of nations, lower obstacles to trade and fewer distortions to competition make nation-specific factors even more important to firm and nation competitive success (Porter, 1990; Lundvall, 1993; Davies, 1996; Archibugi and Michie eds., 1997).

In other words, the current phase of global competition does not affect only firms, but also national and regional systems. In the new environment, whilst market forces are indeed very important, nations have continued to play a significant role in corporate strategies, including those of transnational corporations. Therefore, the structural features of national economies such as production and management organisation, technical infrastructure and other institutional factors, have continued to exert a significant influence on firms' performances. The terms of 'structural competitiveness' and 'national systems of innovations' have been used to assess these national specificities. They point out that differences in national technological capabilities endure. On the other hand, if we assume that uncertainty, bounded rationality and localised learning dominate micro-economic behaviour and the dynamic world of technological change, then at the national level the drive towards standardisation and convergence could be rather limited, and several productive configurations may coexist even over the long run. So, nation states and national economies are still essential elements of economic analysis. The trade specialisation trends of major countries and areas during the past decade can be interpreted in this perspective.

Appendix: SIE, World Trade Data Base

The foreign trade statistics used in this chapter stem from the SIE, *World Trade* data base, which provides detailed information on exports and imports of 83 countries with respect to 450 product groups, 98 sectors, 25 broad commodity groups and five main product categories. The data base includes trade statistics with respect to the 26 OECD countries, the newly industrialising countries (NICs), the other developing countries and the former CMEA countries, and makes it possible to examine and analyse the entire world trade matrix. The source for the basic trade statistics of the SIE *World Trade* database are the tapes of the OECD and UN.

The *SIE* database is organised in different product group classifications at various levels of disaggregation (450 product groups, 98 sectors, 25 categories, five branches) according to the three Standard International Trade Classifications (SITC), *Revised, Revision 2, Revision 3,* defined by the Statistical Office of the UN (1961, 1975, 1985 as to the periods 1961–75, 1978–87, 1988 on).

The broad product group classifications used in this chapter are based on the 450 product groups of the SIE, *World Trade*. A summary list of the product groups included in each class of products is provided below:

1   *Food items and agricultural raw materials* (41 product groups): food – live animals – animal oil and fats – natural rubber – vegetable and animal textile fibres – cork and wood – skins
2   *Fuels* (4 product groups): coal – petroleum oil – gas
3   *Other raw materials* (17 product groups): iron ore – ores of base metals – other crude minerals
4   *Food industry* (36 product groups): meat and meat preparations – dairy products – vegetable and fruit preparations – cereal preparations – sugar preparations – other edible products
5   *Science based* (59 product groups): synthetic organic dyestuffs – radioactive and associated materials – polymerisation and co-polymerisation products – antibiotics and other pharmaceutical products – nuclear reactors – automatic data processing machines and units – telecommunications equipment – semiconductor devices – electronic microcircuits – electronic measuring instruments – electric power machinery and apparatus – internal combustion piston engines – aircraft and associated equipment – medical instruments – optical instruments – photographic apparatus and equipment
6   *Scale intensive* (88 product groups): organic chemicals – inorganic chemical products – other chemical materials and products – medicinal and pharmaceutical products – rubber manufactures – iron and steel – television, radio, other image-sound recorder and reproducers – household type electrical equipment – ships and boats – railway vehicles and equipment – road vehicles
7   *Specialised suppliers* (43 product groups): agricultural machinery – machine tools for working metals – metal working machinery – other machine tools for specialised particular industries – construction and mining machinery – textile and leather machinery – paper and paper-

board machinery – other machinery for specialised particular industries – other general industrial machinery and equipment – electrical equipment and components – measuring, checking, analysing instruments – optical goods – other miscellaneous products

8 *Resource intensive* (18): paper and paperboard – petroleum products – non-metallic mineral manufactures – non-ferrous metal products

9 *Traditionals or supplier dominated* (76 product groups): textile products – articles of apparel and clothing accessories – leather manufactures – footwear – wood manufactures – furniture – paper and printed products – articles of ceramic materials – glass products – miscellaneous manufactures of metal (structures, tools, cutlery and other articles) – jewellery, goldsmiths – imitation jewellery – musical instruments – sporting goods – toys and games – other miscellaneous products

10 **Residuals**: other product groups n.e.s.

Note

The research leading to this paper has been supported by the TSER Project, 'Technology, Economic Integration and Social Cohesion', and the University of Rome 'La Sapienza' within the project 'Crescita e competitività internazionale in un sistema di interdipendenze tecnologiche' (Growth and international competitiveness in a system of technological interdependences).

References

Amendola, G., Guerrieri, P. and Padoan, P.C. 1992. International patterns of technological accumulation and trade, *Journal of International and Comparative Economics*, 2: 173–97. Reprinted in Archibugi and Michie (eds.) 1998.

Archibugi, D. and Michie, J. (eds.) 1997. *Technology, Globalisation and Economic Performance*, Cambridge, Cambridge University Press.

1998. *Trade, Growth and Technical Change*, Cambridge, Cambridge University Press.

Archibugi, D. and Pianta, M. 1992. *The Technological Specialization of Advanced Countries, Report to the EC on Science and Technology Activities*, Boston, Kluwer.

CEPII 1983. *Economie mondiale: la montee des tensions*, Paris, Economica.

Davies, A. 1996. Innovation in large technical systems: the case of telecommunications, *Industrial and Corporate Change*, 4: 321–55.

Dosi, G., Pavitt, K. and Soete, L. 1990. *The Economics of Technical Change and International Trade*, Brighton, Wheatsheaf.

Dosi, G., Freeman, C., Nelson, R., Silverberg, G. and Soete, L. (eds.) 1988. *Technical Change and Economic Theory*, London, Frances Pinter.

Dowrick, S. 1997. Trade and growth: a survey, in Fagerberg, Hansson, Lundberg and Melchior (eds.).

Edquist, C. (ed.) 1997. *Systems of Innovation*, London, Pinter.

Ernst, D. and Guerrieri, P., 1997. International production networks and changing trade patterns in East Asia: the case of the electronics industry, DRUID Working Paper, Department of Industrial Economics and Strategy, Copenaghen Business School.

Fagerberg, J. 1988. International competitiveness, *Economic Journal*, 98: 355–74.

Fagerberg, J., Hansson, P., Lundberg, L. and Melchior, A. (eds.) 1997. *Technology and International Trade*, Cheltenham, Edward Elgar.

Foray, D. and Freeman, C. (eds.) 1992. *Technology and the Wealth of Nations*, London and New York, Pinter and OECD.

Freeman, C. and Soete, L. 1997. *The Economics of Industrial Innovation*, Cambridge, MA, The MIT Press.

Gourevitch, P. and Guerrieri, P. (eds.) 1993. *New Challenges to International Cooperation: Adjustment of Firms, Policies and Organizations to Global Competition*, San Diego, University of California, Graduate School of International Relations and Pacific Studies.

Grossman, G.M. and Helpman, E. 1991. *Innovation and Growth in the Global Economy*, Cambridge, MA, MIT Press.

Guerrieri, P. 1993. Patterns of technological capability and international trade performance: an empirical analysis, in Kreinin (ed.).

　1997. The changing world trading environment, technological capability and the competitiveness of the European industry, Paper presented at the Conference on 'Technology, Economic Integration and Social Cohesion' TSER Project, Vienna, January, 1997.

Guerrieri, P. and Milana, C. 1995. Changes and trends in the world trade in high-technology products, *Cambridge Journal of Economics*, 19: 225–43.

　1998. High-technology industries and international competition, in Archibugi and Michie (eds.).

Guerrieri, P. and Tylecote, A. 1997. Interindustry differences in technical change and national patterns of technological accumulation, in Edquist (ed.).

Haque, I. (ed.) 1995. *Trade, Technology and International Competitiveness*, Washington, The World Bank.

Hood, N. and Vahlne, J.E. (eds.) 1988. *Strategies in Global Competition*, London, Croom Helm.

Ito, T. and Krueger, A.O. (eds.) 1993. *Trade and Protectionism*, Chicago and London, The University of Chicago Press.

Kreinin, M. (ed.) 1993. *The Political Economy of International Commercial Policy: Issues for the 1990s*, London and New York, Taylor & Francis.

Lall, S. 1995. The creation of comparative advantage: country experiences, in Haque, I. (ed.).

Lundvall, B.Å. 1993. User–producer relationships, national systems of innovation and internationalization, in Foray and Freeman (eds.).

Lundvall, B.Å., (ed.) 1992. *National System of Innovation: Towards a Theory of Innovation and Interactive Learning*, London, Pinter.

Nelson, R. (ed.) 1993. *National Innovation System*, New York, Oxford University Press.

OECD, 1992. *Technology and the Economy: The Key Relationship*, Paris, OECD.

Ohmae, K. 1990. *The Borderless World*, New York, Harper.

Oman, C. 1995. The policy challenges of globalisation and regionalisation, *Policy Brief*, n. 11, Paris, OECD.

Patel, P. and Pavitt, K. 1994. The continuing, widespread (and neglected) importance of improvements in mechanical technologies, *Research Policy*, 23: 533–46.

Pavitt, K. 1984. Sectoral patterns of technical change: toward a taxonomy and theory, *Research Policy*, 13: 343–73.

    1988. International patterns of technological accumulation, in Hood and Vahlne (eds.).

Porter, M. 1990. *The Competitive Advantages of Nations*, London and New York, Macmillan.

Rosenberg, N. 1976. *Perspective on Technology*, Cambridge, Cambridge University Press.

    1982. *Inside the Black Box*, Cambridge, Cambridge University Press.

Scherer, F.M., 1982. Inter-industry technology flows in the United States, *Research Policy*, 11: 227–45.

Scherer, F.M. 1992. *International High Technology Competition*, Cambridge, MA, MIT Press.

Schmookler, J. 1966. *Invention and Economic Growth*, Cambridge, MA, Harvard University Press.

Sjoholm, F. 1996. International transfer of knowledge: the role of international trade and geographic proximity, *Welwirtschaftliches Archiv*, 132: 97–115.

Soete, L. 1987. The impact of technological innovation on international trade patterns: the evidence reconsidered, *Research Policy*, 16: 101–30.

Urata, S., 1993. Japanese foreign direct investment and its effect on foreign trade in Asia, in Ito and Krueger (eds.).

Vernon, R., 1979. The product cycle hypothesis in a new international environment, *Oxford Bulletin of Economics and Statistics*, 41: 114–32.

Von Hippel, E. 1988. *The Sources of Innovation*, New York, Oxford University Press.

PART III

Globalisation and economic performance

9 The political economy of globalisation

MICHAEL KITSON AND JONATHAN MICHIE

What is called globalisation is changing the notion of the nation state as power becomes more diffuse and borders more porous. Technological change is reducing the power and capacity of government to control its domestic economy free from external influence.
Tony Blair, Leader of the British Labour Party, speaking to Executives of Rupert Murdoch's News Corporation.[1]

The plain fact is that the nation state as it has existed for nearly two centuries is being undermined. . . . The ability of national governments to decide their exchange rate, interest rate, trade flows, investment and output has been savagely crippled by market forces.
Nigel Lawson, former UK Chancellor of the Exchequer.[2]

Introduction

The process of globalisation – whether just of technology or of the economy more generally – has profound implications for the conduct of economic policy. Yet there is still little clarity over what the term 'globalisation' signifies; over the extent to which the process it denotes has developed; or over the implications of any of this for government economic policy.

The powerless state perspective characterises the world economy as a truly global system which has undermined the ability of national governments to implement effective independent policies (Ohmae, 1990, 1993, 1995).

This view has been challenged, for example, by Hirst and Thompson (1996). However, most such critiques accept the basic premises that, firstly, there has been *some* increase in globalisation – it is only the *extent* of the increase which is questioned; and, secondly, that to the extent that the degree of globalisation *has* increased, the scope for government action is thereby diminished – again, it is only the *degree* to which government policy

163

has become less effective which is disputed.[3] We take a rather different approach. On the first of the above two premises, we have argued elsewhere that there has been some increase in globalisation, but that this process has been both exaggerated and rather unspecified (see Kitson and Michie, 1995a, 1995b). But there is no logical reason for the second premise to necessarily follow from the first; and we would argue that it does not. Certainly, an increase in globalisation does make less effective various national economic policy instruments. But this cannot be read off automatically; there are certain aspects of globalisation which may allow national economic policy to be pursued more effectively. More importantly, the degree of difficulty in pursuing policy at the national level should be separated analytically from the question of its desirability; even if the implementation of policy has become more difficult, this does not in itself necessarily make it any less desirable or important. And there are certainly aspects of policy – such as the creation of international institutional arrangements, or the pursuit of competitive advantage – where policy at the national level has become more important and desirable. If the pursuit of such policy has become more difficult then the appropriate conclusion might be the precise opposite of the one normally asserted or accepted in such discussion. Rather than government intervention having become outdated, it may be that to see through the necessary policy will require more far-reaching and radical intervention on the part of national governments than would have been the case in the previous, easier circumstances.

This chapter thus argues that there are indeed trends towards increased globalisation, and that these changes are having an adverse impact on the economic performance of some countries – there are 'winners and losers'.[4] This indicates a need for increased intervention by nation states to maintain and improve economic performance in an increasingly integrated world economy. Although the analysis in this chapter is primarily concerned with the performance of industrialised countries, many of the processes will also apply to developing countries.

The chapter is organised into three parts. Section 1 considers the trends and patterns of economic globalisation, and of the globalisation of technology. Section 2 considers the link between increased openness – in terms of the growth in international trade – and economic performance. Section 3 considers the implications for national economic policy. We then conclude by considering whether the apparent contradiction between the globalisation of technology, on the one hand, and national systems of innovation, on the other, has any parallels with the literature on the implications of the globalisation of the economy more generally for national economic policy.

Table 9.1. *Growth of world output and world trade, 1870–1990*
(annual % growth rates, calculated peak to peak)

		Output	Trade
Pre-WW1:	1870–1913	2.7	3.5
Inter-war:	1913–37	1.8	1.3
	1913–29	*2.3*	*2.2*
	1929–37	*0.8*	*0.4*
Post-war:	1950–90	3.9	5.8
	1950–73	*4.7*	*7.2*
	1973–90	*2.8*	*3.9*

Sources: Authors' calculations from the following:
World Trade – based on volume of world exports from:
1870–1913 – Lewis (1981), appendix III, table 4;
1913–1950 – Maddison (1962), table 25;
1950–1991 – Wells (1993), appendix.
World Output – based on constant price GDP series from:
1870–1950 – Maddison (1991), table 4.7 (computed from annual growth
rates of sixteen countries);
1950–1990 – Wells (1993), appendix.

1 Trends and patterns in globalisation

The concept of globalisation has been applied to a wide variety of variables
– including social, political and cultural. Here we adopt a narrower focus,
setting the globalisation of technology within the context of economic
globalisation and in particular the growth of international trade.

Economic globalisation

A number of recent studies have suggested that the world economy is no
more open to world trade now than it was before the World War One (Hirst
and Thompson, 1996; Wes, 1996). Although this may be correct in the case
of certain individual nations, it is wrong for the world economy as a whole.
That said, the process of increased global integration has been erratic and
has been punctured by periodic crises, the formation of regional trading
blocs and shifting world economic leadership (see Kitson and Michie,
1995a).
    During the 1870 – 1913 period there was an almost continual increase in
world trade and world output. As shown in table 9.1 world trade increased

Table 9.2. *The growth and volatility of world output and world trade, 1870–1990*

		Output			Trade		
		Mean average growth rate (%)	Mean standard deviation (%)	Coefficient of variation	Average growth rate (%)	Standard deviation (%)	Coefficient of growth
Pre-WW1:	1870–1913	2.8	2.1	0.75	3.6	2.5	0.71
Inter-war:	1924–37	2.1	4.8	2.26	2.2	7.5	3.48
	1924–29	3.7	0.8	0.22	5.7	2.2	0.39
	1929–37	1.3	5.9	4.53	0.5	8.5	16.65
Post-war:	1950–90	3.9	1.8	0.45	5.9	4.6	0.78
	1950–73	4.7	1.6	0.34	7.5	4.2	0.56
	1973–90	3.1	1.6	0.53	4.5	4.9	1.09

Sources: As table 9.1.

by an average of 3.5 per cent per annum whereas world output increased by an average of 2.7 per cent per annum. There were cyclical variations in trade[5] and output and significant differences in national growth rates but only in four years did world trade decline (1885, 1892, 1900 and 1908) and only in three years did world output decline (1876, 1893 and 1908).

The interdependence between world trade and growth is indicated by the high positive correlation between the two variables. Additionally, despite some significant downturns during the early 1890s and at the turn of the century, the world economy was becoming progressively more open. Evidence of the volatility of the growth rates of output and trade is presented in table 9.2 which gives figures on absolute dispersion (the standard deviation) and relative dispersion (the coefficient of variation). The long-term perspective suggests that trade growth during this period was less volatile than during the disrupted period of the 1930s and the post-Bretton Woods period but was relatively more volatile than during the Bretton Woods period itself. Similarly, output growth was less volatile than during the turbulent 1930s but was more volatile than during the entire post-World War Two period, including post-1973.[6]

Discontinuities in growth and trade characterise the interwar period, with the relative stability of the 1920s followed by the turbulence of the 1930s. As shown in table 9.1, during the 1913–29 period world trade grew at an average annual rate of 1.3 per cent, whereas output grew at an average annual rate of 1.8 per cent. Much of this slow growth can be explained by the disruptions and dislocations of World War One. The international trading system was in considerable disarray and only recovered slowly; by 1924 the volume of world trade was only 7 per cent above the 1913 level. From 1924 onwards output and trade grew at a faster rate and experienced less volatility than in the pre-1913 period.

During the 1930s, or more precisely from 1929, the world economy suffered severe disruptions. The Great Depression of 1929–32 was the most severe depression in the world economy since the Industrial Revolution. During these three years world trade collapsed at an average annual rate of 9.9 per cent and world output declined at an average annual rate of 6.2 per cent. The disintegration of the world trading system was reflected in a movement towards a more closed world economy, a reversal of the 1920s trend towards increased openness. From 1932 there was a world recovery, albeit one with large inter-country variations (see Kitson and Michie, 1994). During the period 1932–7, world output grew at an average annual rate of 5.2 per cent and world trade at 5.8 per cent, although this failed to return trade to its 1929 level. For the 1919–37 period as a whole, as shown in tables 9.1 and 9.2, growth of output and trade was very slow and, as expected given the experience of the Great Depression, highly volatile.

During the 1950–90 period world output and trade grew at a faster rate than in any of the previous periods. As shown in table 9.1, world output grew at an average annual rate of 3.9 per cent and world trade grew at an average annual rate of 5.8 per cent. Only in one year (1982) did world output fall;[7] and only in four years did world trade fall (1952, 1958, 1975, 1982).

The post-war period can be broadly divided into two sub-periods. The Bretton Woods period, from 1950 to 1973, and the post-1973 period. The former witnessed a rapid growth of trade (average annual growth of 7.2 per cent) and output (average annual growth of 4.7 per cent), with a significant rise in the openness of the world economy. The openness indicator increased at an average annual rate of 2.4 per cent during this period, three times the increase during the pre-1913 period. In part this can be explained by a catching-up process as the world economy adjusted from the dislocations of World War Two: it was not until 1968 that openness reached the level achieved in 1913. It also reflects, however, the increasing integration of the world economy based on an effective and stable international trading system. This integration promoted openness despite the growing contribution of non-tradable activity to domestic output in advanced economies.[8] As shown in table 9.2, trade and output were less volatile during this period than during any other period apart from the late 1920s. Moreover, comparison with the 1920s is not strictly appropriate as the Bretton Woods period was significantly longer – the stability of the system over 23 years being added testimony to its success.

The collapse of the Bretton Woods system ushered in a period of slower growth of world trade and output. From 1973 to 1990, world trade grew at an average annual rate of 3.9 per cent, around half that achieved in the Bretton Woods period, and output increased at an average annual rate of 2.8 per cent. Within this period there were major setbacks in the mid-1970s and the early 1980s; the former caused by the first OPEC shock and the latter by 'OPEC 2' and the 'monetarist' shock of the deflationary policies being adopted in a number of the leading industrialised countries.[9] The impact of these disruptions was to severely impede the openness of the world economy. The post-World War Two trend towards a more open world economy was halted from the mid 1970s and only resumed from the mid 1980s.

The issue of regionalism requires clarification and elaboration. The key issues are, firstly, to what extent has the degree of regionalism in the world economy increased; secondly, would such regionalism destroy or create trade; and, thirdly, would it distort or promote multilateralism? Regionalism can perhaps best be defined in terms of preferential regional trade agreements (RTAs) amongst groups of countries, or trade within broadly defined geographic regions such as Europe and North America. It does seem to have emerged in the world economy in a significant way in two periods: firstly in the 1930s and then again in the 1980s.

During the early 1930s the chaos in world markets led to an increased use of discriminatory trade policies and the *de facto* formation of trading blocs, usually centred on a dominant country. For countries such as the UK, France, The Netherlands and Italy, a growing proportion of trade during the 1930s was conducted with their respective Empires. Furthermore, currency blocs also grew in importance as countries sought exchange rate stability and made extensive use of exchange rate agreements and discriminatory exchange controls. However, despite the formation of trading blocs – or perhaps because of it, due to the dispersed location of Empires and Colonies – trade did not actually become regionalised on a geographical basis; the world did not see the development of 'natural' trading blocs.

The first post-World War Two wave of regionalism was from the mid 1950s with the establishment of the original European Economic Community (EEC) and European Free Trade Area (EFTA). The 1980s saw pressure for the formation of RTAs led by the United States which negotiated a series of agreements culminating in the formation of the North American Free Trade Area (NAFTA).[10] It is too early to discern the impact of the NAFTA agreement on intra-bloc trade. The evidence for the European Community (EC, now European Union), however, does show a rise in intra-bloc trade since 1960 although most of the increase occurred in the period up to 1973 with a later spurt from the mid 1980s (Lloyd,

1992).[11] The intra-bloc share of the EFTA countries (the original six members) showed a moderate increase up to the mid 1970s, followed by a decline of a similar magnitude.

An alternative measure of regionalisation is the regional share of world trade. Looking at the shares of world imports of the three principal RTA blocs since 1960 shows that the combined shares of the European Community and EFTA have not increased significantly over the period (the total for all three regions jumps upwards in 1989 with the formation of the Canada–United States free trade agreement). The share of the EC/EU has increased but this reflects the expansion of membership (Lloyd, 1992).

In addition to the explicit role of RTAs, regionalism can occur through the increased *geographic* concentration of trade. Attention has been focused on the development of a tripolar world economy dominated by North America, Europe and Japan and the 'Asian Tigers'. There have been contrasting trends in intra-bloc trade since 1960 in these three areas: increasing in Europe and Asia but falling in North America since 1969 (Lloyd, 1992).[12] The share of world imports of the three areas accounted for nearly four fifths of world imports in 1989 – although it is noticeable that this dominance dates at least from the start of the period. The share of Europe has averaged over 40 per cent, although there was a fall from the mid 1970s until the mid 1980s. The share of North America has been relatively stable at around 16 per cent, although there was an increase in the early 1980s. The most significant change has been the rapid growth of the Asian share of world imports, almost doubling over the period. The evidence provides some indication that both RTAs and the development of geographical blocs has led to an increase in regionalism as both a defensive and aggressive response to intensified international competition.

The leading nation in the world economy has shifted during different epochs of international economic development. The pre-World War One era saw Britain, the first industrialised economy, as the dominant economic power. Increasingly, however, its relative position declined – the 'diminished giant' syndrome (Bhagwati and Irwin, 1987) – with the rising economic might of the US, Germany and others as 1914 approached. Table 9.3 indicates that Britain's share of the output of the world's capitalist countries (measured as the aggregate output of Maddison's 16 capitalist countries) declined from 21.5 per cent in 1870 to 15.3 per cent in 1913 whereas the US share rose from 24.5 per cent to 40.8 per cent over the same period.[13] In addition, Britain's share of exports from these countries declined from 37.2 per cent in 1870 to 27.0 per cent in 1913 (table 9.4).[14] During the same period the output of the US increased rapidly so that by 1913 its share of the output of the capitalist countries was more than two and a half times that of the UK. Furthermore, although Britain remained the largest

Table 9.3. *GDP shares of 'world' capitalist countries (% benchmark years)*

	UK	US	Germany	Japan
1870	21.5	24.5	8.6	5.0
1913	15.3	40.8	8.9	5.0
1929	11.8	46.1	7.5	6.2
1950	11.1	51.3	6.5	5.1
1973	7.9	41.5	8.7	13.9
1989	6.9	41.0	7.8	16.7

Notes:
1 'World' is Maddison's 16 capitalist countries.
2 GDP data are measured in 1985 US relative prices and adjusted to exclude the impact of boundary changes.
Source: Authors' calculations from Maddison (1991).

exporter in 1913, its share of total exports was only 8 percentage points greater than that of the US and only 6 percentage points greater than that of Germany.

During the inter-war period Britain attempted to reimpose its hegemony, but its long-run relative decline continued. By 1929 the US share of the capitalist world's GDP was four times that of Britain and it had overtaken Britain as the world's leading exporter.[15] Britain could not maintain its leading role in the international monetary system; indeed, it has been argued that this, combined with the reluctance of the US to assume leadership, resulted in global instability which exacerbated the depth and duration of the great depression (Kindleberger, 1973).[16] What is certainly true is that the post-World War Two 'Golden Age of Capitalism' was underpinned by the strength of the US economy, with the dollar thereby being able to act as the anchor to the international monetary system. As indicated in tables 9.3 and 9.4, by 1950 the US accounted for over half of GDP, and a third of exports, of the capitalist countries. However, the growth of the world economy and the emergence of other economies, in particular Germany and Japan, was to undermine the US's relative position. In 1973, when the Bretton Woods system collapsed, the US share of output had fallen by 10 percentage points since 1950 and its share of exports had fallen to less than the combined total of Germany and Japan.

Table 9.4 indicates that the US share of exports has declined since 1973 whereas the Japanese share has increased significantly. In terms of shares of world manufactured exports, as shown in table 9.5, Japan has certainly

Table 9.4. *Export shares of 'world' capitalist countries (% benchmark years)*

	UK	US	Germany	Japan
1870	37.2	11.0	16.6	0.2
1913	27.0	19.1	21.1	1.2
1950	20.5	32.7	5.6	1.9
1973	8.8	23.5	14.5	9.1
1987	8.4	20.1	14.4	13.4

Notes:
1 'World' is Maddison's 16 capitalist countries.
2 Export data are measured in 1985 prices and exchange rates.
Source: Authors' calculations from Maddison (1991).

caught up with, if not overtaken, the US, and while the European Union (EU) had, as recently as 1980, a share almost double that of Japan, it has since fallen significantly. On this measure, the balance of forces appears now to be very much a tripolar one. Looking at the distribution of world income shows Europe, the US and Japan as the three clear concentrations. Although Japan accounts for a far lower share of world income than does either the EU or the US, Japan's GDP per head was 119 per cent of the EU average in 1990, with a faster growth rate than in either the US or the EU.

Breaking down manufacturing trade into high, medium and low tech, Japan can be seen from the figures reported in table 9.6 not only to have captured a growing proportion of OECD trade, but particularly so in high tech trade, with a concomitant decline in the US's share of total manufacturing trade in the OECD, other than in low tech trade. These changes in relative shares have been accompanied over the past 20 years by a fall in OECD manufacturing employment of 8 per cent. Yet manufacturing employment actually rose in Japan over the same period by 2 per cent and was barely unchanged in the US. It is the EU which has had the big manufacturing job losses, amounting to 20 per cent over the past 20 years, with the worst case being the UK, suffering a 35 per cent fall. This in turn is reflected in the poor EU employment rates and correspondingly high unemployment.

The globalisation of technology

In this section we evaluate trends in the globalisation of technology or 'techno-globalism'. A distinction can be made between three separate pro-

172 Michael Kitson and Jonathan Michie

Table 9.5. *Exports: shares of world exports of manufactures (%)*

	1980	1986	1992
Japan	11.2	14.1	12.3
US	13.3	10.8	12.8
EU	21.9	19.4	17.6
Intra-EU	24.1	22.9	26.1
Rest of world	29.4	32.8	31.2

Source: Kitson and Michie, 1995a.

cesses which are often subsumed within the catch-all general term technological globalisation (on which, see Archibugi and Michie, 1995, 1997). Firstly, the international exploitation of national technological capabilities: firms try to exploit their innovations on global markets either by exporting products which embody them or by licensing the know-how. Secondly, collaboration across borders among both public and business institutions to exchange and develop know-how: firms are expanding their non-equity agreements to share the costs and risks of industrial research (see Hagedoorn and Schakenraad, 1990; 1993). Metcalfe (1995) points out that the scientific community has always been international in scope, although public research centres and academia have recently increased their proportion of cross-border linkages substantially. Thirdly, the generation of innovations across more than one country, which refers particularly to the activities of multinational corporations, as discussed by Cantwell (1995) and Patel (1995).

On the first two of these dimensions to the globalisation of technology, it is hardly controversial that they have increased in importance. Trade and patent flows, international technical agreements and scientific co-authorships have all shown a dramatic increase over the past two decades or so. On the third category of the extent to which multinational corporations have increased their technological operations in host countries, the evidence itself is less well established. Patel (1995), taking into account the patented inventions of more than 500 of the world's largest enterprises, shows that the vast majority of inventions are developed in the firms' home nation. According to him, multinational corporations — the companies which by definition are globally oriented – tend to be loyal to their own home-based country when they have to locate a strategic asset such as technology. However, these results presented by Patel appear at odds with those of Cantwell (1995). From a historical perspective, Cantwell shows that the

Table 9.6. *Shares of OECD trade in manufactures (%)*

| | 1970 | | | | 1980 | | | |
	Total	High tech	Medium tech	Low tech	Total	High tech	Medium tech	Low tech
US	20.3	31.1	21.7	13.4	17.4	26.3	15.4	13.3
Japan	11.0	13.2	8.5	13.2	15.0	21.1	16.9	7.1
Germany	18.9	17.7	23.1	15.0	20.6	16.2	24.7	17.9
France	9.3	7.7	8.5	10.7	10.3	8.7	10.0	12.1
Italy	7.3	5.5	7.1	8.5	8.6	5.1	7.7	12.8
UK	10.4	10.5	11.9	8.9	8.9	10.2	8.5	8.5

Source: Kitson and Michie, 1995a.

share of innovations generated by firms in host countries has increased considerably.

Patented inventions, however, capture the most formalised part of technological knowledge only. Multinational corporations might be keener to decentralise forms of knowledge which do not belong to the core of their business strategy. Companies might be more willing to locate abroad facilities which are less critical to their strategy, such as software, engineering, design and so on. Less-developed countries offer an adequately trained workforce but at salaries which are much lower than in the developed countries while information technologies make the geographical location of high-tech jobs less relevant. This justifies the widespread concern that industrial countries could lose skill-intensive jobs to the benefit of the South.

On what might induce companies to centralise or decentralise their technological activities, Howells and Wood (1993) suggest that the advantages of centralisation include: the benefits of economies of scale and scope which are associated with larger R&D operations; the minimum efficient size which is associated with indivisibilities of certain scientific instruments and facilities; the increased security over in-house research, which amongst other things reduces the risk of competitors copying or leap-frogging in key research fields; and the ability to create a well-established dense local innovation network with higher-education institutes, contract research companies and other support agencies. The main advantages they see associated with decentralisation are: a more effective and applicable R&D effort focused on the actual needs of the business and operational units; improved communications or coupling between R&D and other key corporate functions; less problems in 'programme dislocation' when a project is transferred from R&D to production; and better responsiveness to various local market needs. To this list might be added: to keep a window open on the technological developments of other countries; and to take advantage of the fields of excellence of the host country.[17]

2 Trade and economic performance

From the above it should be clear that the world economy is indeed becoming more integrated, but that the notion of a fully globalised economy is a misleading simplification. The pace and extent of globalisation has varied during different international policy regimes and has been interrupted by intermediate developments, such as the formation of regional trading blocs.

Conventionally, it has been argued that 'globalisation' implies either that it is no longer feasible for individual countries to pursue national trade policies in face of globalised financial markets or that it is unnecessary since trade deficits will only be the result of individuals' decisions to save or dissave, which can be readily financed by global financial markets, and that these trade imbalances will therefore in time be self-correcting.[18] This has been accompanied by a positing of national economic policy objectives as being to seek 'stability' and 'convergence'. Stability is interpreted, perversely, as stability of policy instruments – interest rates, exchange rates, fiscal balances, and so on – despite the fact that stability in these will provoke or exacerbate instability in real economic variables. Convergence is interpreted, again perversely, as the convergence of policy instruments – interest rates, tax rates and government expenditure – to the lowest level, despite the fact that such convergence may generate divergences in real economic variables.

Contrary to the developing orthodoxy, we would argue that increased economic integration increases the need for the active use of economic instruments, including where appropriate unilateral trade policies (see Kitson and Michie, 1995b), in order to target real variables such as output and employment.

More specifically, the distributional impact of exchange rate movements increases as economies become more open on capital and current accounts, with any given exchange rate movement causing a greater redistribution of income within the domestic economy.[19] Additionally, increased international integration may constrain the growth and weaken the economic structure of some trading nations.

Although the hysteresis literature suggests that shocks will affect the growth level and not the growth rate, here we adopt an alternative Kaldorian view, whereby shocks can also affect the growth rate. Kaldor's approach (1970, 1982), incorporating the Harrod foreign trade multiplier (Harrod,

1933), emphasises that the trade cycle reflects fluctuations in export demand. Additionally, he argues that investment is best modelled as an induced component of aggregate demand, being determined by the income changes which are in turn induced by the Harrod foreign trade multiplier. Whereas exports are an injection into the foreign trade multiplier, imports are a leakage. Thus, a high dependence on imports – a high import propensity – may constrain the growth of a domestic economy. Moreover, variations in trade performance in an increasingly integrated world economy may lead to persistent divergences in growth rates, with success in international trade becoming cumulative as increasing demand for net exports allows countries (or, more specifically, the firms and industries within them) to exploit economies of scale, improving their competitiveness and leading to further improvements in their trade performance. Conversely, weaker trading nations may fail to maintain balance of payments equilibrium at a high level of economic activity, with deflationary policies then pursued in an attempt to maintain external balance. The combined impact of poor trade performance and domestic deflation is likely to lead to a cumulative deterioration in relative economic growth as countries fail to exploit the increasing returns associated with a high level of economic activity. These twin processes of virtuous cycles of growth and vicious cycles of decline illustrate that the benefits of trade integration may not be evenly spread (Sawyer, 1994, discusses these processes of vicious cycles and uneven spreading of benefits as among the factors which have made full employment a relatively exceptional state of affairs under capitalism).

A cumulative causation approach may be taken to suggest that economies may be permanently locked-in to a slow or a fast growth path. This would be misleading as well as inconsistent with the 'stylised facts' of growth (Kitson, 1996). Although cumulative processes may generate forces that encourage divergences in growth, other forces may temper or ameliorate such effects. The international transfer of technology may allow the adoption of new techniques – improving the performance of weak economies. Furthermore, successful countries and regions may get 'locked-in' to certain techniques of production or become overcommitted in certain sectors (Setterfield, 1992), constraining their future growth performance – a typical example being the UK's overcommitment to traditional industries at the end of the nineteenth century. Additionally, a change in policy regime may improve the growth path of a relatively weak economy, and if particularly successful may create the conditions for a virtuous cycle of growth. Thus, although a cumulative causation approach indicates the forces that generate divergences in growth, such divergences will be affected, probably bounded, and potentially reversed, by the institutional, policy and technological regime.

With trade integration increasing the potential costs and benefits which will result from one nation's competitive advantage or disadvantage, increasing globalisation makes national institutions and policies more important rather than less. The costs of falling behind are exacerbated.

3 Implications for economic policy

Thus we would argue that increased globalisation of trade and technology increases the need for active government economic, trade, industrial and technology policies. A failure to formulate a cohesive policy framework can lead to an individual country suffering from externally generated shocks and/or being locked into slow growth due to an inability to effectively compete in an increasingly integrated world economy.

A first requirement is a stable macroeconomic policy regime – where stability is judged by real variables, such as output and employment growth rather than stability of nominal variables such as prices of money supply growth (or its new-Keynesian descendent, nominal GDP). Fiscal, monetary and exchange rate policies should aim to ensure a continuous and sustainable expansion of aggregate demand, with flexibility to counteract external shocks. The potential permanent impact of temporary shocks on the output level, which will be particularly important in economies highly dependent on skills and sophisticated capital equipment, indicates the importance of counter-cyclical policies. In addition it shows the danger of deflationary policies to counter inflation which may permanently harm long-run growth potential.

A second requirement is an effective industrial and technology policy. The importance of nation-specific factors in developing technological innovation has been highlighted by Freeman (1987) and Nelson and Rosenberg (1993) amongst others. The concept of a national system of innovation is defined and applied differently (Archibugi and Michie, 1997), although it usually embodies education, innovation and R&D policies, as well as historical and cultural factors. Thus the ability to utilise increasingly globalised technology, will depend on national systems, or as Abramovitz (1986) has stressed, 'social capability'.[20] Metcalfe (1995) differentiates between two broad categories of government action, firstly, financial incentives to companies to attract companies' innovative activities and, secondly, public supply of infrastructures to make a country attractive for the deployment of such activities. The latter approach, which includes investment in education, communications and university–industry partnerships and so on, have increased in importance and are likely to be more effective than the financial incentive approach. The effectiveness of financial incentives may be greater in attracting lower-tech activities which are more cost sen-

sitive and more internationally mobile. Additionally, the positive externalities from a public investment strategy are likely to be greater, an issue
prominent in the new growth theory literature.

A third requirement are policies that enhance social capability. Crafts
(1995), in analysing growth in Western Europe during the period 1950–73,
stresses the importance of institutional reform. Eichengreen (1996) argues
that European countries achieved high growth during the post-World War
Two period through the formation of institutional arrangements that promoted high investment and wage restraint, to the long-term advantage of
firms and workers. Since the collapse of the 'golden age' in the early 1970s
there has been a failure in the industrialised countries to reform institutions
in order to reduce distributive conflict whilst maintaining high investment
and job generation rates.

While globalisation may result in national action having greater payoffs
– and national inaction greater costs – it could still be the case that although
globalisation makes national action more rather than less important, at the
same time it makes it more difficult, or less feasible. Has the process of
globalisation removed discretion over domestic economic management?
Our answer would be no. The state's involvement in domestic economic
activity varies widely – with significant differences in government expenditure, taxation, size of the welfare state, the extent of income distribution
and industrial and labour market policies. Furthermore, there is little evidence that there is any trend towards economic policies converging. Among
the larger economies, the gap between the lowest and highest shares of
government has increased since 1980, and this was during a period when
the average public spending/GDP ratio increased (*The Economist*, 1995).

The aspect of globalisation that has had the greatest impact on domestic
policy has been the internationalisation of capital markets. Yet, even here
the impact has been mixed. The free movement of capital has limited the
scope for independent exchange rate and monetary policies. This has had
benefits – the UK's attempt to maintain an overvalued exchange rate in the
ERM, with all that entailed for output and employment, was scuppered by
the volume of speculative currency flows. Glyn (1995) has argued that the
free movement of capital is likely to constrain an expansionary domestic
programme as the reaction of foreign exchange markets will lead to large
initial depreciation which will 'front-load' the impact on real wages. Such
terms of trade effect on real wages may have adverse effects but this will
depend on the structure of wage bargaining and, in particular, the speed of
response to rising import prices. Furthermore, a large depreciation will
increase the demand for tradables (exports and import substitutes) which
will increase output and employment and may allow real wages to increase
in the medium term. Additionally, an expansionary fiscal policy may be

easier due to increased financial integration allowing countries to finance public borrowing without significant adverse impact on domestic interest rates.

Conclusions

The purpose of this chapter has been to consider the broader economic environment within which technological globalisation and policy need to be analysed. We find several parallels between the processes of economic and technological globalisation. Firstly, both processes – of economic and technological globalisation – tend to be rather poorly defined; when unpicked the processes are found to be much more complex than a simple and single term such as 'globalisation' might imply.[21] Secondly, then, much of the 'globalisation' claims are rather exaggerated (mainly due, no doubt, to the term being rather poorly specified).[22] Thirdly, though, another possible reason for such claims being exaggerated is that some of the developments which have been interpreted as constituting evidence of increased globalisation have rather constituted an increase in regionalisation (see Kitson and Michie, 1995b; and Archibugi and Michie, 1995) – and this increase in regionalisation could be considered to represent in some respects a move away from globalisation. Fourthly, the globalisation that has occurred has not necessarily meant a reduction in national differentiation; on the contrary, it has been accompanied by an increase in technological specialisation (Archibugi and Michie, 1995) and by global winners and losers in terms of economic growth (Kitson and Michie, 1995b). And, fifthly, national economic, industrial and technology policy is made more important rather than less by any increased openness of national economies which means that any loss of competitive advantage is translated all the more rapidly into declining market share, output, employment and living standards. Policy may be more difficult to implement in face of global pressures, but far from implying a need for *less* government policy, such globalisation implies that policy action may need to be *more* interventionist and far-reaching than was the case in the past, if the necessary goals are to be achieved in these more difficult conditions.

Notes

1 Quoted in the *Financial Times*, 20 March 1996.
2 Quoted in the *Economist*, 7 October 1995, p. 15.
3 Thus: 'Many over-enthusiastic analysts and politicians have gone beyond the evidence in *over-stating* both the extent of the dominance of world markets and their ungovernability. . . . we have a myth that *exaggerates* the degree of helplessness in the face of contemporary economic forces. . . . It is *not* the case cur-

rently that radical goals are attainable: full employment in the advanced countries, a fairer deal for the poorer developing countries, and more widespread
democratic control over economic affairs for the world's people.' Hirst and
Thompson, 1996, pp. 6–7, emphasis added – to highlight the fact that the logic
of the 'globalisation is making national governments irrelevant' thesis is not
being challenged, only the degree to which the process has gone. As explained
in the text, we do not accept this logic. It may well be that radical goals are less
attainable today than previously, but to decide whether or not this is so would
require an evaluation of factors other than the degree of globalisation.

4   This chapter is concerned with 'winners and losers' in the context of aggregate
    national economic performance. There is, of course, the related issue of
    'winners and losers' within nations, and how globalisation has affected the
    growth of inequality and unemployment amongst low-skilled workers in the
    industrialised countries (see Wood 1994, 1995; and for a more sceptical view see
    Eatwell, 1995, and Singh and Zammit, 1995; for a related argument to Woods's,
    see Galbraith, 1996, commented on by Michie, 1996).

5   For instance the growth of trade accelerated from the early 1900s to 1913.

6   Eichengreen (1994) examines the volatility of GDP across countries during the
    operation of different exchange rate regimes. He concludes that 'There is no evi-
    dence that output volatility increased with the shift from pegged to floating rate
    regimes after 1972: if anything the opposite may have been true' (p. 172). This
    conclusion may be dependent on Eichengreen's use of standard deviations (of
    detrended series) as the measure of volatility, since the transition to floating
    exchange rates led to lower growth of world output (see table 9.1) and a lower
    mean growth rate for most industrialised countries.

7   As pointed out by Wells (1993), on the more demanding criteria of per capita
    output there are six years of absolute decline.

8   During the post-World War Two period there was an increase in service sector
    activity in both the private and public sectors, much of which was not interna-
    tionally tradable.

9   Japanese economic policy also shifted towards austerity in 1981. It is true that
    the Japanese budget deficit continued to increase, but this was due to depressed
    tax revenue (see Itoh, 1994, p. 37).

10 See Bhagwati (1993) who argues that the US, frustrated at the slow progress of
    the GATT talks, turned to regionalism instead.

11 The intra-bloc share of the original six members of the EC also increased up to
    the early 1960s but subsequently it declined until the early mid 1980s. This pos-
    sibly reflected the trade diversion impact of new members to the bloc.

12 The intensity of intra-regional trade index constructed by Anderson and
    Norheim (1993, table 2.2), for various benchmark years, shows a continuous
    rise for Western Europe during the post-World War Two period, a rise for
    North America until 1979 followed by a subsequent decline, and a decline for
    Asia since 1958. The apparent contradiction of the latter with the intra-bloc
    share evidence is probably due to the intensity index adjusting for the fast
    growth of the Asian economies.

13 These data do not cover the whole world economy. They are useful, however, in

providing internally consistent comparisons over time of the changing shares of output between the group of countries covered.

14 As with the GDP data, the export data series will underestimate the total of world exports. Using more comprehensive series (Lewis, 1981), the share of UK merchandise exports is seen to have declined from 18.9 per cent in 1870 to 13.7 per cent in 1913. Although these shares are lower, the rate of decline is very similar.

15 Maddison's (1962) figures for the whole world economy indicate that in 1929 the US had 14.7 per cent of world export markets whereas the UK had 8.6 per cent.

16 This argument has been challenged by Eichengreen (1992) who argues that the problems of the interwar monetary system were primarily due to lack of cooperation amongst central banks rather than the absence of an effective hegemonic power.

17 An extensive survey of companies' headquarters and host facilities has identified the type of work undertaken in overseas R&D laboratories (Pearce and Singh, 1992). The most frequent activities carried out in host countries are to derive new production technology and to adapt existing products to the local markets to make them accepted by local communities. Even the taste of Coca-cola, the most typical standardised product of the global economy, is not quite the same in the USA, Japan and Italy (see Ohmae, 1990).

18 For a discussion and criticism of this idea that trade deficits have been made unimportant, see Coutts and Godley (1992) and McCombie and Thirlwall (1992).

19 See Frieden (1994, p. 82) who also argues that it is the internationally oriented economic groups within any country which will in general prefer fixed exchange rates, while domestically based groups will prefer floating rates.

20 The level of social capability will vary over time and across countries. Moreover, the notion of 'social capability' is itself open to many interpretations; some believing it can be increased by rectifying market failures and improving incentive structures, others stressing macroeconomic stability, institutional reform and improved regulation.

21 For an analysis of the various processes involved in economic 'globalisation' see Kitson and Michie (1995a); and for a suggested taxonomy for analysing the globalisation of technology, see Archibugi and Michie (1995).

22 This is argued with regard to economic globalisation in Michie (1996) and with regard to technological globalisation in Archibugi and Michie eds., (1997).

References

Abramovitz, M. 1986. Catching up, forging ahead and falling behind, *Journal of Economic History*, 46: 385–406.

Anderson, K. and Backhurst, R. (eds.) 1993. *Regional Integration and the Global Trading System*, Hemel Hempstead, Harvester Wheatsheaf.

Anderson, K. and Norheim, H. 1993. History, geography and regional economic integration, in Anderson and Backhurst (eds.).

Archibugi, D. and Michie, J. 1995. The globalisation of technology: a new taxonomy, *Cambridge Journal of Economics*, 19: 121–40. Reprinted in Archibugi and Michie (eds.), 1997.

  1997. Technological globalisation or national systems of innovation?, *Futures*, 29: 121–37.

Archibugi, D. and Michie, J. (eds.) 1997. *Technology, Globalisation and Economic Performance*, Cambridge, Cambridge University Press.

Arestis, P. and Marshall, M. (eds.) 1994. *The Political Economy of Full Employment*, Aldershot, Edward Elgar.

Arestis, P., Palma, G. and Sawyer, M. (eds.) 1996. *Markets, Unemployment and Economic Policy: Essays in Honour of Geoff Harcourt*, London, Routledge.

Bhagwati, J. 1993. Regionalism and multilateralism: an overview, in Melo and Panagariya (eds.).

Bhagwati, J. and Irwin, D. 1987. The return of the reciprocitarians: US trade policy today, *The World Economy*, 10: 109–30.

Cantwell, J. A. 1995. The globalisation of technology: what remains of the product cycle model?, *Cambridge Journal of Economics*, 19: 155–74. Reprinted in Archibugi and Michie (eds.), 1997.

Carlin, W. and Soskice, D. 1990. *Macroeconomics and the Wage Bargain*, Oxford, Oxford University Press.

Commission of the European Communities 1993a. *Employment in Europe, 1993*, COM(93) 314, Luxembourg, Office of Official Publications of the European Communities.

  1993b. *European Social Policy, Green Paper*, COM(93) 551, Luxembourg, Office of Official Publications of the European Communities.

Coutts, K. and Godley, W. 1992. Does Britain's balance of payments matter any more?, in Michie (ed.).

Crafts, N. F. R. 1995. The golden age of economic growth in Western Europe, 1950–1973, *Economic History Review*, 48: 429–47.

Crafts, N. F. R. and Toniolo, G. (eds.) 1996. *Economic Growth in Postwar Europe*, Cambridge, Cambridge University Press.

Eatwell, J. 1995. The international origins of unemployment, in Michie and Grieve Smith (eds.).

Economist (The) 1995. The myth of the powerless state, 7 October, 15–6.

Eichengreen, B. 1992. *Golden Fetters: The Gold Standard and the Great Depression, 1919–39*, Oxford, Oxford University Press.

  1994. History of the international monetary system: implications for research in international macroeconomics and finance, in Van Der Ploeg (ed.).

  1996. Institutions and economic growth after World War II, in Crafts and Toniolo (eds.).

Freeman, C. 1987. *Technology Policy and Economic Performance*, London, Pinter Publishers.

Freeman, C. and Soete, L. (eds.) 1990. *New Explorations in the Economics of Technical Change*, London, Pinter.

Freiden, J. A. 1994. Exchange rate politics; contemporary lessons from American history, *Review of International Political Economy*, 1: 81–103.

Galbraith, J. 1996. Uneven development and the destabilization of the north: a Keynesian view, *International Review of Applied Economics*, 10: 107–20.

Glyn, A. 1995. Social democracy and full employment, *New Left Review*, May/June, 33–55.

Grassman, S. and Lundberg, E. (eds.) 1981. *The World Economic Order: Past and Prospects*, London and Basingstoke, Macmillan.

Hagedoorn, J. and Schakenraad, J. 1990. Inter-firm partnerships and cooperative strategies in core technologies, in Freeman and Soete (eds.).

1993. Strategic technology partnering and international corporate strategies, in Hughes (ed.).

Harrod, R. 1933. *International Economics*, Cambridge, Cambridge University Press.

Hirst, P. and Thompson, G. 1996. *Globalization in Question*, Cambridge, Polity Press.

Howells, J. and Wood, M. 1993. *The Globalisation of Production and Technology*, London, Belhaven Press.

Hughes, K. (ed.) 1993. *European Competitiveness*, Cambridge, Cambridge University Press.

Itoh, M. 1994. Is the Japanese economy in crisis, *Review of International Political Economy*, 1: 29–51.

Kaldor, N. 1970. The case for regional policies, *Scottish Journal of Political Economy*, 17: 337–48.

1982. Limitations of the *General Theory*, *Proceedings of the British Academy*, 68: 32–48.

Kindleberger, C. 1973. *The World in Depression, 1929–1939*, London, Allen Lane.

Kitson, M. 1996. The competitive weaknesses of the UK economy, in Arestis, Palma and Sawyer (eds.).

Kitson, M. and Michie, J. 1994. Depression and recovery: lessons from the interwar period, in Michie and Grieve Smith (eds.).

1995a. Trade and growth: a historical perspective, in J. Michie and J. Grieve Smith (eds.).

1995b. Conflict, cooperation and change: the political economy of trade and trade policy, *Review of International Political Economy*, 2: 632–57.

Lewis, A. 1981. The rates of growth of world trade, 1830–1973, in Grassman and Lundberg (eds.).

Lloyd, P. J. 1992. Regionalisation and world trade, *OECD Economic Studies*, Spring, 7–44.

Maddison, A. 1962. Growth and fluctuations in the world economy, 1870–1960, *Banca Nazionale del Lavoro Quarterly Review*, 15: 127–95.

1991. *Dynamic Forces in Capitalist Development*, Oxford, Oxford University Press.

McCombie, J. and Thirlwall, T. 1992. The re-emergence of the balance of payments constraint, in Michie (ed.).

Melo, J. and Panagariya, A. (eds.) 1993. *New Dimensions in Regional Integration*, Cambridge, Cambridge University Press.

Metcalfe, J. S. 1995. Technology systems and technology policy in an evolutionary framework, *Cambridge Journal of Economics*, 19: 25–46. Reprinted in Archibugi and Michie (eds.), 1997.

Michie, J. 1996. Creative destruction or regressive stagnation?, *International Review of Applied Economics*, 10: 121–6.

Michie, J. (ed.) 1992. *The Economic Legacy: 1979–1992*, London, Academic Press.

Michie, J. and Grieve Smith, J. (eds.) 1994. *Unemployment in Europe*, London, Academic Press.

1995. *Managing the Global Economy*, Oxford, Oxford University Press.

Nelson, R. R. (ed.) 1993. *National Innovation Systems*, New York, Oxford University Press.

Nelson, R. R. and Rosenberg, N. 1993. Technical innovation and national systems, in Nelson (ed.).

Ohmae, K. 1990. *The Borderless World: Management Lessons in the New Logic of the Global Market Place*, London, Collins.

1993. The rise of the region state, *Foreign Affairs*, Spring, 78–87.

1995. Putting global logic first, *Harvard Business Review*, January/February, 119–25.

Patel, P. 1995. Localised production of technology for global markets, *Cambridge Journal of Economics*, 19: 141–54. Reprinted in Archibugi and Michie (eds.), 1997.

Pearce, R. D. and Singh, S. 1992. *Globalizing Research and Development*, Houndmills, Macmillan.

Sawyer, M. 1994. Obstacles to the achievement of full employment in capitalist economies, in Arestis and Marshall (eds.).

Setterfield, M. 1992. A long run theory of effective demand: modelling macro-economic systems with hysteresis, Ph.D. thesis, Dalhouise University, Canada.

Singh, A. and Zammit, A. 1995. Employment and unemployment: north and south, in Michie and Grieve Smith (eds.).

Van Der Ploeg, F. (ed.) 1994. *The Handbook of International Macroeconomics*, Oxford, Blackwell.

Wells, J. 1993. Factors making for increasing international economic integration, Unpublished Manuscript, Cambridge, University of Cambridge.

Wes, M. 1996. Globalisation: winners and losers, Commission on Public Policy and British Business, IPPR Issue Paper No. 3.

Wood, A. 1994. *North–South Trade, Employment and Inequality: Changing Fortunes in a Skill-Driven World*, Oxford, Oxford University Press.

1995. How trade hurts unskilled workers, *Journal of Economic Perspectives*, 9: 57–80.

10 The geographical sourcing of technology-based assets by multinational enterprises

JOHN H. DUNNING AND CLIFFORD WYMBS

1 The changing nature of foreign direct investment

Until about a decade ago, the received theory of foreign direct investment (FDI)[1] asserted that firms established foreign value-added activities in order to exploit their home-based competitive (or ownership-specific (O)) advantages, and to benefit from the internalisation of cross-border intermediate product markets. To be sure, there was some *natural* resource seeking foreign direct investment (FDI), designed to gain access to agricultural products, raw materials and minerals not available, or not available on such advantageous terms, in the investing country. Multinational enterprises (MNEs) also invested in developing countries to take advantage of low cost and/or more productive unskilled or semi-skilled labour. However, in each of these cases, as with market and efficiency seeking FDI, the main objective of the investing firms was to seek out the location specific assets of foreign countries, which could be used in conjunction with their own mobile O specific assets, which, in turn, were assumed to reflect the availability and quality of *created* assets in their home countries.

World economic events of the last decade – particularly the globalisation and liberalisation of markets, a new generation of technological and organisational advances and the emergence of third world countries as significant sources of FDI – have changed the economic environment for MNE activity. While, as with exports and licensing arrangements, international production continues to be a means of capturing economic rent on the O advantages of the investing companies, increasingly firms are investing abroad to protect or augment their core competencies. In such cases, they are 'buying into' foreign created assets (notably technological capacity, information, human creativity, and markets), some of which are proprietary to particular foreign firms and others which are more generally accessible to corporations but immobile across geographical space.[2]

Most frequently, the modality of created asset seeking FDI takes the form of the acquisition of foreign firms, rather than greenfield investment. Since the early 1980s, about three-fifths of all intra-triad FDI has taken the form of mergers and acquisitions.[3] At the same time, there has been a spectacular increase in cross-border non-equity strategic alliances, especially within the knowledge and information-intensive sectors (Hagedoorn, 1996). The recognition that firms cannot fully reach their global objectives without cooperating with other economic entities, particularly in foreign countries, has led to the coining of the term *alliance capitalism* to describe the kind of market economy now emerging (Dunning, 1995, 1997). More than anything, created asset-seeking FDI reflects the widening geographical sources of knowledge capital throughout the world, but particularly within the advanced industrial countries. It is prompted both by the fact that the supply of many products is requiring multiple and very different kinds of knowledge, and by the need of firms to share the costs, and/or increase the rate, of innovative and related activities to maintain, or advance, their global competitive positions.

2 MNEs technological activities in host countries: some evidence

Scholarly opinion about the significance of the foreign sourcing of the competitive advantages of firms is divided. In their earlier work, Raymond Vernon (1966) and Richard Caves (1971) both contend that the competitive advantages of firms largely reflected the resource competencies and market conditions of their home countries. More recently, Michael Porter (1990), has vigorously avowed the view that firms need a strong home base from which to launch and upgrade their global activities, although he also acknowledges that firms may not only have multiple home bases but some of these may be outside their countries of origin. Porter's concept of the home base essentially relates the need of corporations to cluster their asset-creating activities in those countries and, indeed, in regions or districts within countries which exhibit a competitive advantage in these activities.[4] Hence, it is quite consistent that a UK pharmaceutical company may have its home base for research and development in tropical diseases, for example, in Malaysia, or a computer software company may have its home base in a region of low labour costs such as Bangalore in India, or for a Japanese company to locate its home base for bio-technology R&D in California.

Other scholars – notably Rugman (1991), Rugman ed. (1993), Rugman, Broeck, and Verbeke eds. (1995) and Dunning (1992) – have been less concerned with the geographical allocation of a firm's asset-creating value added activities, which is frequently designed to capture the economies of scale or take advantage of location-bound specialised resources and capabilities (Dunning, 1993), than with the extent to which its presence in a foreign country enables it to augment its existing global competitive advantages. This it may do both by a feedback of information and knowledge, experience and expertise created within its network of subsidiaries, and by tapping into the knowledge and information created by other firms or of non-market institutions in the regions or countries in which their subsidiaries are located. Such knowledge augmentation may result from both formal bilateral alliances with foreign suppliers, customers and competitors (Rugman, 1995; D'Cruz and Rugman, 1993), and from being part of an agglomeration of interrelated knowledge creating and learning activities, e.g., in the form of techno-cities, science parks, R&D consortia and industrial clusters.[5]

Over the years, there have been a large number of attempts to assess the extent to which firms perceived they gained a competitive advantage by tapping into foreign located created assets. In the late 1950s and 1960s, several studies showed that there was a sizeable feedback of knowledge and information from foreign subsidiaries to their parent company.[6] In one of the first post-World War Two surveys on FDI in the USA, Ajami and Ricks (1981) found that the search for advanced technical and management know-how was one of the key factors which was then attracting FDI to the US. Later studies, e.g., Pearce and Singh (1991), Pearce and Papannastassiou (1995) and Kim and Lyn (1990) have supported this contention, with respect to FDI in both the United States and Europe.

More recently, Kuemmerle (1996), in a survey of 32 leading MNEs in the pharmaceutical and electronics industries found not only that a sizeable proportion of R&D was undertaken outside their home countries, but that, between 1980 and 1995 this proportion had risen. A study of corporate patenting in the United States of 167 of the largest European and American Industrial firms over the period 1901–90 confirms that over the last decade a rising proportion of foreign technological activity has been designed to provide a further source of technology that can be utilised internationally (Cantwell and Piscitello, 1996, pp. 29–30). In their investigation of Japanese FDI in the US, Kogut and Chang (1991) found that Japanese firms were attracted to R&D intensive sectors – particularly via the establishment of joint ventures. Earlier, Kogut (1990) had concluded that one of the main reasons for Japanese FDI in the biotechnology and electronics sectors in the US had been to tap into US technological advantage. David Teece (1992) came to the same conclusion with respect to FDI in Silicon Valley in California; while Paul Almeida (1997) suggests that, relative to their indigenous counterparts, foreign firms tend to be more concentrated in US regions which are knowledge intensive.

These data are confirmed by more macro-data on patents and R&D expenditures. Cantwell and Hodson (1991) have shown that the proportion of patents registered in the US by the foreign subsidiaries of the world's largest industrial enterprises increased on average from 20 per cent in 1970 to 41.5 per cent in 1987. Such ratios significantly varied both between sectors and countries, but it can be concluded that the contribution of subsidiaries to the technological advantages of their parent organisations was inescapable.

The proportion of R&D expenditures of US MNEs accounted for by their foreign affiliates rose from 7.5 per cent in 1977 to 13.2 per cent in 1993 (see the results of the US Department of Commerce survey in Dalton and Serapico, 1995), while that of Swedish MNEs rose from 14.0 per cent in 1978 to 24.7 per cent in 1994 (IUI, 1996); and that of Japanese MNEs from 1.44 per cent in 1989–90 to 2.51 per cent in 1992–3 (Kumar, 1996). The percentage of total R&D expenditure accounted for by foreign affiliates rose from 7.5 per cent in 1977 to 15.0 per cent in 1992 (Dunning and Narula, 1995). Data on the percentages of R&D expenditure in the UK by foreign owned firms tell a similar story for Pearce and Singh (1992).

Finally, mention might be made of some current research by Birkinshaw and Hood (1996) which, after reviewing a large number of contemporary studies on the product and process activities of foreign subsidiaries, concludes that there is a distinct correlation between the age and experience of foreign subsidiaries and their likely contribution to the competitive advantages of the organisations of which they are part.

3 A survey of 150 of the world's largest industrial enterprises

Our own contribution to the debate on the sourcing of technological advantages by MNEs is based upon the opinions of business executives (usually the director of foreign operations) of some 150 of the world's largest industrial enterprises. These opinions were obtained by way of a questionnaire completed in 1994 and 1995.[7] Between them, these enterprises accounted for about 40 per cent of the total FDI stock of all enterprises in the manufacturing and petroleum industries in 1993–4. Some details of their industry and country distribution are set out in tables 10.1 and 10.2. Earlier papers by one of the authors (Dunning 1996; Dunning and Lundan, 1997) gave some general results of this survey. This chapter is concerned with the perceived significance of FDI as a modality for the sourcing of the *technological* assets of the investing firms.

In table 10.1, industrial sectors are grouped by level of technology deployed, sales, and degree of multinationality are reported for each sector.[8] Two separate measures are reported for multinationality, one based on an average of the percentage of the global assets and employment of the sample firms accounted for by their foreign subsidiaries and the other on the latter's propensity to engage in foreign R&D activity.

Table 10.1. *Distribution of 150 leading industrial MNEs by sector, 1994–5*

Sector	No. of companies	Global sales (Bln$)	Sales %	Degree of multinationality Assets and employ*	R&D*
High technology					
Aerospace	5	73.1	2.9	6.4	2.7
Pharmaceuticals	6	43.9	1.8	49.7	28.4
Chemicals	16	189.9	7.6	50.5	23.4
Computers	9	213.9	8.6	28.4	8.5
Electronics	20	389.1	15.6	38.9	24.8
Total	56	909.9	36.4	34.8	17.5
Medium technology					
Industrial equipment	8	73.8	3.0	38.4	11.0
Motor vehicles	12	580.0	23.2	34.3	7.5
Petroleum	14	498.4	19.9	47.8	24.3
Total	34	1,152.2	46.1	40.2	14.3
Low technology					
Food and drink	22	246.7	9.9	46.7	30.5
Paper	10	39.0	1.6	24.4	8.1
Building materials	5	16.4	0.7	48.0	39.7
Metal and metal proc.	14	107.3	4.3	36.3	22.8
Other	9	28.5	1.1	57.3	45.6
Total	60	437.9	17.5	42.5	29.3
Total all sectors in 1994–6	150	2,500.0	100.0	40.3	22.0

Note:
* 'Assets and employment' and 'R&D' totals for each technology grouping are averages of industry values.
Source: Survey conducted by the authors in 1994–5.

Within the *high-technology sectors* (HTS) grouping, aerospace companies are shown to have the lowest percentage of foreign value added activity – viz 6.4 per cent assets and employment and 2.7 per cent R&D. These low totals are directly related to the strategic nature of the industry and its close ties with national governments. The computer sector, with the next lowest foreign assets and employment of 28.4 per cent and R&D ratio of 8.5 per cent, is partially explained by the United States and Japanese dominance of this sector. There are strong agglomerative economies associated with research pockets located in the United States, most notably Silicon Valley in California; and there is also a tendency for the majority of

Table 10.2. *Distribution of 150 leading industrial MNEs by region or country of origin, 1994–5*

Region/country	No. of countries	Global sales (Bln$)	Sales %	Degree of multinationality	
				Assets and employ*	R&D*
Developed countries	134	2,455.4	98.2	42.3	22.8
Large European	46	959.9	38.4	49.6	31.0
of which Germany	13	359.6	14.4	43.6	23.1
UK + UK/net	23	400.3	16.0	58.0	36.7
Other	10	200.0	8.0	36.9	28.3
Small European	20	131.1	5.2	55.0	33.1
of which Sweden	7	32.0	1.3	68.5	53.0
Switzerland	5	68.9	2.8	59.9	33.2
Other	8	30.2	1.2	40.2	16.3
United States	34	728.1	29.1	36.1	13.2
Japan	26	606.4	24.3	27.0	5.8
Other developed countries	8	30.0	1.2	31.3	18.3
Developing countries	16	44.7	1.8	20.1	13.9
Total all countries in 1994–5	150	2,500.0	100.0	40.5	22.0

Note and Source: As for table 10.1.

Japanese R&D, other than scanning activities, to be located in Japan. At the other end of the spectrum are firms in the pharmaceutical sector which have over 28 per cent of their R&D facilities and 50 per cent of their assets and employment located outside their home countries. This finding is consistent with research of Kuemmerle (1996) and demonstrates the need in this industry for global knowledge augmentation to remain competitive. Similar patterns are observed in the chemical and electronic sectors.

Turning to firms in the *medium-technology sectors* (MTS), auto production (as reflected in assets and employment) is more likely to be located near end product markets, while R&D is located near home production. Somewhat surprisingly, in view of quite recent penetration of foreign markets by Japanese firms, a Japanese MNE had the highest foreign R&D component of over 20 per cent. Due to the nature of its product and refining processes, petroleum companies recorded the highest levels of both measures of multinationality.

In the *low-technology sectors* (LTS), the above average degree of multinationality associated with the food and drink and building materials sectors primarily reflects the importance of having products both tailored to end user requirements and made near their point of final consumption. On the other hand, paper is more a commodity product, and research is mainly located near the home production area.

Table 10.2 classifies our sample firms by their country of nationality. MNEs headquartered in developed countries accounted for an overwhelming percentage of global sales (viz 98.2 per cent). More specifically, firms from large European countries accounted for 38.4 per cent of sales, those from smaller European countries for 5.2 per cent, United States companies for 29.1 per cent and Japanese companies accounted for 24.3 per cent of sales.

Though approximately ten percentage points lower than the United States and 15 percentage points lower than their large European counterparts, the Japanese asset and employment multinationality of Japanese firms' average of 27.0 per cent is more similar to these countries than its relative R&D percentages. In 1993–4 Japanese firms undertook only 5.8 per cent of their R&D expenditures outside of the border, while their equivalent percentages for the United States and large European firms were 13.2 per cent and 31.0 per cent respectively. In general, Japanese firms appear to use foreign R&D for global scanning purposes, rather than to replicate their domestic innovative activities or to engage in specialised R&D best suited to the resource capabilities of most countries.

Firms from smaller European countries, e.g., Sweden and Switzerland and the UK recorded the highest degree of both indices of multinationality, while Germany had near average levels for assets and employment and R&D (22.0 per cent).

In table 10.3 we present a frequency distribution of the foreign located R&D of the sample firms, classified by their degree of technological intensity. It reveals that on average in 1993–4 foreign-based R&D accounted for 22.0 per cent of global R&D by the 106 MNEs (who accounted for 54.6 per cent of sales) which provided data on the subject. The MTS sector appears to be underrepresented when one looks at the sales of the respondent firms answering the questions; however, no such problems were accounted for in the other two categories.

As expected, within the HTS and the MTS categories, the more technology intensive MNEs also engaged in proportionately the most foreign R&D. This holds for the number of firms, sales revenues and R&D percentage. The results recorded from firms in the LTS were somewhat unexpected. The surveyed firms foreign R&D percentage was 27.2 per cent – a figure considerably more than that recorded by firms in the HTS and MTS (18.2 per cent and 14.8 per cent respectively – this evidence is however consistent with the data reported in the chapter by Pavitt and Patel, in this volume).

Table 10.3. *Percentage of R&D undertaken outside home country by technology grouping*

Percentage of foreign located R&D	High technology			Medium technology			Low technology			All technologies		
	Sales (Bln$)	%	No	Sales (Bln$)	%	No	Sales (Bln$)	%	No	Sales(Bln$)	%	No
Under 2.5	19.40	0.78	2	111.00	4.44	4	24.47	0.98	10	154.87	6.19	16
2.5–4.9	111.65	4.47	8	37.60	1.50	2	25.60	1.02	5	174.85	6.99	15
5.0–9.9	139.00	5.56	3	36.04	1.44	3	3.70	0.15	1	178.74	7.15	7
10.0–19.9	73.60	2.94	9	117.30	4.69	9	24.96	1.00	4	215.86	8.63	22
20.0–39.9	204.87	8.19	11	8.10	0.32	2	100.75	4.03	7	313.72	12.55	20
40.0–59.9	198.01	7.92	8	7.00	0.28	1	19.60	0.78	8	224.61	8.98	17
60%–	0.00	0.00	0	47.20	1.89	2	55.80	2.23	7	103.00	4.12	9
Total	746.53	29.86	41	364.24	14.57	23	254.88	10.20	42	1,365.65	54.63	106
No R&D data	163.37	6.53	15	787.96	31.52	11	183.02	7.32	18	1,134.35	45.37	44
Grand total	909.90	36.40	56	1,152.20	46.09	34	437.90	17.52	60	2,500.00	100.00	150

Percentage of firms responding to the R&D question: 70.67
Overall average R&D percentage: 22.01
High-technology average* 18.2
Medium technology average* 14.8
Low-technology average* 27.2

Note:
*Average values represent all firms in the particular technology sector.
Source: As for table 10.1.

One explanation could be that many LTS are multi-domestic requiring research to be conducted near the sources of production and/or consumption.

Finally, we would observe that there is a close correlation – of +0.70 – between the degree of multinationality of a firm (percentage of global assets and employment accounted for by their foreign affiliates) and the proportion of their global R&D undertaken outside their national boundaries. The correlation coefficient for firms in the above-average technology intensive sector was + 0.68; for those in the average technology-intensive sector, +0.56; for those in the below-average technology-intensive sectors +0.75.

4 The hypotheses and methodology

The main instrument for obtaining the data analysed in this chapter was a questionnaire circulated in 1994 and 1995 to the 500 largest industrial firms listed by *Fortune* in August 1993.[9] In that questionnaire, four sets of questions were asked about the geographical sourcing of technological assets. In each of the four questions, the respondent was asked to rank, on a scale of 1 to 7, his or her perception of the importance of FDI or cross-border alliances in the sourcing and/or augmenting of assets. The respondent was informed that a rank of 1 would indicate that he or she perceived all the advantages were derived from their firm's domestic operations and none from their foreign operations. By contrast, a rank of 7 would indicate that the respondent perceived all the advantages were derived from their firm's foreign operations; while a rank of 4 would indicate that home and foreign sourcing of technological advantages were equally balanced.

The four sets of questions referred to:

(1) The access to:
   (1a) *professional, scientific and administrative personnel* and
   (1b) *process and product technology* and *innovative capacity*. Separate ranks were requested for each of these created assets, and these were then averaged.
   (1c) *organisational structures and competencies* and *managerial capacity* and *competitiveness*. Again, separate ranks were obtain and averaged.
(2) The impact of consumer demand on:
   (2a) the *upgrading of product quality* and
   (2b) *making for more product innovation*. The results were averaged.
(3) The effect of inter-firm rivalry (i.e., is your main competition from domestic or foreign owned firms?)
(4) The perceived value of local technological links with:

(4a) *related firms* (industry agglomerative economies associated with cluster of suppliers, customers, competitors, etc.)

(4b) *universities and/or public or semipublic bodies*, e.g., research consortia in the host countries, in relation to those in the home country.

In each case, it is worth noting (although we did not ask the firms to give us information on this point) that any augmenting of knowledge or motivation to upgrade technological competitiveness might result either directly from the activities engaged in by the foreign subsidiaries, or from the ability of such subsidiaries to tap into external sources of knowledge by being part of a cluster of related activities (Porter, 1990).

A fifth question of interest concerned the relationship between modality of international involvement and the sourcing of technological advantages. In particular, we wished to test the hypothesis that, *ceteris paribus,* deeper forms of cross-border involvement, e.g., FDI and strategic alliances, are more likely to generate a feedback of technical knowledge and expertise than that of shallower forms of involvement, e.g., exports and sub-contracting. This we did by seeing whether the firms in our sample, which perceived FDI as a critical mode for acquiring technological advantages, also ranked the foreign sourcing of these related assets more highly than those which perceived that their main mode of augmenting such advantages was by non-equity alliances and/or exports.

In two earlier papers (Dunning, 1996; Dunning and Lundan, 1997), it was demonstrated that the degree of multinationality of a firm was by far the most significant contextual variable affecting the extent to which firms perceived that they acquired competitive advantages from their foreign activities. In some cases, too, the country of origin of the MNEs was seen to be significant. However, neither of these papers considered how the sourcing of technological advantage might vary according to industrial sector. This being so, in the first part of our field study, described in this section, we present a series of tables which set out the perceived significance of the foreign sourcing of the four kinds of technological advantage earlier identified, classified by the main industry of the respondent firms – as identified by the respondents. In table 10.4, we relate the sourcing of technological advantage of all firms according to 13 industrial sectors. In tables 10.5 and 10.6 we performed an in-depth look at the degree of multi-nationality within each industry and how it affects the sourcing of technological advantage. (Table 10.5 presents this information based on an assets and employment measure of multinationality, while table 10.6 uses R&D criteria). In tables 10.7, 10.8, 10.9, 10.10 and 10.11, we adopt a rather different procedure by setting out the ranking of technological advantage according to the perceived significance of three modalities of international involvement in acquiring competitive advantage.

Table 10.4. *The sourcing of technological advantage of sample firms by industrial sector*

Sector	Access to assets			Consumer demand			Linkages	
	(1a) Human resources	(1b) Tech & R&D cap.	(1c) Managerial & org.	(2a) Product quality	(2b) Product development	(3) Inter firm rivalry	(4a) Related firms	(4b) Education
High technology								
Aerospace	2.17	2.20	2.07	2.50	2.00	4.80	2.80	1.80
	(0.66)	(1.10)	(1.22)	(1.22)	(0.71)	(2.17)	(0.45)	(0.84)
Chemicals	3.34	2.59	3.83	3.66	3.44	4.81	4.38	3.56
	(1.05)	(0.66)	(0.89)	(0.98)	(1.03)	(1.05)	(1.15)	(0.81)
Computers	3.07	3.11	3.15	3.33	3.78	4.56	3.78	2.67
	(0.93)	(1.24)	(1.49)	(1.00)	(1.09)	(1.67)	(1.09)	(0.87)
Electronics	3.26	2.88	3.58	3.61	3.63	4.70	4.35	3.47
	(0.89)	(0.81)	(1.21)	(1.33)	(1.38)	(1.78)	(1.50)	(1.47)
Pharmaceuticals	3.72	3.58	3.78	3.25	3.50	4.33	4.50	3.83
	(1.43)	(1.74)	(1.24)	(0.99)	(1.22)	(1.86)	(1.22)	(1.17)
Medium technology								
Industrial equipment	2.98	2.44	3.33	2.88	2.75	4.88	3.00	2.63
	(0.97)	(1.27)	(0.84)	(1.12)	(1.04)	(1.64)	(0.93)	(0.92)
Motor vehicles	3.33	3.00	3.67	3.00	3.17	3.75	3.83	3.67
	(1.14)	(1.31)	(1.15)	(1.52)	(1.90)	(1.66)	(1.03)	(1.58)
Petroleum refining	2.58	2.68	2.57	3.08	3.25	5.07	3.93	3.14
	(0.80)	(0.97)	(0.96)	(1.06)	(1.41)	(1.49)	(1.21)	(0.77)

Low technology

Food, drink, tobacco	3.49	3.11	3.80	3.27	3.50	4.41	4.64	3.60
	(1.60)	(1.73)	(1.76)	(1.53)	(1.65)	(1.97)	(1.76)	(1.79)
Paper	3.06	3.22	2.89	4.28	4.11	4.33	3.67	2.67
	(1.32)	(1.28)	(1.36)	(1.62)	(1.76)	(1.66)	(1.66)	(1.32)
Building materials	3.40	3.30	3.67	3.80	4.00	5.00	4.80	4.00
	(0.91)	(1.20)	(1.11)	(1.30)	(1.58)	(1.87)	(1.10)	(1.58)
Metals & metal prod.	2.92	2.68	3.05	3.29	3.43	4.64	4.21	3.23
	(1.04)	(1.17)	(1.21)	(1.01)	(1.28)	(1.15)	(1.12)	(1.09)
Other	3.37	3.39	3.26	3.81	4.00	4.56	3.89	3.56
	(1.38)	(1.54)	(1.37)	(1.19)	(1.31)	(2.19)	(1.62)	(1.51)

Note:

Figures represent average respondent scores ranging from a rank of 1 (all advantage derived from domestic operations of the firm and none from its foreign operations) to a rank of 7 (all advantages derived from foreign operations of the firm and none from its domestic operations). Figures in brackets represent the standard deviation around each of the arithmetic means.

Source: As for table 10.1.

Table 10.5. *The sourcing of technological advantage of sample firms by industrial sector and degree of multinationality of sales and assets*

Sector		(1a) Human resources	(1b) Tech & R&D cap.	(1c) Managerial & org.	(2) Overall	(2a) Product quality	(2b) Product development	(3) Inter-firm rivalry	(4a) Related firms	(4b) Education
		Access to assets			Consumer demand				Linkages	
High technology										
Aerospace	Low	1.66	1.50	1.50	2.17	1.50	1.50	4.00	2.50	1.50
	High	2.75	3.00	2.67	3.83	3.75	2.50	6.50	3.00	2.50
Chemicals	Low	3.33	2.62	3.67	3.54*	3.38*	3.25	4.75	4.00	3.38
	High	3.45	2.64	4.10	4.33*	4.21*	3.85	5.00	4.86	3.71
Computers	Low	2.67*	3.00	2.39**	3.00	3.00	3.67	5.17	3.33	2.50
	High	3.89*	3.33	4.70**	4.11	4.00	4.00	3.33	4.69	3.00
Electronics	Low	3.14	2.68	3.48	3.87	3.50	3.70	3.91**	3.82	3.91
	High	3.56	3.25	3.87	4.29	3.94	3.75	5.88**	5.12	5.88
Pharmaceuticals	Low	2.72*	2.50**	2.89*	2.78*	2.67	2.67	4.33	3.67	3.33
	High	4.72*	4.67**	4.67*	3.78*	3.83	4.33	4.33	5.33	4.33
Medium technology										
Industrial equipment	Low	2.67	2.12	3.00	2.50	2.50	2.50	4.00	2.50	2.25
	High	3.29	2.75	3.67	2.83	3.25	3.00	5.75	3.50	3.00
Motor vehicles	Low	3.50	3.25	3.83	3.22	3.25	3.33	3.33	3.83	4.00
	High	3.13	2.60	3.53	2.73	2.60	2.80	4.00	3.80	3.20
Petroleum refining	Low	2.45	2.57	2.38	2.76	2.79	3.14	5.00	3.86	3.00
	High	2.75	2.91	2.72	3.53	3.50	3.20	5.33	4.00	3.17

Low technology

Food, drink, tobacco	Low	2.65**	2.06**	3.07*	2.70**	2.72*	2.89*	3.78**	3.78**	2.88*
	High	4.26**	4.11**	4.37*	4.33**	4.00*	4.11*	5.44**	5.44**	4.56*
Paper	Low	2.95	3.50	2.67	4.50	4.25	4.00	3.75	2.75	1.75**
	High	3.46	3.38	3.33	4.08	4.12	4.00	4.50	4.25	3.75**
Building materials	Low	3.17	3.17	3.44	3.78	3.33	3.67	4.67	4.67	4.00
	High	3.75	3.50	4.00	4.67	4.50	4.50	5.50	5.00	4.00
Metals & metal prod.	Low	2.57*	2.64	2.67	3.19	3.36	3.86	5.29**	4.29	3.00
	High	3.53*	3.00	3.67	3.83	3.58	3.33	4.00**	4.17	3.40
Other	Low	2.83*	2.38**	3.08	3.75**	3.25	3.50	3.75**	3.25**	3.00*
	High	4.60*	4.83**	4.22	5.22*	4.75	5.00	6.67**	5.67**	5.00*

Note:

Figures represent average respondent scores ranging from a rank of 1 (all advantage derived from domestic operations of the firm and none from its foreign operations) to a rank of 7 (all advantages derived from foreign operations of the firm and none from its domestic operations). High and low sector means were statistically compared using a t-test to determine if significant differences existed.

* Significant at the 0.10 level.

** Significant at the 0.05 level.

Source: As for table 10.1.

Table 10.6. *The sourcing of technological advantage of sample firms by industrial sector and degree of multinationality of R&D*

Sector		Access to assets			(2) Overall	Consumer demand		(3) Inter-firm rivalry	Linkages	
		(1a) Human resources	(1b) Tech & R&D cap.	(1c) Managerial & org.		(2a) Product quality	(2b) Product development		(4a) Related firms	(4b) Education
High technology										
Aerospace	Low	1.67	1.50	1.50	2.17	1.50	1.50	4.00	2.50	1.50
	High	2.83	4.00	2.30	4.67	4.00	2.00	6.00	3.00	1.00
Chemical	Low	3.50	2.69	3.83	3.54*	3.50	3.25	5.25	4.25	3.50
	High	3.26	2.57	3.90	4.33*	4.07	3.86	4.42	4.57	3.57
Computers	Low	3.46	3.75	3.42	3.00	3.00	3.25	5.50	4.00	2.50
	High	3.00	2.00	3.67	3.33	3.50	3.00	2.00	3.00	3.00
Electronics	Low	2.81	2.57	3.10	4.05	3.71	4.00	5.00	4.00	2.86
	High	3.61	3.33	3.89	4.11	3.75	3.50	5.83	5.17	3.33
Pharmaceuticals	Low	2.08*	1.75*	2.30**	2.17	2.00*	2.00	4.50	3.50	3.00
	High	5.25*	5.50*	5.00**	4.00	4.00*	4.50	4.50	6.00	5.00
Medium technology										
Industrial equipment	Low	2.62	2.12	3.00	2.50	2.50	2.50	4.00*	2.75	2.50
	High	3.91	3.50	4.17	3.17	4.00	3.50	6.50*	3.00	2.00
Motor vehicles	Low	2.87	2.50	3.33	2.53	2.60	2.60	3.00	3.40	3.60
	High	4.38	3.83	4.56	4.33	4.17	4.70	4.33	4.66	4.33
Petroleum refining	Low	2.07	2.00	2.13	2.17	2.25	2.25	4.80	3.40	3.20
	High	2.58	2.75	2.50	3.33	3.12	3.25	5.26	3.75	2.50

Low technology

Food, drink, tobacco	Low	2.62**	2.10**	2.93**	2.73	2.80	3.10	3.60**	3.80**	2.50
	High	4.08**	3.75**	4.50**	3.83	3.58	3.67	5.67**	5.00**	4.40
Paper	Low	2.17	2.83	1.78	4.33	4.33	4.33	3.67	3.33	2.00
	High	4.00	4.00	3.89	4.33	4.00	3.67	4.33	4.00	3.33
Building materials	Low	3.00	3.00	3.00	3.00	3.00	3.00	3.50	4.00	2.50
	High	3.67	3.00	4.00	5.33	5.00	5.00	7.00	6.00	5.00
Metals & metal prod.	Low	2.30*	2.40	2.40	2.73**	2.80**	2.80**	5.00	4.40	2.40*
	High	3.50*	3.10	3.60	4.00**	3.94**	4.20**	4.00	4.40	4.00*
Other	Low	2.89	2.50*	3.22	4.11	3.67	4.00	3.00**	3.67	3.33
	High	4.73	5.00*	4.67	4.83	4.75	5.00	6.50**	5.50	5.50

Note:

Figures represent average respondent scores ranging from a rank of 1 (all advantage derived from domestic operations of the firm and none from its foreign operations) to a rank of 7 (all advantages derived from foreign operations of the firm and none from its domestic operations). High and low sector means were statistically compared using a t-test to determine if significant differences existed.

* Significant at the 0.10 level.

** Significant at the 0.05 level.

Source: As for table 10.1.

Table 10.7. *The sourcing of technological assets of sample firms by country and degree of multinationality: (a) sales and assets*

		Developed	Large Europe	Germany	UK net	Other Lr. Euro	Small Europe	Sweden	Switzerland	Other small E.	United States	Japan	Other developed	Developing
Access to assets	Low	2.92	2.99	3.10	3.15	2.97	3.20	3.96	3.94	2.75	3.04	2.30	2.58	2.03
	High	3.67	3.53	3.69	3.86	2.71	4.11	3.50	4.58	3.70	3.65	2.87	4.00	3.11
Consumer demand	Low	3.57	3.65	3.86	3.78	3.20	4.00	6.00	5.00	4.75	3.67	2.80	5.33	2.83
	High	4.49	4.81	4.17	5.73	5.00	4.44	4.00	2.50	6.00	3.71	3.00	5.00	4.00
Inter-firm rivalry	Low	4.27	4.91	5.14	5.33	3.60	5.60	5.50	6.33	7.00	4.21	3.20	4.50	4.33
	High	5.10	5.77	5.67	6.27	6.00	5.10	5.33	2.50	5.50	4.11	2.90	4.00	4.33
Linkages	Low	3.31	3.35	3.36	3.42	3.60	3.90	4.25	3.83	5.13	3.04	3.15	2.30	3.33
	High	4.22	4.18	4.50	4.82	4.00	4.70	4.33	5.00	4.25	3.95	3.30	5.00	3.58
Overall	Low	3.53	3.74	3.86	3.94	3.34	4.21	4.29	4.75	5.14	3.46	2.86	3.14	3.13
	High	4.34	4.55	4.51	5.17	3.98	4.62	4.75	3.65	4.91	3.86	3.03	4.50	3.81
Population	(m)	770.9	308.8	80.6	73.0	155.2	53.3	8.7	6.9	37.7	253.1	124.5	30.8	376.4
GNP/ capita	($000)	22.6	20.1	23.0	18.4	19.5	23.3	27.0	36.1	20.1	23.2	28.2	19.8	3.7
GNP	(Bln$)	17,460	6,219	1,856	1,343	3,020	1,240	235	249	756	5,882	3,510	609	1,387

Note:
Figures represent average respondent scores ranging from a rank of 1 (all advantage derived from domestic operations of the firm and none from its foreign operations) to a rank of 7 (all advantages derived from foreign operations of the firm and none from its domestic operations).
Source: As for table 10.1.

Table 10.8. *The sourcing of technological assets of sample firms by country and degree of multinationality: (b) R&D*

		Developed	Large Europe	Germany	UK net	Other Lr. Euro	Small Europe	Sweden	Switzerland	Other small E.	United States	Japan	Other developed	Developing
Access to assets	Low	3.21	3.21	3.56	3.13	2.50	3.40	4.00	3.94	3.06	3.01	1.98	2.17	1.80
	High	3.52	3.52	3.47	3.98	3.13	4.25	3.83	4.58	3.77	3.31	2.67	3.56	3.30
Consumer demand	Low	3.71	3.71	4.00	4.33	2.25	4.17	6.00	5.00	4.00	3.27	2.29	6.00	3.00
	High	4.94	4.94	4.40	5.00	6.50	4.57	5.00	2.50	4.33	4.13	2.67	4.67	3.30
Inter-firm rivalry	Low	3.50	4.83	5.50	5.00	4.00	5.88	6.00	6.33	5.00	4.07	2.43	4.50	4.30
	High	5.24	5.80	5.40	6.22	5.25	5.13	5.00	2.50	7.00	4.33	3.17	4.00	2.30
Linkages	Low	2.66	3.44	4.08	3.60	3.13	4.13	4.83	3.83	4.33	3.07	2.50	1.33	2.50
	High	4.42	4.28	3.90	4.67	3.25	5.00	4.50	5.00	5.00	3.50	3.83	4.67	3.67
Overall	Low	2.88	3.80	4.28	4.00	2.97	4.43	5.18	4.75	4.10	3.36	2.30	3.54	2.91
	High	4.42	4.59	4.29	4.95	4.15	4.77	4.58	3.65	5.03	3.80	3.08	4.22	3.04
Population	(m)	770.9	308.8	80.6	73.0	155.2	53.3	8.7	6.9	37.7	253.1	124.5	30.8	376.4
GNP/ capita	($000)	22.6	20.1	23.0	18.4	19.5	23.3	27.0	36.1	20.1	23.2	28.2	19.8	3.7
GNP	(Bln$)	17,460	6,219	1,856	1,343	3,020	1,240	235	249	756	5,882	3,510	609	1,387

Note:
Figures represent average respondent scores ranging from a rank of 1 (all advantage derived from domestic operations of the firm and none from its foreign operations) to a rank of 7 (all advantages derived from foreign operations of the firm and none from its domestic operations).
Source: As for table 10.1.

Table 10.9. *Importance of FDI as a means of accessing foreign technological advantage, 1994–5*

Sector	FDI – not important					FDI – important				
	Number of firms	Sales (Bln$)	Sector sales/ total sales (%)	Asst & em/ sector (%)	R&D/ sector (%)	Number of firms	Sales (Bln$)	Sector sales/ total sales (%)	Asst & em/ sector (%)	R&D/ sector (%)
High technology										
Aerospace	4	42.9	19.4	8.2	2.5	1	30.2	1.3	1.0	3.0
Chemicals	2	18.2	8.2	37.3	22.5	13	146.7	6.5	52.1	22.2
Computers	2	7.6	3.4	30.0	7.0	7	206.3	9.2	27.9	9.3
Electronics	5	28.7	13.0	39.8	28.2	15	360.4	16.0	38.5	22.6
Pharmaceuticals	1	3.4	1.5	54.0	36.0	5	40.5	1.8	48.9	25.8
Total (sum/average)	14	100.8	45.5	33.8	19.2	41	784.1	34.9	41.9	16.6
Medium technology										
Industrial equipment	1	2.3	1.0	85.0	–	7	71.5	3.2	31.7	11.0
Motor vehicles	1	30.0	13.5	20.0	3.0	11	550.0	24.5	36.1	8.1
Petroleum	2	34.1	15.4	7.5	0.0	12	464.3	20.6	55.2	31.3
Total (sum/average)	4	66.4	30.0	37.5	1.5	30	1,085.8	48.3	41.0	16.8
Low technology										
Food and drink	4	12.7	5.7	16.5	0.3	17	229.6	10.2	55.2	40.6
Paper	3	17.7	8.0	17.2	1.5	5	21.3	0.9	28.0	10.8
Building materials	1	4.0	1.8	62.5	50.0	4	12.4	0.6	44.4	34.5
Metal and metal proc.	4	17.2	7.8	37.8	26.0	10	90.1	4.0	35.6	20.9
Other	4	2.7	1.2	52.0	49.0	5	25.9	1.1	59.4	43.3
Total (sum/average)	16	54.2	24.5	37.2	25.4	41	379.3	16.9	44.5	30.0
Total all sectors	34	221.4	100.0	31.7	18.3	112	2,249.2	100.0	43.6	23.9

Note:
For each technology category (HTS, MTS, LTS), sector percentages for asset and employment and R&D are averaged. For the 'Total all sectors' row, a weighted average (by number of firms) is calculated.
Source: As for table 10.1.

Table 10.10. *Importance of alliances as a means of accessing foreign technological advantage, 1994–5*

Sector	Alliances – not important					Alliances – important				
	Number of firms	Sales (Bln$)	Sector sales/ total sales (%)	Asst & em/ sector (%)	R&D/ sector (%)	Number of firms	Sales (Bln$)	Sector sales/ total sales (%)	Asst & em/ sector (%)	R&D/ sector (%)
High technology										
Aerospace	1	30.2	3.3	1.0	3.0	4	42.9	2.8	8.2	2.5
Chemicals	8	66.9	7.3	52.1	20.9	7	98.0	6.3	47.3	24.1
Computers	1	1.6	0.2	30.0	4.0	8	212.3	13.7	28.2	9.4
Electronics	2	0.8	0.1	45.5	45.5	18	388.3	25.1	38.1	21.0
Pharmaceuticals	–	–	–	–	–	6	43.9	2.8	49.7	28.4
Total	12	99.5	10.8	32.2	18.4	43	785.4	50.7	34.3	17.1
Medium technology										
Industrial equipment	4	44.8	4.9	44.0	11.0	4	29.0	1.9	32.8	11.1
Motor vehicles	4	158.9	17.3	33.8	4.7	8	421.1	27.2	35.1	9.2
Petroleum	7	345.7	37.6	55.3	21.3	7	152.7	9.9	41.6	26.8
Total	15	549.4	59.7	44.3	12.3	19	602.8	38.9	36.5	15.7
Low technology										
Food and drink	13	186.0	20.2	48.2	31.1	8	56.3	3.6	44.3	29.2
Paper	6	19.2	2.1	34.7	16.7	3	19.8	1.3	11.5	1.8
Building materials	4	12.5	1.4	39.9	29.5	1	3.9	0.3	80.5	60.0
Metal & metal proc.	5	43.7	4.7	58.2	46.0	9	63.6	4.1	22.6	9.5
Other	3	10.3	1.1	53.8	10.0	6	18.2	1.2	58.2	54.5
Total	31	271.7	29.5	47.0	26.7	27	161.8	10.4	43.4	31.0
Total all sectors	58	920.6	100.0	46.3	23.4	89	1,550.0	100.0	37.1	20.4

Note:
For each technology category (HTS, MTS, LTS), sector percentages for asset and employment and R&D are averaged. For the 'Total all sectors' row, a weighted average (by number of firms) is calculated.
Source: As for table 10.1.

Table 10.11. *Importance of trade as a means of accessing foreign technological advantage, 1994–5*

Sector	Trade – not important					Trade – important				
	Number of firms	Sales (Bln$)	Sector sales/total sales (%)	Asst & em/sector (%)	R&D/sector (%)	Number of firms	Sales (Bln$)	Sector sales/total sales (%)	Asst & em/sector (%)	R&D/sector (%)
High technology										
Aerospace	4	67.4	3.8	3.2	2.7	1	5.7	0.9	16.0	–
Chemicals	9	86.6	4.8	54.4	18.6	6	78.3	11.8	42.2	28.8
Computers	6	154.0	8.6	28.1	11.0	3	59.7	9.0	29.0	3.5
Electronics	6	60.2	3.4	46.9	38.3	14	329.0	49.4	35.1	16.25
Pharmaceuticals	5	29.8	1.7	50.0	28.4	1	14.1	2.1	48.4	–
Total (sum/average)	30	398.0	22.2	36.5	19.8	25	486.8	73.1	38.7	16.2
Medium technology										
Industrial equipment	6	67.8	3.8	31.8	11.2	2	6.0	0.9	58.0	10.0
Motor vehicles	9	566.0	31.5	33.8	4.4	2	11.2	1.7	35.5	14.0
Petroleum	10	422.7	23.6	60.3	34.8	4	75.7	11.4	20.0	3.3
Total (sum/average)	25	1,056.5	58.9	42.0	16.8	8	92.9	13.9	37.8	9.1
Low technology										
Food & drink	16	202.0	11.3	44.5	28.0	4	35.5	5.3	57.7	38.0
Paper	7	34.7	1.9	22.5	11.2	1	2.0	0.3	27.5	1.0
Building materials	3	8.9	0.5	43.2	29.5	2	7.5	1.1	55.2	60.0
Metal & metal proc.	8	71.3	4.0	38.9	20.9	6	36.0	5.4	32.1	26.0
Other	6	23.2	1.3	45.5	26.0	3	5.3	0.8	73.0	75.0
Total (sum/average)	40	340.1	19.0	38.9	23.1	16	86.3	13.0	49.1	40.0
Total all sectors	95	1,794.6	100.0	40.9	21.2	49	666.0	100.0	41.4	24.0

Note:
For each technology category (HTS, MTS, LTS), sector percentages for assets and employment and R&D are averaged. For the 'Total all sectors' row, a weighted average (by number of firms) is calculated.
Source: As for table 10.1.

The second part of our empirical work attempts to quantify the significance of groups of contextual variables as determinants of the geographical sourcing of technological advantages. Here we shall consider four dependent variables, which correspond to the four technological advantages that we identify above; and in each case, for each of the firms in the sample. We regress these advantages against four contextual variables, which we hypothesise may be expected to influence the geographical sourcing of these advantages. These contextual variables are:

(i)   Degree of multinationality of the firm. We used two indices of multinationality viz (a) the average of proportion of assets and employment accounted for by foreign affiliates and (b) the average percentage of global R&D conduced outside home countries of firms. We would hypothesise in each case that there would be a positive relationship between the sourcing of technological assets and the degree of multinationality.

(ii) Sales of the firm. Here we hypothesise that there would be a positive relationship and expect that larger firms have the resources to seek out and better exploit foreign technological assets.

(iii) Degree of technological intensity of industry (measured by R&D as a percent of sales). Here we hypothesise that there is justification for both a positive or negative relationship and expect a positive relationship for science-based sectors like pharmaceuticals and negative relationship for sectors which are multi-domestic in nature, e.g., food and drink. *A priori*, the strength of these competing forces cannot be determined.

(iv) Size of firm's home country (measured by population). Here we would hypothesise that there would be negative correlation between this variable and the extent to which firms acquire new or augment existing assets from foreign sources.

(v)   Income of firm's home country. Here we again would hypothesise a negative relationship as we would expect firms from wealthier nations to have less need of foreign technological assets than firms from poorer nations.

This gives us eight regression equations, using two separate measures of (i).

5 Findings: based on technology intensity

In table 10.4, we set out data on the sources of technological assets according to the industry of the respondent firms. Bearing in mind that our earlier studies had concluded that the degree of multinationality was the most significant variable determining the sourcing of assets, this table provides the respondents' scores for the sourcing of technological assets by individual industry. Standard deviations are also reported so that statistical comparisons can be made between industries; between types of competitive advantage; and between groups of firms based on the level of technology. Because of the large number of relationships set out, we confine our observations to the more significant of those identified.

Types of technological advantage   Overall, almost three quarters (75/104) of the mean responses in table 10.4 were within the 3.0 to 4.9 range. Only the inter-firm rivalry dimension had sector averages greater than the above range. In fact, regardless of sector, inter-firm rivalry consistently scored the most important 'foreign' influence in upgrading technological assets. Out of the 12 sectors here, motor vehicles was the only one that had a value below 4.0. The next most important dimension, viz linkages with local firms, indicates that firms seek external rather than internal sourcing to obtain competitive advantage. This result is consistent with the intentions of Porter's (1990) findings that firms seek out areas of agglomerative economies associated with industry clusters in order to gain and/or maintain competitive advantage. One half of the sectors (6/12) had an average score of 4.0 or higher for the linkage dimension. With regard to the direct access to asset dimension, firms consistently reported deriving greater advantage from foreign managerial and organisational attributes than from foreign technology and R&D and human resources.

Sector comparisons   Overall, there was no clear suggestion that (apart from pharmaceuticals) HTS firms perceived they gained more advantage from foreign sources than others, rather the converse. However there was the greatest variability within the HTS, the highest and lowest values for the entire sample being recorded for the foreign sourcing of technological assets range. It ranged from 3.6 in the case of the pharmaceutical industry to 2.2 in the case of the aerospace industry. Statistical differences are observed at the 0.05 per cent level between the aerospace sector and most others. The aerospace industry is closely aligned with government activities and, as might be expected, we find that its firms look mostly to domestic sources to obtain their needed technology. Pharmaceutical firms (3.8) significantly differed from those in petroleum refining (2.6) with regard to managerial and organisational capabilities. Pharmaceuticals (4.3) also differed from those in the industrial equipment sector (4.9) with regard to inter-firm rivalry. In both cases, pharmaceuticals derived a greater portion of their technological assets from foreign sources. With regard to inter-firm rivalry, on average, firms in all industrial sectors viewed foreign competition to be a more important inducement to raising technological standards than domestic competition.

Technological advantages and asset and employment multinationality

In table 10.5, we sought to quantify the amount and direction of firm variability as it relates to the foreign sources of competitive advantage for each sector. Because of considerable firm size variation ($0.39bln. to $138.2bln.) and home country differences (GNP ranged from $42 to $5,882bln.), we expected this level of disaggregation to prove particularly revealing. Because the study's objective is to assess the competitive advantage derived from foreign source assets, we believed that the degree of multinationality[10] of a firm would make an ideal variable to create two sub-populations for each source of competitive advantage for each sector. Multinationality in this table is defined to be the average percentage of a firms' assets and employment deployed in foreign countries. Mean values were computed for each of the sources of the four groups of technological advantage identified in the previous section. These mean values were then statistically compared to determine if there are significant differences between the HM and LM firms.

High-technology sectors (HTS) Within the HTS, the extent to which firms believe that they gain technological advantage from their foreign operations varies a great deal, e.g., within the aerospace sector values' range from 1.50 to 6.50. On average, apart from aerospace firms, all the HM firms perceived they gained upwards of 40 per cent of their technological advantage as a direct result of their foreign operations. The aerospace category revealed no statistical differences for any broad grouping of competitive advantage, e.g., access to assets; consumer demand influences; inter-firm rivalry; and external linkages. This finding could be attributed to the fact that all firms in this sector recorded low degrees of multinationality and that governments encourage homogeneity in the sector. Similarly, both HM and LM firms cited that they derived the majority of their advantages associated within the access to assets, consumer demand and the linkages categories from domestic sources. For the inter-firm rivalry category – as might be expected – HM firms rated their main competition as coming from foreign firms.

Within the chemical industry, the product quality criteria (3.38 LM and 4.21 HM) and the overall measure of consumer demand (3.54 LM and 4.33 HM) showed significant differences, while no significant differences were observed for the other three categories. HM firms, on average, rated efficient production, upgrading product quality and creating more product innovation as originating from foreign rather than domestic activity. By contrast, LM firms cited competitive advantage as stemming primarily from their domestic operations. Firms in both the HM and LM groups perceived they derived the majority of their technology advantage from domestic sources, but cited competition and linkages with foreign firms as yielding significant competitive gains.

Within the computer industry, only two variables – viz managerial and organisational capabilities (4.70) and linkages to related firms (4.69) – out of the nine tested had scores that indicated HM firms received the majority of their competitive advantages from foreign sources. Partially explaining these findings is that computer firms with a significant foreign deployment of assets are attracted to areas like Silicon Valley and learn from varied managerial practices around the world. Relative to their HM counterparts, LM computer firms viewed that inter-firm rivalry (5.17) was more likely to be derived from foreign sources.

Within the electronic industry, two classes of firms appear with respect to their perception of the source of inter-firm rivalry. HM firms (5.88) sense that the vast majority of their competition comes from foreign-owned firms, while LM (3.91) firms see other domestic firms as their greatest rivals.

Within the HTS, pharmaceutical firms show the greatest difference between the HM and LM categories. Each of the access to assets variables shows HM firms seeing the vast majority of their technological advantages coming from foreign sources, while the low multinationality firms see the opposite: absolute differences ranged from 3.00 to 1.78, and all were significant. HM firms also indicate that about one-half of consumer demand factors, contributing to their global competitive strengths, emanate from foreign sources, while LM firms perceive more of it coming from domestic sources (a score of approximately 2.70).

Medium-technology sectors (MTS)   In the MTS, there were no significant differences in the rankings assigned by the HM and LM firms, and with the exception of inter-firm rivalry, the average response to each question indicated that firms received the majority of their competitive advantages from domestic sources. One possible explanation for this rather unexpected similarity is that the auto and petroleum industries are mature industries, and made up of large firms which tend to closely imitate each others' behaviour.

Low-technology sectors (LTS)   In the LTS, the food, drink and tobacco industry displays the greatest difference between HM and LM firms. In fact, there are significant differences between every variable, with HM firms obtaining one-half or more of their technological advantages from foreign sources, while LM firms derive most of their advantages from their home location. Some of the most pronounced differences occurred for the variables technological capabilities (2.07), product quality (1.28), inter-firm rivalry (1.66) and inter-firm linkages to related firms (1.66). A possible explanation is that at one end of this group are firms from developing countries which are small and which focus on quasi-monopolies in internal markets, while, at the other end, are large firms which manufacture and sell products in consuming countries throughout the world.

Paper companies' HM and LM firms had significant differences only for the education variable (1.75 LM and 3.75 HM). Firms with greater multi-nationality also appear to have increased their ability to tap into foreign-based environmental agencies and research consortia.

Metal and metal products showed significant differences for the variables skilled workers (2.57 LM and 3.53 HM) and inter-firm rivalry (5.29 LM and 4.00 HM). Like computers, LM firms' value for inter-firm rivalry was greater than those of HM firms. This could result because HM firms may be larger in size and have somewhat protected home markets, while LM firms may be selling most of their products in competitive international markets. There were no significant differences observed for the building materials category.

(b) Technological advantages and R&D multinationality

The above exercise was repeated in table 10.6 but the percentage of foreign R&D was substituted for the percentage of foreign assets and employees as a measure of multinationality.[11] With this new criteria, we were able to test two alternative hypotheses. The first is that more foreign-based R&D reduces the need for external foreign resources; and the second that more R&D is a way of tapping into such resources.

High-technology sectors (HTS)   Within the HTS, aerospace, computers and electronics had no significant differences between HM and LM firms. In the chemical sector, HM and LM firms exhibit significant differences in the sourcing of competitive advantage with regard to consumer demand attributes. This is a similar finding to that shown in table 10.5. The pharmaceutical sector exhibits significant differences between HM and LM firms for all the access to assets categories, as in table 10.5. However, the absolute differences are much more pronounced in table 10.6. The absolute difference between HM and LM firms is 3.20, approximately 50 per cent greater than the absolute difference recorded when assets and employment were used as a measure of multi-collinearity. In fact, the biggest difference for the entire table occurred for the technology variable (1.75 LM and 5.50 HM).

Medium-technology sectors (MTS) With one exception – inter-firm rivalry in the industrial equipment sector (4.00 LM and 6.50 HM) – no significant differences were recorded for industrial equipment, motor vehicles and petroleum refining.

Low-technology sectors (LTS) In table 10.6, consumer demand values for HM firms were considerably lower than their counterparts shown in table 10.5. For example, the overall mean for HM food, drink and tobacco value was 3.83 as compared with 4.33 in table 10.5. This suggests that a firm which derived considerable value from foreign consumer demand operations might not have answered the R&D question. For metal and metal products, HM and LM firms had significant differences for the overall consumer demand categories (2.73 HM and 4.00 LM) and the other two sub-categories. The R&D measure of multinationality better identified significant differences than that of assets and employment for the consumer demand and linkages categories. HM firms derived just over one-half of their competitive advantage from foreign countries for these variables, while low R&D firms were much more domestic country focused. No significant differences were recorded for the paper and building materials categories.

   Overall, the evidence suggests that more R&D is a way of tapping into foreign resources. This is particularly true for the pharmaceutical sector (thus confirming the findings of Kuemmerle, 1996), but there are some exceptions, most noticeably computers. Also inter-firm rivalry shows fewer differences than shown in table 10.5 between HM and LM firms.

6 Findings: based on geography

Earlier in this chapter we hypothesised that the extent to which a firm might derive its technological advantages from foreign sources was likely to be negatively associated with a country's income level and with its size, as measured by its population. In fact, as table 10.7 reveals, first world MNEs, other than those from Japan, consistently ranked their propensity to source their technological assets outside their home countries higher than those from developing countries. The contrasts were particularly noticeable between developing and small European MNEs. One reason for this may be that, as table 10.2 has shown, in all our country groupings, the former tends to be the least multinational and the latter the most multinational, both in respect of assets and employment and R&D. The differences also seem to be most marked in respect of access to foreign assets, and least marked in respect to consumer demand pressures and inter-firm rivalry (especially in the case of LM firms).

Relating the sourcing of technological advantages to the population of the country confirms that MNEs from smaller countries are more likely to rely upon foreign countries, than are those from larger countries.[12] Again however, Japanese firms seem to be outliers in that, while their home country boasts a larger population than that of any of the European countries, the benefits perceived by the former to be derived from their foreign operations are consistently below those acknowledged by their European counterparts.

Among developed countries, the foreign sourcing of technological advantages for Japan appears very different from the rest of the countries and regions. Japanese firms, on average, are perceived to derive most of their technological advantages from their home country. This is particularly true for the categories access to assets and consumer demand, where firms from the rest of the world consistently indicate that over one-half of their technological advantage is derived from foreign sources, while Japanese firms, including the HM group, indicate that between a quarter and a third are so procured. Large European MNEs appear to be most similar to their United States counterparts in securing their managerial and technological skills (access to assets variable) from foreign countries. Also, as expected, small European MNEs obtained greater technological advantage from foreign sources than any of the other groupings. Table 10.7 also reports indicators for country and region size (population) and economic activity (GNP) as possible weights to the high and low measures. (Note, country totals were reported only if a firm answered a questionnaire.) The United States and large European countries are about the same size and represent about two thirds of the economic activity.

Table 10.8 demonstrates that the difference between developed and developing countries in the sourcing of foreign technological advantage are even more pronounced when R&D, rather than assets and employment, are used to measure multinationality. Once again, for firms from developed countries, Japanese firms appear to gain the least amount of technological advantages from foreign sources in the developed country category. Within the low R&D category for the variable access to assets, Japanese firms reported an extremely low average of less than 2.0.

7 Findings: based on mode of involvement

We now turn to consider how far the mode of international involvement appears to influence the extent to which firms perceive they access and/or augment their technological assets from foreign sources. Tables 10.9, 10.10 and 10.11 respectively measure the importance of FDI, strategic alliances and trade in firms gaining competitive advantage. The focal modality was deemed of above-average importance for a firm if the respondent assigned it a rank of 5, 6 or 7, and deemed of below-average importance if a rank of 1, 2, 3 or 4 was given.

For every industry in table 10.9 except aerospace, FDI was viewed by the great majority of firms as a critical modality for enhancing their technological capabilities. Sales associated with firms which believe FDI is important are ten times greater than for firms which do not believe it is important. Even excluding aerospace from the HTS, the old, well-established MT industries of industrial equipment, motor vehicle and petroleum have the greatest requirements for FDI. This is consistent with the findings of Birkinshaw and Hood (1996) that there is a distinct correlation between the age and experience of foreign subsidiaries and their likely contribution to the global competitive advantage of their parent companies. In most cases, the percentage of foreign R&D undertaken by firms that view FDI as important is higher than those that do not. Somewhat surprisingly, the same statement cannot be made for the degree of multinationality which is much more industry specific. The degree of multinationality, whether measured by assets and employment or R&D, did not vary according to the importance attached by firms to FDI as a means of accessing foreign assets or markets.

In table 10.10, the significance of non-equity alliance relationships are analysed. On average, the firms that ranked alliances as being of above-average importance had a lower percentage of their assets and employment located in foreign countries and a higher percentage of their R&D in foreign countries. Based on the ratio of firms which view alliances as relatively important to those which do not, the HTS of (4/1) aerospace, (8/1) computers, (18/2) electronics and (6/0) pharmaceuticals, and MT industry of (8/4) motor vehicles, all have ratios greater than 2, and benefit the most from tapping into the tangible and intangible assets of foreign countries via alliances. Revenues from firms in these sectors that view alliances as of above-average importance are approximately ten times greater than the ones that do not. The chemicals (7/8), industrial equipment (4/4) and petroleum (7/7) sectors all have ratios of approximately 1 and also benefit from alliances. The one surprising result was for firms in the metal and metal products sector, where the two multinationality measures for those which regarded alliances of above-average importance were approximately 50 per cent (22.6 per cent/58.2 per cent) and 20 per cent (9.5 per cent/53.8 per cent) of those which ranked the importance of alliances at 4 or less.

Table 10.11 shows that approximately three quarters of the firms accounting for approximately 73.6 per cent of the revenues view trade as relatively unimportant in tapping into tangible and intangible assets of foreign countries. Firms in the HTS that view trade as unimportant have higher levels of assets and employment in foreign markets than those firms

Table 10.12. *Assets by mode of sourcing*

	Technological assets			Organisational assets		
	FDI	Alliances	Trade	FDI	Alliances	Trade
HTS						
Aerospace	2.25	2.25	2.00	2.00	2.08	3.00
Chemicals	2.54	2.57	2.92	3.90	3.81	3.78
Computers	3.13	3.13	3.50	3.08	3.08	4.33
Electronics	2.77	2.81	2.68	3.82	3.65	3.14
Pharmaceuticals	3.30	3.58	4.00	3.47	3.78	4.00
MTS						
Industrial equipment	2.57	2.00	2.25	3.24	2.92	3.17
Motor vehicles	3.09	3.19	1.75	3.67	3.92	2.17
Petroleum	2.92	2.79	2.50	2.81	2.52	2.00
LTS						
Food and drink	3.44	4.00	2.62	4.04	4.75	4.00
Paper	2.60	3.17	2.00	2.30	3.11	2.00
Building materials	3.13	3.00	2.75	3.58	4.00	3.67
Metal & metal proc.	2.40	2.00	2.58	2.77	2.54	3.11
Other	3.20	3.83	5.00	3.20	3.78	4.67

	Quality and innovation assets			Linkage to foreign bodies		
	FDI	Alliances	Trade	FDI	Alliances	Trade
HTS						
Aerospace	4.00	2.63	3.50	3.00	1.75	3.00
Chemicals	3.73	3.93	3.33	3.53	3.43	3.83
Computers	3.44	3.44	4.00	2.50	2.50	3.00
Electronics	3.47	3.44	3.04	3.53	3.28	3.07
Pharmaceuticals	3.10	3.25	4.00	3.80	3.83	4.00
MTS						
Industrial equipment	3.00	2.62	2.00	2.43	2.50	3.00
Motor vehicles	3.14	2.75	3.25	3.82	3.75	2.50
Petroleum	3.00	3.43	2.50	3.25	3.00	3.00
LTS						
Food and drink	3.47	3.62	2.75	3.59	3.62	3.50
Paper	4.10	2.67	2.00	2.60	3.00	4.00
Building materials	3.75	5.00	4.00	4.25	5.00	4.50
Metal & metal proc.	3.20	2.94	3.25	2.90	2.88	3.00
Other	2.70	4.08	4.75	3.60	4.00	5.50

Note: Figures represent average respondent scores ranging from a rank of 1 (all advantage derived from domestic operations of the firm and none from its foreign operations) to a rank of 7 (all advantages derived from foreign operations of the firm and none from its domestic operations).
Source: As for table 10.1.

that view trade as important. Firms in the LTS show the exact opposite relationship, with higher levels of assets and employment in foreign countries associated with the importance of trade. In the MTS, the petroleum industry exhibits the same characteristics of the HTS, while the motor vehicle and industrial equipment firms are more like those in the LTS. The trade relationship is not as clear with regard to the R&D measure of multinationality. Within each of the segments (HTS, MTS and LTS), the importance and non-importance of trade is sector, rather than technology level, dependent. The electronics segment presents a unique situation in that it is the entry where a greater number of firms view trade as important than view it as unimportant (14/6).

Taking the data set out in tables 10.9, 10.10 and 10.11 as a whole, it can be shown that FDI and alliances appear as substitute modalities for acquiring foreign technological assets, while for electronics FDI, alliances and trade appear as complements to one another. For firms the computers, electronics, pharmaceuticals, industrial equipment, motor vehicles, petroleum and metal and metal products both strategic alliances and FDI are important modes of acquiring competitive advantage. Trade, as measured by the percentage of global sales accounted for by exports, is perceived to be very important in acquiring competitive advantage in the chemicals, electronics, petroleum and building materials sectors.

In table 10.12, the average ranking of sources of competitive advantage for access to assets, consumer demand and inter-firm linkages are reported for respondents that view each modality of investments as important. For example, the average score of the access to assets variable in the chemical industry for the respondents who thought strategic alliances were important was 2.57. From tables 10.9, 10.10 and 10.11, 76.7 per cent, 60.5 per cent and 34.0 per cent respondents replied that FDI, strategic alliances and trade were important.

Among the respondents who viewed FDI as important, those from the food and drink sector recorded the highest average scores of 3.44 and 4.04. As shown in table 10.1, the food industry has a large percentage of its assets and employment in foreign locations and these are leveraged to augment these global competitive positions. Similarly the paper industry scored the highest for quality and innovative assets, and the building materials industry the highest for linkage to foreign institutions. The building industry has to set its standards according to those required by countries in which it operates, and because of this, a high score here is not surprising.

Of the respondents who viewed alliances as most important, those in the food and drink sector maintained that their principal foreign competitive advantage was in their access to technological and organisational assets. Firms in the building materials sector maintained that they gained important benefits from linkages to foreign institutions, consumer demand for high quality products and from tapping into foreign innovatory assets.

Of the respondents who viewed trade as an important mode of gaining technological advantages, those in the building material sector obtained the greatest benefit from linkages to foreign institutions, those in the pharmaceutical sector gained the greatest advantage from technological assets, those in the computer sector achieved the most benefit from organisational assets and those in the computer, pharmaceutical and building materials sectors benefited the most from consumer linkages.

8 Findings: multivariate analysis

Up to this point, we have provided descriptive statistics on the importance of FDI, cross-border alliances and trade as a means of accessing foreign technological assets; and also of how the importance of foreign sourcing varies by industry and degree of multinationality of the sourcing firm. This section recasts some of the bivariate data into multiple regression equations. The dependent variable is the propensity of individual firms to source their technological assets from foreign countries and the independent variables are the contextual variables identified earlier (see Exhibit 1 for variable definitions in the context of the regression equations.) The hypotheses setting out the expected relationships between these two sets of variables are identified in section 4.

To more fully understand how firms source technological assets from foreign countries, specific relationships associated with created assets, consumer demand and linkages were tested. Because of the variety of factor conditions associated with these variables and the desire to isolate specific relationships, two independent measures were used. The first focused on firms sourcing competitive advantages from foreign technology-based assets associated with professional and scientific personnel and product and process innovations; while the second measured how firms perceived they augmented their domestic competencies by applying foreign learned organisational and managerial practices. The third relationship tested the amount of competitive advantage obtained by firms who had operations in foreign countries with sophisticated consumers; while the fourth helped assess the gains derived by firms being part of a foreign cluster of related firms and/or near a foreign research institution.

The four contextual variables use firm-level, industry-level and country-level measures to explain each of the above sources of competitive advantage. The firm-level variables are the degree of multinationality and firm sales. Multinationality, as in the descriptive statistics section, is measured in two ways, i.e., employment and assets (MEA) and R&D (MRD), and its

Exhibit 1

Dependent variables (variable names in parentheses)

* Created assets:	1	Technology dependent (**INN**)
	2	Organisational based (**ORG**)
* Consumer demand:	3	(**CONS**)
* Linkages:	4	(**LINK**)

Independent variables

Firm size
* Degree of multinationality (variable names in parentheses)

	(1a)	Average of foreign employment and assets (**MEA**)
	(1b)	Share of R&D (**MRD**)
* Size of firm	2	Firm sales (**SIZE**)

Industry level

* R&D intensity	3	Ratio of sector R&D to sales (**RDI**) (measured at a sectoral level)

Country level

* Size of home country	4	Gross National Product (**GNP**)
* Population of home country	5	Population (**POP**)

relationship with each dependent variable is estimated separately. As indicated earlier, we would expect a positive relationship between the multinationality variables, MEA and MRD, and all of the above dependent variables because the greater the assets and employment and R&D outside the home country the greater the likelihood a firm's technological capabilities will come from foreign sources. However, we would also expect that MRD would have a stronger relationship than MEA in the estimation of the advantages derived from a firm's access to foreign technological assets, because MRD is likely to be more directly related to those assets. Alternatively, we would expect the percentage of foreign assets and employment to better explain how a firm gains competitive assets from organisational creative assets because MEA is more closely aligned with managerial rather than scientific pursuits. Because MRD and MEA had a correlation coefficient of approximately +0.70, these variables were entered into the regression equations independently.

With respect to the SIZE of firm variable, the literature suggests that large firms are more likely to engage in FDI than smaller firms.[13] However, the same literature is not specific as to which size firms most intensively use their foreign assets to gain competitive advantage. Though a weak positive relationship is expected, the above ambiguity will hinder the identification of a significant relationship with any foreign sources of competitive advantages.

It is difficult to offer a single hypothesis about the relationships between the industry variable (RDI) and the sourcing of foreign technological advantage. In table 10.4, LTS firms were shown a higher percentage of their creative assets from foreign sources than HTS firms. MTS firms had the lowest percentages. However, there was considerable variability within the HTS, MTS and LTS; in fact, firms within the pharmaceutical sector perceived they gained the greatest amount of technologically created assets from foreign sources. A case could be made for the effect being in either direction, and a two-tailed t-test is therefore required to assess this relationship.

The population variable, (POP), and the size of home country variable, (GNP), measure country-level effects. It is expected that the larger the population of the home country of the respondent firm, the less likely it would need to seek out foreign sources of competitive advantage. A similar relationship is expected for GNP. Firms from larger home countries are hypothesised to be less dependent on foreign sourcing for competitive advantage.

Regression model

Initially, all the identified explanatory variables (except that only one measure of multinationality – MRD or MEA – was included in each equation due to multi-collinearity concerns) were regressed against each of the dependent variables. Next, for each dependent variable, the equations representing the two levels of multinationality were compared. If the equations associated with the MEA measure proved superior, then these equations were re-estimated to identify and retain only significant variables. If the equations associated with MRD proved superior then an additional step was required. Because fewer firms responded to the R&D question than the asset and employment questions, the equation with MEA had to be reestimated with a smaller sample and then compared with the MRD equation. Then the superior equation was re-estimated and only significant variables were identified and reported.

Model results

Overall the two measures for multinationality, MRD and MEA had correlation coefficients with the dependent variables ranging from +0.37 to +0.50 and +0.34 to +0.46, respectively. As stated previously MRD and

MEA had a +0.70 correlation coefficient. All the other independent variables had correlation coefficients of less than +0.20 with the dependent variables. Among the independent variable, only POP and GNP had correlation coefficients greater than 30 per cent. The bottom line of this preliminary bivariate analysis is that the multinationality variables are likely be the main explanatory variables in the following four models.

Our previously stated belief that foreign MRD was superior to MEA in explaining *firms sourcing competitive advantages from foreign technology assets*, i.e., professional and scientific personnel and product and process innovations, was confirmed. Also, a positive relationship was observed for the RDI variable and this indicated that the greater the R&D as a percentage of sales for a sector, the greater the perception of executives that they derived gains in competitiveness from foreign sources of professional personnel and product technology. Even using a two-tailed t-test this relationship proved significant at the 0.05 level. Indeed, these two variables explained over 21 per cent of the variation in the foreign technology asset variable. The third most important variable, population of the home country (POP), though not significant, exhibited a negative relationship consistent with our earlier hypothesis.

N	Dependent variable	Independent variables	Coefficients std. error	Probability >	R^2-Adj.
102	INN	RD	0.0245 (0.004)	0.0001	0.2124
		RDI	0.0299 (0.030)	0.0026	

Moreover, foreign assets and employment was the only significant variable that explained how firms gained *competitive advantage by accessing foreign learned organisational and managerial practices*. As we earlier asserted, foreign assets and employment, rather than the percentage of R&D, are more closely related to firms gaining competitive advantage by learning from foreign organisational and managerial practices (ORG). The next most important variable, size of firm (SIZE), had a negative sign, contrary to our relatively weak assertion for this variable.

N	Dependent variable	Independent variables	Coefficients std. error	Probability >	R^2-Adj.
135	ORG	MEA	0.0231 (0.004)	0.0001	0.1919

Turning now to the third relationship, only the two multinational variables proved significant in explaining the sourcing of competitive *advantage by firms who had operations in foreign countries with demanding or sophisticated consumers.* In this case, the R^2 for MEA was less than that of MRD; however, when we ran MEA with the same number of firms as MRD, the former's R^2 was almost 25 per cent more. The next most important variable, GNP, was consistent with the hypothesised negative sign.

N	Dependent variable	Independent variables	Coefficients std. error	Probability >	R^2-Adj.
98	CONS	MEA	0.022 (0.005)	0.0001	0.1604

The fourth relationship tested the amount of competitive advantage a firm gained *from being part of a foreign clusters of firms and/or near a foreign research institution.* Once again, MEA proved to be the major explanatory variable. One would expect that the greater amount of these assets deployed in foreign countries, the greater the likelihood that executives would believe they would gain competitive advantage from foreign clusters of activity. The population variable (POP) proved significant and with expected negative sign. The interpretation here is simply that the bigger your home market the less likely you are to seek out foreign clusters of innovative activity in your sector. Almost 43 per cent of the variation in the linkage variable was explained by these two explanatory variables.

N	Dependent variable	Independent variables	Coefficients std. error	Probability >	R^2-Adj.
99	LINK	MEA	0.022 (0.005)	0.0001	0.4298
		RDI	–1.899 (1.047)	0.0050	

In conclusion, specific relationships associated with created assets, consumer demand and linkages were estimated and tested for significance. As expected the level of multinationality was the most significant contextual variable in each case. In the INN (equation 1) and LINK (equation 4), two contextual variables RDI and POP proved significant.

9 Conclusion

The results of this study clearly indicate that the degree of multinationality of a firm is significantly associated with the perception that firms augment their global technological advantages from foreign sources. This they do via a feedback of information and knowledge, experience and expertise created within its network of subsidiaries and/or by tapping into the knowledge and information created by other firms or of non-market institutions. In depth analysis of the relationship between the degree of multinationality of some 150 large industrial MNEs and several different technological advantages enables us to identify several interesting industry and geographical specific differences in their technology-based competitive advantages. For example, pharmaceutical firms obtain more of their competitive advantage from foreign sources than any other sector. Alternatively, the aerospace sector, relies the most on domestic sources to gain competitive advantage. First world MNEs, apart from those from Japan, consistently ranked their propensity to source their technological assets outside their home countries higher than those from developing countries.

The study has also confirmed that 'deeper' forms of foreign involvement, e.g., FDI and alliances, are likely to generate a greater feedback of technical knowledge than shallower forms of involvement, e.g., export and sub-contracting.

The regression results confirmed the important role that the degree of multinationality plays in explaining the extent of which firms source their technological assets from foreign locations. As expected, the R&D measure of multinationality explained more variation in the dependent variable associated with technology-based created assets and the asset and employment measure of multinationality was superior for the other dependent variables. Also as expected a significant negative relationship was confirmed between a home country's population and the sourcing of competitive advantage from foreign industry clusters.

The policy implications of the findings of this chapter are straightforward. Governments need to recognize that firms engage in foreign activities both to exploit their existing technology-based competitive advantages and to protect, or augment, these advantages. There is also a strong suggestion that the foreign operations of firms become a significant component of the world economy, that technology, organisational skills and other tangible assets are likely to be transferred across national boundaries, not only from the investing firms to their subsidiaries but from the subsidiaries back to the investing firms. This is particularly likely to be the case where MNEs, e.g., Asea Brown-Boveri, Unilever, IBM, etc., operate multiple home bases.

This being so, it behoves governments to pursue as liberal policies towards both inward and outward FDI as their macro-organisational strategies allow. At the same time, they need to create and sustain the kind of domestic political and economic environments, which allow both its own firms to become strong contestants in the global marketplace and to attract high value FDI into their domestic arenas.

Appendix 1: characteristics of the sample

The sample consists of a total of 150 responses from 135 firms. For those that provided multiple responses, the statistics on the size and degree of transnationality, as well as industry classification, follow those of the largest corporate unit. Apart from size and degree of transnationality, all other multiple responses are treated as unique individual responses in the analyses. Of the 150 responses to the survey, 111 came from firms that are ranked in the Fortune 500 largest industrial enterprises (*Fortune* 1994). The remaining firms were contacted to improve the industrial and/or geographic representation of the data. These firms are all among the largest MNEs in their respective home countries. The identity of one firm in the sample was concealed and therefore that firm could not be classified by industry. However, values for the other variables used in the various classifications were obtained.

Notes

1 As set out in Caves (1996) and Dunning (1993).
2 Sometimes between countries and sometimes within countries.
3 For further details see UNCTAD (1995 and 1996).
4 Excellent examples include the watch industry of Switzerland, the cork industry in parts of Portugal, the cutlery industry in Solingen (Germany), the financial services industry in the City of London, and the multi-media industry in Lower Manhattan, New York.
5 See especially examples given by Enright (1994). For an examination of different kinds of sub-national spatial clustering and how being part of each may generate intra-cluster knowledge accumulation and transfer see Markusen and Gray (1996).
6 See especially Dunning (1958), Safarian (1966), Brash (1966), Reddaway *et al.* (1968) and Deane (1970).
7 For further details see appendix 1.
8 High-technology sectors (HTS) are defined as those in which the average R&D expenditure as a percentage of sales in the US was at least 4 per cent, and in which scientists and engineers employed in R&D as a percentage of total employment were 2 per cent or more. Medium-technology sectors (MTS) are defined as those in which the corresponding ratios vary between 2 per cent and 3.9 per cent, respectively; and low-technology sectors (LTS) are defined as those with ratios under 2 per cent and under 1 per cent, respectively. More specifically, HTS include aerospace, computers, chemicals, electronics and pharmaceuticals; MTS include industrial equipment, motor vehicles and petroleum refining; and LTS include beverages, building materials, food, metal products, paper, publishing and printing, rubber and plastics, textiles and tobacco.
9 See appendix 1 for a description of the sample firms.
10 High multinationality (HM) firms are defined as those located at and above the industry's median value of the percentage of its assets and employment accounted for by the foreign affiliates of its constituent firms. Low multinationality (LM) firms are those located below the industry's median value of the percentage of its assets and employment accounted for by the affiliates of its constituent firms.
11 Because the R&D question had less responses than the asset and employment questions, the number of observations in some categories were quite small. This

resulted in high standard deviations relative to their means and non-significant results, even though the absolute differences between HM and LM appear large relative to the absolute differences in table 10.5.

12   And especially so in the case of access to assets, inter-firm rivalry, and linkages.

13   See, e.g., Dunning (1993), chapter 6.

References

Ajami, R. A. and Ricks, D. A. 1981. Motives for the American firms investing in the United States, *Journal of International Business Studies*, 7: 25–46.

Almeida, P. 1996. Knowledge sourcing by foreign multinationals: patent citation analysis in the US semi-conductor industry, Washington, Georgetown University (mimeo).

    1997. Knowledge sourcing by foreign multinationals: patent citation in the US semi-conductor industry, *Strategic Management Journal* (forthcoming).

Anand, J. 1997. Foreign direct investment and the sourcing of technological advantage: evidence from the bio-technology industry, *Journal of International Business Studies* (forthcoming).

Bartness, A. and Cerny, K. 1993. Building competitive advantage through a global network of capabilities, *California Management Review*, 34: 78–103.

Birkinshaw, J. and Hood, N. 1996. Development processes in multinational subsidiaries, Stockholm School of Economics and Strathclyde University (mimeo).

Brash, D. T. 1966. *American Investment in Australian Industry*, Canberra, Australian University Press.

Cantwell, J. A. 1989. *Technological Innovation and Multinational Corporations*, Oxford, Basil Blackwell.

Cantwell, J. A. and Hodson, C. 1991. Global R&D and UK competitiveness, in M. Casson (ed.).

Cantwell, J. A. and Piscitello, L. 1996. The diversification and internationalization of corporate technology: from a strategic choice historically to a complementary technology today, Reading and Milano, Reading University and Politecnico di Milano (mimeo).

Casson, M. (ed.) 1991. *Global Research Strategy and International Competitiveness*, Oxford, Basil Blackwell.

Caves, R. 1996. *Multinational Enterprises and Economic Analysis*, Cambridge, Cambridge University Press.

Caves, R. E. 1971. Industrial corporations: the industrial economics of foreign investment, *Economica*, 38: 1–27.

Dalton, D. H. and Serapico, M. G. 1995. *Globalizing Industrial Research and Development*. Washington US Department of Commerce, Office of Technology Policy, Asia Pacific Technology and Programs.

Deane, R. S. 1970. *Foreign Investment in New Zealand Manufacturing*, Wellington, Sweet and Maxwell.

Dunning, J. H. 1958. *American Investment in British Manufacturing Industry*, London, George Allen and Urwin, reprinted by Arno Press, New York.

    1992. The competitive advantage of nations and TNC activities, *Transnational Corporations* 1: 135–68.

1993. *Multinational Enterprise and the Global Economy*, Harlow, Addison Wesley.

1995. Reappraising the eclectic paradigm in the age of alliance capitalism, *Journal of International Business Studies,* 26: 461–91.

1996. The geographical sources of the competitiveness of firms: Some results of a new survey, *Transnational Corporations,* 5: 1–29.

1997. *Alliance Capitalism in Global Business*, London and New York, Routledge.
Dunning, J. H., Kogut, B. and Blomstrom, M. 1990. *Globalization of Firms and the Competitiveness of Nations*, Lund, Lund University Press.

Dunning, J. H. and Lundan, S. 1997. The technological sourcing of competitiveness of multinational enterprises: an econometric analysis, Reading, University of Reading (mimeo).

Dunning, J. H. and Narula, N. 1995. The R&D activities of foreign firms in the US. *International Studies of Management and Organization*, 25: 39–73.

D'Cruz, J. R. and Rugman, A. M. 1993. Business networks, telecommunications and international competitiveness, *Development and International Cooperation*, 9: 223–61.

Enwright, L. M. 1994. Regional clusters and firm strategy, paper presented to Prince Bertil Symposium on *The Dynamic Firm, The Role of Regions, Technology, Strategy and Organization*, Stockholm June.

Fortune 1994. *Fortune*'s Global 500: The world's largest industrial corporations, 130: 137–90.

Hagedoorn, J. 1996. Trends and patterns in strategic partnering since the early seventies, *Review of Industrial Organization,* 11: 601–16.

IUI 1996. *A Survey of Swedish MNCs 1965–94*, Stockholm, Industrial Institute for Economic and Social Research (IUI).

Jaffe, A. B., Trajtenberg, M. and Henderson, R. 1993. Geographical localization of knowledge spillovers as evidenced by patent citations, *Quarterly Journal of Economics*, 108: 577–98.

Kim, W. S. and Lyn, E. O. 1990. Foreign direct investment theories and the performance of foreign multinationals operating in the US, *Journal of International Business Studies*, 21: 41–54.

Kogut, B. 1990. The permeability of borders and the speed of learning across countries, in Dunning, Kogut and Blomstrom.

Kogut, B. and Chang Sea Jin 1991. Technological capabilities and Japanese direct investment in the United States, *Review of Economics and Statistics*, 73: 401–13.

Kumar, N. 1996. Determinants of location of overseas R&D activity of US and Japanese multinational enterprises, Maastricht, UN University, Institute for New Technology (mimeo).

Kuemmerle, W. 1996. The drivers of foreign direct investment into research and development: An empirical investigation, Boston, Harvard Business School Working Paper No. 96:062.

Markusen, A. and Gray, M. 1996. Industrial clusters and regional development in New Jersey, Newark, Rutgers University Center for International Business Education and Research Working Paper No. 96.002, September.

Pearce, R. D. and Papannastassiou, M. 1995. R&D Networks and innovation: decentralized product development in multinational enterprises, Reading,

Department of Economics Discussion Papers Series B Vol. VII No. 204 October.

Pearce, R. D. and Singh, S. 1991. The overseas laboratory, in M. Casson (ed.).

1992. *The Globalization of Research and Development*, London, Macmillian.

Porter, M. E. 1990. *The Competitive Advantage of Nations*, New York, The Free Press.

Reddaway, N. B., Potter, S. T. and Taylor, C. T. 1968. *The Effects of UK Direct Investment Overseas*, Cambridge, Cambridge University Press.

Rugman, A. M. 1991. Diamond in the rough, *Business Quarterly*, 55: 61–4.

1995. The Theory of the Flagship Firm, Toronto University of Toronto (mimeo).

Rugman, A. M. (ed.) 1993. *Management International Review*, Spring, 33, No. 2 (Special Edition on Michael Porter's Diamond of Competitive Advantage).

Rugman, A. M., Broeck, J. Vanden and Verbeke, A. (eds.) 1995. *Beyond the Diamond: Research in Global Management,* Greenwich, CT, JAI Press.

Rugman, A. M. and D'Cruz, J. R. 1995. The five partners business network model, paper presented to conference on *The Multinational Enterprise in the 21st Century*, Taipei, Chinese Culture University, November.

Safarian, A. E. 1966. *Foreign Ownership of Canadian Industry*, Toronto, University of Toronto Press.

Teece, D. J. 1992. Foreign investment and technological development in Silicon Valley, *California Management Review*, 2: 88–106.

UNCTAD 1995. *World Investment Report 1994: Transnational Corporation and Competitiveness*, New York and Geneva, United Nations.

1996. *World Investment Report 1995: Transnational Corporations Investment, Trade and Industrial Policy Arrangements*, New York and Geneva, UN.

US Department of Commerce (vd) *Surveys of Current Business* and *Benchmark Surveys dealing with Outward Foreign Direct Investment*.

Vernon, R. 1966. International investment and international trade in the product cycle, *Quarterly Journal of Economics,* 80: 190–207.

11 Innovation as the principal source of growth in the global economy

JOHN CANTWELL

1 Introduction

I will divide my discussion into three sections. First, I will explain why innovation matters to the growth and competitiveness of firms and wider economies, and to the trade balances of national economies. I argue that with globalisation, innovation is exercising a steadily increasing influence upon economic performance. I advance this argument in the context of two very different perspectives on profits and economic growth, each of which can be found in the extensive historical literature on these issues.

Second, I deal with a possible counter-argument, which says that in a global world the rewards from innovation cannot be kept by the originators within national boundaries, and therefore it becomes less important as a source of profits and growth. This is known in the literature as the 'appropriability' argument – the view that it is difficult for innovating firms or countries to appropriate a full return on their investments in innovation. I show instead how, in the light of a newly emerging consensus among economists about the nature of technological change (a consensus especially, although not exclusively, among non-neoclassical economists), the appropriability argument has been overplayed, and need not be of undue concern.

Third, I contend that national systems of innovation and states continue to have an important role to play in a global economy. Far from collapsing with globalisation (as some writers have imagined), national systems of innovation have been consolidated, and I explain why. There is also a role for policy support for innovation by national states, despite the fact that the justification for that policy cannot rest entirely on the appropriability argument, as it has done traditionally in the economics literature since about 1960. I assess how the conventional justification for innovation policies needs to be altered, taking into account the ways in which globalisation has changed the agenda for states and for policy makers.

2 Growth and competitiveness – two views on the origins of profits

Two schools of economic thought can each be grouped together with respect to alternative views on the origins of profits in a capitalist economy. According to the first such school, profits derive from a search for lower wage costs (either through lower wage rates, or by increasing the intensity of work), and from positions of market power (facilitating higher prices in final product markets, and lower prices in markets for the intermediate products used as inputs). The two are often linked, where for example work is 'put out' to a contractor who is obliged to sell at low prices, and manages to do so by setting low wage rates and poorer working conditions. This perspective on profits dominates much of the economics literature – it is common to most mainstream macroeconomists and industrial economists, to neo-Ricardians, and to most twentieth-century Marxist economists.

In this perspective, multinational corporations (MNCs) as well as states stand to lose from global competition. Their protected markets are eroded and costs are driven ever lower (to the lowest common denominator) by international competition, and so profits are everywhere squeezed. The obvious reaction is to pass the squeeze on to others – to workers and contractors, whose security of contract is weakened. This is the perspective as well of the financial markets – to 'make the assets sweat' and to maximise their current value. Overall, this is a zero sum game, in which the gains are limited and of a one-off kind, like in a national context the revenues from privatisation. In classical terms, profits are generated primarily in the realms of exchange and distribution, although there are then consequences for the way in which production is organised.

In the second view profits derive instead from innovation. This is the perspective of Schumpeter and of modern evolutionary economists, but it has strong classical antecedents, especially in the work of Smith and Marx. In this case innovative MNCs and states in the most dynamic centres gain, and not necessarily at the expense of others. Innovation is a positive sum game, in which the gains need not be limited or of a one-off kind. In classical terms, profits are created in production and through continual advances in production, not in the spheres of exchange or distribution – although here, going the other way around, innovation has consequences for the way in which markets are organised.

By and large, the Schumpeterian perspective on the creation of profits is shared by innovative companies based in the most dynamic centres, and by the more internationally integrated MNCs, particularly in sectors at the leading edge of innovation. Note also that the scope for dynamism is not a function of the existing level of productivity or technological capability, although it may be a positive function of the degree of openness of an economy (since the greater incentive to export and compete in world markets increases companies' dynamism). Japan, Korea and other economies of the Far East have been generating higher rates of innovation than the United States, although they began from lower levels of capability. For these purposes innovation is defined as the creation of new products and processes, even where these are not at some notional 'technology frontier'. Innovation consists primarily of the accumulation of tacit capability (a process sometimes termed technological accumulation), which capability is embodied in social organisation (mainly in firms), and which is to this extent tied to production in a particular location by a specific set of firms.

So, in this second view of the origin of profits, what is the mechanism by which innovation leads to a higher share of profits, and hence to greater competitiveness and economic growth? I have modelled this mechanism as a process by which wage increases tend to follow productivity increases (including product as well as process improvements that raise the value of products per worker), but with a lag (Cantwell, 1989, 1992). Owing to this lag, the faster the rate of innovation or productivity growth, the higher is the share of profits in income. However, if wages do track productivity they will still increase faster with innovation. As in the classical tradition of Smith and Ricardo, a faster rate of economic growth pulls up wages. With innovation, living standards rise despite the low share of wages in income – as remarked earlier, creating profits through innovation is a positive sum game.

I believe that both historical and recent evidence accords very well with this model. In the most innovative capitalist societies (Japan, Korea, Germany, etc., in the post-war period) productivity and output growth is relatively high, and wages rise faster than elsewhere. The model also suggests that these innovative economies have a tendency towards trade surpluses. One way of explaining this is that import growth follows export growth, just as wages follow productivity; yet another way of looking at this idea is that the propensity to save out of profits is higher than the propensity to save out of wages, so that a greater share of profits in income is associated with a higher overall propensity to save out of income. All these features (exports leading imports, and high savings ratios) also characterise the more dynamic economies.

Of course, in practice profits are generated in both the ways I have outlined here, which could therefore be seen simply as different parts of a broader story. In the first case the focus is on lowering wage costs relative to the value of output per worker with some given technology; while in the second case the objective is to increase productivity by changing the methods of production. The two may be connected, and some writers have emphasised these connections – such as in the discussions of Ricardo and Marx of the impact on wages of the introduction of machinery. I think it can be argued that the second type of profits have always been more important in the longer term than the first (consider, for example, the displacement of the traditional Indian textile industry with its low wages by the rise of the Lancashire cotton mills), but I would contend that with globalisation the second kind of profits have become even more important relative to the first. To extend the arguments advanced earlier, MNCs have lost profits of the first kind since privileged positions in various individual markets have been swept away as these markets have become steadily more internationally interdependent, but MNCs have increased opportunities for creating profits of the second kind through internationally integrated strategies for innovation (Cantwell, 1994).

There is other evidence in favour of this view, apart from the trend towards internationally integrated MNC networks and greater affiliate specialisation since the 1960s which has, by increasing the potential for the innovative creativity of affiliates within their respective corporate groups, given MNCs in most industries a new source of higher profitability and growth (Cantwell and Sanna-Randaccio, 1993). One such piece of additional evidence is the new and continuing concerns over 'competitiveness', which can be attributed to the frailty of the first kind of profits in a global economy, as isolated pockets of market power are increasingly challenged. The central feature of globalisation is a qualitative increase since the late 1960s in the degree of international interdependence between locationally dispersed production facilities.

The importance of competitiveness at a national level is observed in the persistence of trade imbalances in the form of surpluses in the more highly innovative economies (Japan) and deficits in the less innovative (the US and the UK). To be sure, these trade imbalances are explained partly by factors other than differences in industrial competitiveness – divergent macroeconomic policies and trade policies, financial factors and currency movements have all played a role – but it is striking how these imbalances have persisted since 1982, during a period when policies and exhange rates have changed quite considerably. Moreover, in the long run the causality seems to run the other way, as witnessed by the trend appreciation of the Japanese yen and depreciation of the US dollar and the pound sterling, leaving aside the substantial shorter-run fluctuations in all currency values (in the model referred to earlier, currency appreciation may act as a partial substitute for a faster rise in wages in local currency units in the more dynamic economy).

One response to the erosion of profits of the first kind has been an ever-more desperate search for new profits of this kind, through various means of financial restructuring, sub-contracting agreements and the re-negotiation of contracts. Likewise, the current fashion for 'labour market flexibility', if by this is meant the use of contractual flexibility as a means of lowering wages relative to the hours and the intensity of work, as opposed to the creation of greater functional flexibility through the development of facilities for re-training workers for new tasks. However, ultimately these one-off gains offer little way out. The longer-term response must surely be directed principally towards increased efforts for innovation. In this respect internationalisation tends to have an extremely beneficial longer-term impact on development, by shifting the focus from the first kind to the second kind of profits, whatever the deficiencies might be of the sometimes more immediate impact of the greater intensity of re-contracting in a less-regulated environment.

Thus, for example, the new wave of strategic alliances between MNCs has been far more oriented towards joint technological development and inter-firm cooperation in learning, and has been relatively less motivated by the joint exercise of market power, by comparison with the international cartels of the interwar years (Hagedoorn and Schakenraad, 1990; Cantwell and Barrera, 1998). The growing pressures of international competition imply that in a dynamic (as opposed to a static) setting, surviving firms must be increasingly committed to the continuous upgrading of their own capability base, and hence to technological improvement. The distinction between the orthodox kind of profits and the Schumpeterian innovative kind is also analogous to the distinction between static profit maximisation (organising transactions so as to increase current efficiency and market power), and the evolutionary search for higher profits, a somewhat unpredictable search that leads to some mistakes and blind alleys and hence some failures even among 'rational' agents (Nelson and Winter, 1982). The immediate static impact of greater competition is the re-organisation of contracts and the re-distribution of income, which might be explained along the lines of the economists' standard conception of profit maximisation, while the dynamic impact is that firms must search for higher profits over time through innovation, a search that takes place around an inter-firm variety of viable alternative paths.

3 Capturing the returns to innovation

It should be clear already that my definition of innovation and of technology is a rather broad one. Until quite recently, most of the post-war literature had accustomed economists to thinking of technology in much narrower terms, as akin to knowledge or information, often generated in large firms through the research and development (R&D) function. When the exclusive focus of attention is on this element of technology, the 'appropriability' argument comes immediately to the fore, as to whether firms (and the countries in which they are situated) can appropriate a full return on their investments in the creation of such knowledge or information, which can be traded and otherwise dispersed into the public domain. This information-like element of technology thus has the characteristics of a latent public good (Nelson, 1992), since information is costly to create, but once created it may be transferred to others at close to zero marginal cost, and it is non-depletable no matter how much more widely it is used. Since in most cases the patent system provides only a rather ephemeral way of protecting knowledge and ensuring that it is exploited solely privately (Levin, Klevorick, Nelson and Winter, 1987), this gives rise to the classic problem identified by Nelson (1959) and Arrow (1962) – that the social rate of return on investments in research and knowledge creation may exceed the private rate of return, leading to an underinvestment by private firms in research and hence in innovation. As I noted at the beginning, this problem would be accentuated if knowledge were also to flow increasingly easily and cheaply across national boundaries, since there would then be little point in national governments trying to correct for the underinvestment as they would end up simply subsidising free riders in other countries (the problem would recur at an international level).

In the standard account, the difficulties of appropriating a full economic rent from investments in knowledge creation have to do firstly with uncertainties over the outcome of research, uncertainties over the ultimate value of knowledge or the associated devices at any given stage of development, and the ease with which imitators can replicate the results at lower (and perhaps at low marginal) cost. The difficulty that even experts in the field may have in forecasting the results of R&D projects, and in predicting the commercial value of inventions, implies that it is troublesome for those engaged in research or invention to ensure that they are fully rewarded for their efforts through contracts with other parties who, prior to the completion of a deal, lack information on the true value of what they are purchasing. Moreover, secondly, because of technological interrelatedness, even if the private value of a particular invention could be established in advance, its creation will contribute to a wider pool of knowledge, and hence there are likely to be external benefits from the wider usage of this latent public good element of any new technology.

Hence, there are both microeconomic and macroeconomic perspectives on the 'appropriability' problem. From the microeconomic or business perspective, the difficulties that commercial inventors have in realising a full return on their investments in new knowledge creation (due to the difficulties in ascertaining the value of an invention in advance), may give rise to a closer vertical integration between R&D and downstream production facilities within the firm. Yet from the macroeconomic or public policy perspective, because the social benefits of R&D exceed the privately appropriated benefits (due to external spillovers associated with the latent public good properties of knowledge, as well as the problems of valuation at the firm-level), there may be an underinvestment in new knowledge creation from a social point of view.

While no doubt there is an issue here, once technology is defined more broadly to include in addition a second element – namely, tacit capability – the 'appropriability' problem appears to have been greatly exaggerated, and it needs to be understood in a rather wider context. In a more general (non-neoclassical) framework, the concept of the 'ease of appropriability' relates not mainly to restrictions on knowledge flows between firms (the efficacy of the patent system, the use of secrecy etc.), but instead to the difficulties of learning in a locally specific environment, and of imitating learning processes when moving between different institutions and between different technological traditions. The new literature on technological change emphasises that it is an evolutionary and path-dependent process, which takes the form of the steady accumulation of tacit capability (through learning processes in production), rather than a sequence of discrete acts of knowledge creation (subsequently capitalised upon through changes in production). Thus, what is appropriated by firms is essentially a return on advances in tacit capability acquired through learning, rather than a return on the creation of particular items of knowledge. The knowledge generating function is instead to be seen primarily as an input into the learning process, the benefits of which depend mainly upon the contribution made to the problem-solving activity through which the firm consolidates its tacit productive capability, as opposed to the (uncertain contractual) value of any inventions.

The inspiration for this new view of technology is essentially twofold, and comes firstly from Rosenberg's (1976, 1982) thorough investigation of the history of technological change, which has shown it to be a cumulative and incremental process of problem-solving in production (a view that again can be traced back to Marx, Smith and the classics). Secondly, the theoretical articulation of the new approach was provided by Nelson and Winter (1982), who suggested that the evolution of tacit capability was encapsulated in the organisational routines of firms' production teams.

In the evolutionary perspective on technological change, the two elements of technology are strictly complementary, in that they cannot be used in an operational production system other than in combination with one another. Thus, potentially public technological knowledge and skills (which also has a tacit component, which is understood only by individual practitioners trained and experienced in the activity in question, and so this component of know-how overlaps with the economist's notion of individual 'human capital') can only be effectively exploited by firms that accumulate the requisite tacit capability (which is acquired through a collective learning process within the firm, and thus becomes embodied in a form of social organisation). For this reason, knowledge cannot be used at zero marginal cost by firms that did not create it, as they must make their own investments in tacit capability. Where one firm imitates another, or borrows knowledge from another by agreement (as in cross-licensing arrangements), the recipient firm will incur costs that are an inverse function of the degree of relatedness between the technological profiles of the companies in question. When a firm imitates another in a different field the costs of learning and establishing its own tacit capability in a new area are sometimes sufficiently high that the costs of imitation exceed the original costs of innovation in the initial firm (Mansfield, Schwartz and Wagner, 1981), which might occur if the imitating company had a very different technological history and an experience that was distant from or unrelated to that of the original innovator.

As in the conventional story, in the new evolutionary approach too, we can distinguish between the microeconomic and the macroeconomic perspectives on the problems of technological learning (of which the 'appropriability' issue is just one). At the firm level, the cost of learning rises the more unrelated is a new technology to the existing capabilities of the firm. Thus, the cost of imitating a rival or even a collaborator is higher, the greater is the difference between the technological traditions of the companies concerned. Since technological traditions are always to some extent differentiated, each firm can exploit some sphere of competence relative to others, but firms whose achievements are particularly distinctive will be able to capture the highest returns. Firms invest in knowledge creation (in large companies, formalised in R&D), so as to be able to tailor the search for new knowledge to the specific needs that arise from their own problem-solving in production, and so as to be able to better understand what is relevant to their own requirements from the knowledge being generated outside the firm, and then to be able to properly assimilate it.

At the public policy level, if firms have limited learning capabilities (say, in a given field outside their existing areas of competence or specialisation) then they will be reluctant to invest in new knowledge creation, which they would find difficult to incorporate into new tacit capability, and hence difficult to capture a return on. However, using this argument the ease of knowledge spillovers between firms is likely to be inversely related with the extent of underinvestment in knowledge creation, and not positively related as in the conventional account. The greater the availability of external knowledge sources from other companies and from the science base (supported by the local government through universities and other public research establishments), the more likely that an individual firm's investment in commercial research will succeed in providing (or suitably identifying and refining) the knowledge inputs needed to help extend and improve its own tacit capability. From this viewpoint, apart from supporting basic research as well as education and training, governments have an important role in actively encouraging knowledge diffusion through intercompany collaborative agreements, licensing and the like.

Note further that these different views on the 'appropriability' issue imply a significant difference of opinion over the form of the connection between appropriability and profits, which relates back to our earlier discussion of arguments about the origins of profits. In the orthodox market-based interpretation, the 'ease of appropriability' is a variant of the market power notion of the origins of profits, and has to do with the ability (or inability) of the firm to earn a return on its investment in new knowledge creation through contracts with downstream users of inventions. In contrast, in the alternative evolutionary formulation the 'ease of appropriability' of a return on technology creation has to do with the difficulties confronting problem-solving activities in production, which are the learning activities that lead to the formation of firm-specific capabilities, and thus to profits. The more difficult it is to raise productivity and improve product quality the higher the potential return to innovative firms, but also the more such firms come to depend upon an innovative environment of intensive knowledge flows between firms and (at least in the science-based industries) knowledge flows between firms and universities.

From this new perspective, innovation and imitation are complements rather than substitutes, since in order to imitate others firms must innovate by creating their own tacit capability, and by adapting any publicly available knowledge to suit their own specific requirements, including the adjustment of methods to the distinctive and unique aspects of their tacit capability. In addition to the costs they must bear, imitators are not free riders, because in the course of the learning process by which they create new tacit capability, they will also normally generate new knowledge of their own, and thereby make their contribution to the public pool. Even in terms of the R&D function as such, firms (at least large firms) that wish to imitate others usually cannot escape their share of the costs. For one thing, because the two elements of technology are complementary, when they are absorbing knowledge production companies need knowledge inputs that are tailored to the specific nuances of their own problem-solving activity, and this is normally most easily obtained from an R&D facility under their own direct control (and in turn, as a result, the knowledge and skills generated by that R&D facility are generally most relevant to the development of production in the same firm) (Cantwell, 1994). For another thing, corporate research has a dual role – apart from creating new knowledge and skills, it is necessary as a means of monitoring knowledge created in the environment outside the firm, and in understanding what parts of that knowledge may be relevant and useful to the firm (Cohen and Levinthal, 1989).

The most innovative firms are also generally the best imitators, and those that make the best use of the knowledge being created in the external environment generally make the greatest contribution to knowledge themselves. Indeed, the very distinction between innovation and imitation is really quite blurred (Cantwell, 1992). Thus, the model that focused upon the returns to single and discrete acts of knowledge creation overplayed the appropriability problem (Mowery and Rosenberg, 1989). Another way of looking at the new approach is as a criticism of the so-called 'linear model', which depicts a simple causal chain running from invention (knowledge creation) to innovation and then to diffusion. In practice, there is a continual interaction between learning in production (innovation) and research and science, but on the whole there tend to be more linkages that run from technology in production to research and to science than the other way round (Rosenberg, 1982, 1994). An illustration is the way in which new instruments and computer technology have completely transformed the nature of scientific enquiry in recent years (such as in the use of more powerful telescopes in astonomy, the use of instruments which enable experiments to be done at a microscopic level, and the use of computer simulations and graphics in virtually every branch of science). Moreover, practical technological advances have sometimes led to new areas of science. Thus, Edison's work on light bulbs led to the discovery of the electron, Marconi's practical discovery of the possibility of international radio transmissions encouraged research on electromagnetic waves, while the Wright brothers' success in demonstrating the feasibility of aircraft construction led subsequently to scientific theories of aerodynamics which explained how their technology worked.

Of course, the mutual interaction between the formation of technological capabilities through problem-solving activity in production and the creation and diffusion of knowledge and skills still does not quite explain the incentive for investing in a local research system and a science base as a means of encouraging a higher level of private investment in corporate R&D and innovation. Instead, it might be argued that in a global economy research and production may become locationally separated, with the linkages between the two sustained at a greater geographical distance – with some of the knowledge inputs into learning coming from afar, either within the multinational firm, or when monitoring external sources of potentially relevant new knowledge. There is a grain of truth in this argument, at least with respect to basic research and scientific advance, which might feed into (and draw upon the fruits of) applied research, development and production in a different location. However, a good deal of recent empirical work has now shown that the intensity of linkages between science and technology still tends to decline with geographical distance (Jaffe, Trajtenberg and Henderson, 1993; Hicks, Ishizuka, Keen and Sweet, 1993; Feldman, 1994; Audretsch and Feldman, 1994; Audretsch and Stephan, 1994). The linkages between science, research and technology have remained essentially localised owing to the importance of face-to-face contacts in communicating the results of complex learning processes which embody a tacit element.

There is one other point that should be mentioned when considering the ability of firms to capture the returns on innovation. That is, to exploit the knowledge and skills created by research, firms require not only suitably matching tacit capability in production, but also complementary or co-specialised assets which lie downstream in product distribution and marketing (Teece, 1986). The direction taken by problem solving in production, and the consequent agenda set for allied research facilities, may well depend upon the nature of these co-specialised assets, and the types of product diversification they would either facilitate or restrain.

4 Globalisation, national systems of innovation and national policies

If the 'appropriability' argument in its usual form is not quite as convincing as it has been held to be, it is necessary first to briefly re-consider the case for technology policies in general. In the new thinking just described, firms often do capture a return even on the basic R&D they perform, which return is sufficient to provide them with an incentive to conduct such research, provided that it is suitably integrated with the development of their tacit capability in production. This is because the generation of new knowledge and skills through commercial R&D is designed as an input into the processes of problem solving and learning in production, and these learning processes create tacit capabilities or firm-specific technological competence, on which a return is earned. Therefore, if firms are investing in the upgrading of their productive capabilities they require new knowledge inputs, and do so increasingly as the level of technological sophistication of their production rises, such that practical technological problem solving will 'call forth' investments in R&D. However, the same research would not provide an adequate return for less able, or for smaller and more narrowly specialised companies, since they lack the technological competence and the breadth of learning or search activity in production needed to exploit it. For this reason, the development of tacit technological capability tends to lead to the emergence of corporate R&D, as we have observed in the recent experience of Korea and Taiwan.

Thus, the problem is not so much a failure in the market for the knowledge and skills created by R&D, but rather a lack of the tacit capability that is needed to exploit such knowledge. If local firms lack capability and innovativeness they are unable to use this knowledge and these skills effectively, which prevents them from appropriating more fully the potential returns on research, and this in turn reduces the volume of R&D that is privately initiated and financed by industry. Hence, an under-investment in knowledge creation from a social point of view is primarily due to an institutional failure rather than a market failure, in that a lack of the dynamic social organisation associated with capability formation in firms reduces their incentive to invest in research, and restricts their ability to exploit what opportunities do arise from the new knowledge and skills which emerge in the firm's external environment. It might be argued that such a lack of innovation relative to invention and external knowledge creation, and relatedly an under-investment in corporate R&D, have been particular features of post-war Britain. This problem would not be solved by a better working of the markets for knowledge, since the intensity of the creation and use of knowledge by firms does not depend mainly upon the characteristics of the market for the exchange of knowledge. Instead, once an institutional structure is in place that encourages learning and the upgrading of corporate capabilities, new markets for knowledge exchange between firms are likely to be established, which in turn would stimulate further investments in corporate research.

There is still a role for policy in this view. By supporting education and training systems, governments help to lower the costs and facilitate the creation of tacit capability in firms. That is, governments can help to address the problem of the development of more sophisticated systems of production, which at root is a problem of institutions (or, if you wish, of institutional failure), and not essentially a problem of the malfunctioning of markets. Likewise, by supporting public research, the universities and the science base, governments indirectly encourage firms to invest in their own R&D to be able to tap into a more extensive external network of research, and thereby to increase the returns on their own R&D through suitably adapting their underlying tacit capability. In this event public research is not replacing some 'missing' private research, but instead public research acts as a catalyst for the widening of private research, which in turn supports the preservation of a more sophisticated tacit capability in production. Thus, what innovative companies expect most from local universities is not research with immediate commercial applications in their own sector (which they would normally prefer to conduct in-house), but rather a wider base of knowledge creation and skills with which their own facilities can interact (Pavitt, 1994).

There are two implications of the argument that technology policy should be directed mainly to fostering the formation of tacit capabilities in firms, rather than trying to correct for deficiencies in the market for knowledge. First, firms rather than governments will tend to lead the process of innovation and capability formation, and firms should not be seen as passive actors responding to the external provision of knowledge and skills. However, of course, governments do help to put into place a set of complementary institutions which encourage innovation and knowledge diffusion, especially through their support of education, training and the science and research infrastructure. For a detailed discussion of how governments might help to assist institutions in confronting the difficulties of technological learning (as opposed to improving the workings of markets for knowledge) in a developing country context, see Lall (1997). Second, it is still worth governments backing the local establishment of basic research facilities, even if some of the knowledge generated has spillover benefits abroad, since the greatest and most immediate impact will be concentrated locally, owing to the tendency for the linkages between science and technology to be geographically localised, as has been shown in the literature using patent citations mentioned earlier (such as Jaffe, Trajtenberg and Henderson, 1993; Audretsch and Feldman, 1994; Frost, 1996; Almeida and Kogut, 1997).

The problem of institution building tends to be better addressed in national systems of innovation in which governments are more geared towards the support of science and technology (with the vocal backing of innovative local companies!), as opposed to purely market-based systems. This is especially true in the modern technological paradigm grounded in information and communication technology, computerisation, and flexible (more complex) production systems, in which the local linkages between science and technology have become more intensive than they were in the past, and increasingly run across a wide range of formerly separate disciplines. While there need not be 'market failure' in the usual sense, it is inappropriate to follow a laissez-faire ideology in which the public support of research is focused upon the areas of the most direct market potential for local companies. To illustrate the point, a mainstream chemical company increasingly needs to draw on knowledge and skills in many diverse areas, such as electronics and biotechnology, in order to further develop its own production systems, even if it has no intention of entering the markets that are most directly connected with the principal products of these fields.

The national system of innovation is the network of institutions in the public and private sectors of each country that support the initiation, modification and diffusion of new technologies (Freeman, 1987, 1995). The nationally distinctive features of the system are represented in the particular sectoral patterns of strength or tacit capability that has been developed in private firms in each country (Nelson ed., 1993; Patel and Pavitt, 1994). The globalisation of technological innovation in MNCs, in the sense of an international integration of geographically dispersed and locally specialised activities, tends to reinforce and not to dismantle nationally distinctive patterns of development or national systems of innovation (Cantwell, 1995). Contrary to what is sometimes alleged, globalisation and national specialisation are complementary parts of a common process, and not conflicting trends (as argued as well by Archibugi and Pianta, 1992, and Archibugi and Michie eds., 1997). The incentive to organise affiliate specialisation is the desire to tap into the locally specific and differentiated stream of innovation in each centre, but by specialising in accordance with these local strengths the latter are reinforced. As remarked already, the creation of tacit capability is localised and embedded in social organisations (Nelson and Winter, 1982), and this organisational distinctiveness has a location-specific as well as a firm-specific dimension. The particular path of innovation followed in each country or region has historical origins (Rosenberg, 1976, 1982). In the period of globalisation since the late 1960s the general tendency has been for MNCs to become more technologically diversified as they establish newly integrated technological systems, while countries or locations have become more specialised in their technological activity (Cantwell, 1993).

Despite the continuing significance of national systems of innovation (Nelson ed., 1993), there is no doubt that the role of the nation state is changing in the newly emerging global economy. The state is being undermined as an independent economic authority. It is not necessarily less important as a player in world economic affairs, but it cannot now act or formulate policy in isolation. Although I will not dwell upon it here, among the consequences are that new international institutions need to be created, the role of existing international institutions needs to be re-defined, and new international agreements between countries are needed. Here instead, I will conclude by briefly commenting upon the ways in which globalisation has changed the agenda for national policy.

To return to the arguments of the two different schools of thought on profitability and growth which I identified previously, I suggested that with globalisation, national policies must be increasingly oriented towards the second type of strategy for growth rather than the first. From the perspective of the first school, states can attract the investments of MNCs by lowering domestic wage costs and establishing protected markets or allowing the companies some degree of local market power. In doing so, states also thereby have the authority to bargain with MNCs to ensure that a 'fair' share of the returns on investments is retained locally. However, the scope for states to behave in this fashion is now diminished if the country wishes to participate in the international integration of activity being organised by MNCs elsewhere. Even if the strategy succeeds, it is likely to reduce local dynamism, as occurred in the import-substituting regimes of Latin America. It is also worth noting the failure of Poland and a number of African countries to attract much investment on the basis of the supposed appeal of low wages, in economies in which the prospects for productivity growth are limited.

Following the second school of thought, according to which innovation is the basis of profits, states are best advised to maintain a good local infrastructure and to encourage local institution building, and to facilitate local inter-company networks for cross-licensing and other schemes for the mutual enhancement of technological development. This type of strategy is increasingly likely to appeal to MNCs when they consider whether to extend capacity, and if so where. In this case, an industrial policy role remains for national governments, even in a global economy. There are certainly still problems for states, but they are not the problems that are often traditionally perceived from the standpoint of the first perspective, such as a loss of bargaining power *vis-à-vis* MNCs. The problems are rather (among others) how to facilitate the most appropriate pattern of national specialisation, or in other words how best to build upon established local strengths in innovation, and how to encourage a greater international coordination of productive activity in such a way as to improve the ability to learn locally from what is being done elsewhere, in other parts of the region or the world.

Note

I am grateful to Daniele Archibugi for helpful comments on an earlier draft of this chapter.

References

Almeida, P. and Kogut, B. 1997. The exploration of technological diversity and the geographic localization of innovation, *Small Business Economics*, 9: 21–31.

Archibugi, D. and Michie, J. 1997. Technological globalisation and national systems of innovation: an introduction, in Archibugi and Michie (eds.) 1997.

Archibugi, D. and Michie, J. (eds.) 1997. *Technology, Globalisation and Economic Performance*, Cambridge, Cambridge University Press.

Archibugi, D. and Pianta, M. 1992. *The Technological Specialization of Advanced Countries*, Dordrecht, Kluwer Academic Publishers.

Arrison, T. S., Bergsten, C. F., Graham, E.M. and Harris, M. C. (eds.) 1992. *Japan's Growing Technological Capability: Implications for the US Economy*, Washington DC, National Academy Press.

Arrow, K. J. 1962. Economic welfare and the allocation of resources for invention, in Nelson (ed.).

Audretsch, D. and Feldman, M. P. 1994. Knowledge spillovers and the geography of innovation and production, London, Centre for Economic Policy Research Discussion Papers, no. 953, May.

Audretsch, D. and Stephan, P. E. 1994. How localised are networks in biotechnology?, Berlin, Wissenschaftszentrum Berlin für Sozialforschung Discussion Papers, FS IV 94–9, July.

Cantwell, J. A. 1989. *Technological Innovation and Multinational Corporations*, Oxford, Basil Blackwell.

Cantwell, J. A. 1992. Japan's industrial competitiveness and the technological capabilities of the leading Japanese firms, in Arrison, Bergsten, Graham and Harris (eds.).

1993. Corporate technological specialisation in international industries, in Casson and Creedy (eds.).

1994. Introduction, in Cantwell (ed.).

1995. The globalisation of technology: what remains of the product cycle model?, *Cambridge Journal of Economics*, 19: 155–74, Reprinted in Archibugi and Michie (eds.) 1997b.

Cantwell, J. A. (ed.) 1994. *Transnational Corporations and Innovatory Activities*, London, Routledge.

Cantwell, J. A. and Barrera, M. P. 1998. The localisation of corporate technological trajectories in the interwar cartels: cooperative learning versus an exchange of knowledge, *Economics of Innovation and New Technology*, 6: 212–29.

Cantwell, J. A. and Sanna-Randaccio, F. 1993. Multinationality and firm growth, *Weltwirtschaftliches Archiv*, 129: 275–99.

Casson, C. and Creedy, J. (eds.) 1993. *Industrial Concentration and Economic Inequality: Essays in Honour of Peter Hart*, Aldershot, Edward Elgar.

Cohen, W. M. and Levinthal, D. 1989. Innovation and learning: the two faces of R&D, *Economic Journal*, 99: 569–96.

Feldman, M. P. 1994. *The Geography of Innovation*, Dordrecht, Kluwer Academic Publishers.

Freeman, C. 1987. *Technology Policy and Economic Performance: Lessons From Japan*, London, Frances Pinter.

1995. The 'National System of Innovation' in historical perspective, *Cambridge Journal of Economics*, 19: 5–24. Reprinted in D. Archibugi and J. Michie (eds.) 1997b.

Freeman, C. and Soete, L. L. G. (eds.) 1990. *New Explorations in the Economics of Technical Change*, London, Frances Pinter.

Frost, T. 1996. From exploitation to exploration: the geographic sources of subsidiary innovations and the evolutionary theory of the multinational enterprise, Stockholm, paper presented at the EIBA Annual Conference, December.

Hagedoorn, J. and Schakenraad, J. 1990. Inter-firm partnerships and cooperative strategies in core technologies, in Freeman and Soete (eds.).

Hicks, D., Ishizuka, T., Keen, P. and Sweet, S. 1993. Japanese corporations, scientific research and globalization, Brighton, Science Policy Research Unit, University of Sussex (mimeo).

Jaffe, A. B., Trajtenberg, M. and Henderson, R. 1993. Geographical localisation of knowledge spillovers, as evidenced by patent citations, *Quarterly Journal of Economics*, 58: 577–98.

Lall, S. 1997. Coping with new technologies in emerging Asia, paper prepared for the Asian Development Bank's 'Emerging Asia' study, January.

Levin, R. C., Klevorick, A. K., Nelson, R. R. and Winter, S. G. 1987. Appropriating the returns from industrial research and development, *Brookings Papers on Economic Activity*, 3: 783–820.

Mansfield, E., Schwartz, M. and Wagner, S. 1981. Imitation costs and patents: an empirical study, *Economic Journal*, 90: 907–18.

Mowery, D. C. and Rosenberg, N. 1989. *Technology and the Pursuit of Economic Growth*, Cambridge, Cambridge University Press.

Nelson, R. R. 1959. The simple economics of basic scientific research, *Journal of Political Economy*, 67: 297–306.

1992. What is 'commercial' and what is 'public' about technology, and what should be?, in Rosenberg, Landau and Mowery (eds.).

Nelson, R. R. (ed.) 1962. *The Rate and Direction of Inventive Activity*, Princeton, N J, Princeton University Press.

1993. *National Innovation Systems: A Comparative Analysis*, Oxford, Oxford University Press.

Nelson, R. R. and Winter, S. G. 1982. *An Evolutionary Theory of Economic Change*, Cambridge, MA, Harvard University Press.

Patel, P. and Pavitt, K. L. R. 1994. National innovation systems: why they are important, and how they might be measured and compared, *Economics of Innovation and New Technology*, 3: 77–95.

Pavitt, K. L. R. 1994. Try business class worldwide, *Times Higher Educational Supplement*, 18 November, p. 14.

Rosenberg, N. 1976. *Perspectives on Technology*, Cambridge, Cambridge University Press.

1982. *Inside the Black Box: Technology and Economics*, Cambridge, Cambridge University Press.

1994. *Exploring the Black Box: Technology, Economics and History*, Cambridge, Cambridge University Press.

Rosenberg, N., Landau, R. and Mowery, D.C. (eds.) 1992. *Technology and the Wealth of Nations*, Stanford, Stanford University Press.

Teece, D. J. 1986. Profiting from technological innovation: implications for integration, collaboration, licensing and public policy, *Research Policy*, 15: 285–305.

12 The policy implications of the globalisation of innovation

DANIELE ARCHIBIUGI AND SIMONA
IAMMARINO

Introduction

Globalisation is not a single phenomenon, but a catch-all concept to describe a wide range of forces. The importance of globalisation is currently the focus of a vivid controversy. On the one hand, there are those who maintain that globalisation has effectively contaminated the greater part of economic life (Ohmae, 1990; Chesnais, 1994; Barnet and Cavanagh, 1994; Brecher and Costello, 1994; Perraton *et al.*, 1997); on the other, there are those who take a more sceptical view (Ruigrok and van Tulder, 1995; Michie and Grieve Smith, 1995; Hirst and Thompson, 1996). However, the terms of the debate are often unclear as three issues, which although related should be kept separate, are not well clarified.

The first is to establish the importance of global forces in social life (does globalisation exist or not?). This requires the identification of the different types of globalisation and an estimate of their weight according to geographical location, industrial sectors and social groupings. The second refers to the value judgement attributable to globalisation (is a global society a good or a bad thing?). Answers to this type of question can only be given by clarifying the actors of reference. Finally, the third issue refers to the viability of national policies enabling the modification of the inertial tendencies produced by globalisation (are there any policies which can regulate globalisation?). As these policies are mainly implemented at a national level, the debate on globalisation must necessarily be judged with reference to the effectiveness of the policies implemented by national governments.

In this chapter, we attempt to critically assess the concept of globalisation as applied to innovation. Our intention is to define its implications for national policies. In section 2 we present a taxonomy of the globalisation of innovation based on three categories: international exploitation, global generation and global collaboration on innovation. This taxonomy, which

242

has already appeared in previous work (Archibugi and Michie, 1995, Archibugi and Michie eds., 1997a), is considered here in the light of the debate which it has triggered, as we believe that it constitutes a useful filter through which to interpret not only the size of the phenomenon (see Iammarino and Michie, 1997; Archibugi and Iammarino, 1998), but also the bearing of public policies on each of the ongoing processes. In fact, in the following two sections, we shall analyse the impact that each category of the globalisation of innovation might have for single countries, with the specific intention of exploring the public policy implications. In the concluding section 5, we identify some directions for further research on the debated topic.

A taxonomy of the globalisation of innovation

During the past few years, too many heterogeneous phenomena have been included in the term 'globalisation of innovation' and this has made the concept's explanatory power lose its potency. Thus we have attempted (Archibugi and Michie, 1995, Archibugi and Michie eds., 1997a) to escape from the maze of the globalisation of innovation by identifying three main categories. These are: (a) the international exploitation of technology produced on a national basis; (b) the global generation of innovations; (c) global technological collaborations.

The unit of analysis to which this taxonomy refers is either the innovation or the innovative research project. The intention is to list the ways in which economic institutions produce and exploit individual innovations and/or innovative projects. The three categories are complementary and not mutually exclusive, both at the firm and country level. Firms, especially large ones, generate innovations in all the different ways described here. From a historical point of view, these categories emerged in three successive stages, even though the second and the third added to rather than substituted for the oldest one. The categories of this taxonomy are included in table 12.1.

The first category includes innovators' attempts to obtain economic advantages through the exploitation of their own technological competence in markets other than the domestic one. This includes innovations developed both by firms and by individual inventors. We have preferred to label this category as 'international' rather than 'global' as the actors introducing the innovations preserve their national identity, even when the innovations are diffused and sold in multiple countries. In the majority of cases, the first market in which a specific innovation is exploited is the one it was developed in: even firms which strongly tend towards foreign markets use the internal markets as a 'laboratory' for their products in order to sample the reactions of consumers and the quality of the products.

Table 12.1 *A taxonomy of the globalisation of innovation*

Categories	Actors	Forms	Evidence	
			Stocks	Flows
International exploitation of nationally produced innovations	Profit-seeking firms and individuals	Exports of innovative goods. Cession of licences and patents. Foreign production of innovative goods internally generated	Very high	Constant increase over last century
Global generation of innovations	Multinational firms	R&D and innovative activities both in the home and the host countries. Acquisitions of existing R&D laboratories or green-field R&D investment in host countries.	Low to medium	Slow increase over time
Global techno-scientific collaborations	Universities and public research centres	Joint scientific projects. Scientific exchanges, sabbatical years. International flows of students.	Rather significant	Increase over last decades
	National and multinational firms	Joint-ventures for specific projects Productive agreements with exchange of technical information and/or equipment.	Low	Sharp increase in recent years

Source: Adapted from Archibugi and Michie, 1995.

The most direct method for firms to appropriate the results of their innovatory activity in foreign markets is to export the products in which the innovations are directly or indirectly incorporated. Another significant way of exploiting innovations in foreign markets is through foreign direct investment (FDI). The conditions allowing international production are known: availability of capital and a willingness to geographically exploit ownership, technological and organisational advantages are required on behalf of the investing firm (see Dunning's (1993) wide ranging treatment). Economic and institutional stability and a minimal level of economic development, or, in other words, location advantages, are required on behalf of the host country. The concession of both licences and patents, and the extension to foreign countries of patents released in the country where the innovation took place, are further types of international exploitation of national technological capacities. It should be remembered that this first category only includes the productive activity operated in host countries which does not entail the creation of additional local technological capacity: if this were to be the case, we would be moving from the first to the second category of this taxonomy.

The second category is the global generation of innovations, which includes innovations conceived on a global scale from the moment they are generated. Only innovations created by multinational enterprises (MNEs) are included in this category. With very few exceptions (such as Shell and Unilever), it is easy to identify the country of origin of such companies, so much so that to some they appear as national enterprises with multinational operations (Hu, 1992).

The authentic global generation of innovations requires organisational and administrative skills that only firms with specific infrastructure and a certain minimum size can attain. Such firms, although limited in number, play a crucial role in the generation of innovations: a few hundred large firms are responsible for 75 per cent of industrial R&D and more than 60 per cent of patents spread in foreign markets (Patel and Pavitt, 1991; Dunning, 1993).

In recent times, a third type of globalisation of innovative activities has made a forceful entry on the scene. This, in some ways, is intermediate to the two preceding categories. We have witnessed an increasing number of agreements between firms for the communal development of specific technological discoveries (Hagedoorn and Schakenraad, 1993). Such collaborations often take place among firms of the same country, but in many cases they involve firms located in two or more different countries, thus emerging as authentically global. These forms of collaboration for technological advances have promoted a variety of mechanisms for the division of costs and the exploitation of results. In a way, the necessity to reduce innovation costs has created new industrial organisation forms and new ownership structures, which today are expanding beyond the simple technological sphere (Mytelka ed., 1991; Dodgson, 1993).

It was not the private sector that discovered this form of knowledge transmission. The academic world has always had a transnational range of action: knowledge is traditionally transmitted from one scholar to another and thus disseminated without always requiring pecuniary compensation. However, different motivations are to be found between the academic and the entrepreneurial communities to this day and these lead to different attitudes towards international cooperation.

Each of the three categories of the globalisation of innovation identified here is also characterised by the existence of a specific international regime. Elaborating on what has been proposed by the literature on international regimes (cf., for example, Strange, 1988; Stopford and Strange, 1991), it is possible to identify for each of the three categories described three main types of interaction: those between firms, those between governments and those between firms and governments. Table 12.2 summarises the competitive and cooperative conditions for each of the three dimensions of the globalisation of innovation, which will be considered separately in the following sections.

The impact of the globalisation of innovation on national economies

The answer to one of the questions previously raised, i.e., whether the globalisation processes are positive or negative, seems, in practice, to be conditional on a number of factors. The advantages, just as the costs, of the tendency towards an increase in the weight of global processes can be substantial and strictly depend upon the characteristics of the participating actors and of their interactions. It is necessary to bear in mind that the dimensions of globalisation summarised in the taxonomy have not affected the various areas of the world at the same time and with the same intensity. In fact, the expansion of global forces has remained limited to the more developed part of the world up to now, so much so as to have been defined a process of 'triadisation', in other words, of increasing polarisation of economic and innovative activities between the Triad economies – that is, Europe, North America and the Pacific Rim countries led by Japan (Chesnais, 1994; Kitson and Michie, in this volume).

The most evident changes implied by the increasing globalisation are the tougher and increased competition and the greater collaboration between actors, both across and within national boundaries. These changes, however, even though polarised in the most developed part of the world, might have an adverse impact on the economic and innovative performance

Table 12.2. *The regimes of the globalisation of innovation – interactions*

Categories	Interactions		
	Firm/firm	Government/government	Government/firm
International exploitation of nationally produced innovations	Strong competition to acquire market shares.	Strong economic rivalry and protection of national production.	Support to national champions and barriers to imports.
Global generation of innovations by MNEs	Competition for areas of economic influence. Rivalry to preserve the expertise and prevent imitation.	Strong rivalry to attract and to acquire high-tech and R&D investments.	Continuous negotiation for S&T investments and for public incentives to innovation.
Global techno-scientific collaborations	Collusive agreements between firms. Increased competition among inter-firm cartels.	Bi-lateral and multi-lateral technical-industrial agreements Control of monopolistic cartels bi-lateral alliances against other nations.	Support to national firms to increase their international scope and the associated learning.

of some countries and regions, leading to a higher risk of 'winners and losers'. Based on an analysis of the effects of the globalisation processes on national and local systems, it can be argued that the current tendencies do not seem to uniquely indicate a greater convergence towards higher levels of economic and technological activity within the group of most advanced countries, and even less so within the regions that constitute them. Considering each of the three aspects of globalisation separately, it is possible to outline the differences in the impact they may have on national economies and on the agents representing them, firms in particular. An attempt to summarise such differences is made in table 12.3.

International exploitation of technology

The processes of market internationalisation and of the multinationalisation of productive activities are certainly the oldest ones in the globalisation phenomenon, and thus the ones that have been most studied. The expansion of market dimensions and their progressive integration have rendered the competition that firms in various countries and world regions must face ever more aggressive, both in domestic and in foreign markets.

The dynamic effects of trade have been increasingly dependent on technology and innovation. The proof of the importance of non-price factors in competitiveness (Thirlwall, 1979; Kaldor, 1981), identifiable principally in national technological capabilities, has anticipated the intense debate on technology as an 'endogenous' determinant of economic growth which has developed since the second half of the 1980s (for a survey see Fagerberg, 1994). The dynamics of the increasing specialisation assume a crucial role in affecting countries' growth, as technological innovation does not occur evenly in the different sectors of the economy. Therefore, one pattern of specialisation is by no means as good as another: countries specialised in fast growing sectors (mainly high-tech) not only may experience faster growth, but they are likely to further reinforce their strength in the international division of labour, due to the cumulative character of technological progress (Lucas, 1988). On the other hand, it has been argued that market size and R&D are both positively correlated with specialisation in high-tech sectors and competitiveness, via internal and external spillover effects (Grossman and Helpman, 1991). The exploitation of national technological competence might thus turn out to exacerbate the strengths and weaknesses of countries and to lead to economic divergence. Several studies have addressed the issue of convergence from the viewpoint of efforts devoted by industrialised nations to technological expertise (Archibugi and Pianta, 1992, 1994; Patel and Pavitt, 1994). At the country level, a limited but

Table 12.3. *The regimes of the globalisation of innovation – implications for the national economies*

Categories	Implications for the national economy		Tendency towards convergence/divergence
	Inwards flows	Outwards flows	
International exploitation of nationally produced innovations	Low learning in consumption goods. Medium learning in capital goods and equipment.	Expansion of the market and the areas of influence. Maintenance of national technological advantages.	Limited but significant economic convergence (GDP per capita) Technological divergence across countries.
Global generation of innovations by MNEs	Acquisition of technological and managerial capabilities. Increased dependence on the strategic choices of foreign firms.	Missing technological opportunities for the internal market. Strengthening of the competitive position of national firms. Tapping into the expertise of the host locations.	Increasing regional/local divergence both in economic and innovation variables.
Global techno-scientific collaborations	Increase of techno-scientific flows. For developed countries, diffusion of their knowledge. For developing countries, acquisition of knowledge and learning opportunities.		Technological convergence across countries.

significant convergence in GDP per capita has been found. The patterns of technological convergence, however, do not emerge strongly, and in some cases divergence has occurred over the last decades.

Hence, it seems that openness in trade and the internationalisation processes, instead of reducing international differences through a more rapid diffusion of technology, are leading to economic convergence of countries which are becoming, at the same time, more dissimilar in their technological performance (Cantwell, 1995; Vertova, 1997). What are the possible effects of this increasing technological specialisation?

It is possible to maintain that among industrialised countries the opportunities to successfully exploit national technological capacities depend increasingly on the relative size of the respective domestic markets. On the one hand, large countries, such as the United States, have the advantage of a greater domestic profitability of innovation and of decidedly ampler spillover effects (Fagerberg, 1996). On the other hand, smaller countries, such as Switzerland, Holland and the Scandinavian countries, can exploit the greater concentration of their industries in a few strong sectors, and thus be in a position to act as global players, thanks also to the smaller fragmentation of their economic and political interests. Medium-sized economies, such as Italy, could have to face expensive restructuring processes of their productive apparatus; within the global competition framework, they would be unable to maintain a complete industrial matrix but also, given their size, they would not be content with 'niche' technology specialisations.

The growing competitive pressure implied by the globalisation process, however, is not limited to trade liberalisation between countries, since FDI flows have been increasingly featuring as complements to trade flows, actually overtaking them in importance as means of exploiting national competitive and technological capacities. The complementary relationship between FDI and trade tends to intensify their impact, possibly causing virtuous and vicious circles both in the investor's home country and in the host location (Cantwell, 1987). MNEs increasingly assimilate and integrate with national and regional systems of innovation: their impact, however, depends crucially on the sectoral profile of the home and host economy. In trying to exploit their competitive advantage, firms relocating their production activity abroad may (but will not necessarily) improve the local industrial capacity through more intense competition in the local market and the transfer of technology associated with the investment. The impact could be either 'driving' or 'enfeebling' with respect to the national technological and industrial base, depending on the pattern of sectoral specialisation and on the comparative 'strengths' of both investing and local firms (Iammarino and Michie, 1997).[1]

Global generation of innovation

Multinational enterprises are undoubtedly the most important actors in the worldwide generation of technology and innovation. The location of innovative activities of multinational enterprises in host countries is often linked to the location of their productive activity but, however strong the correspondence between productive activities and R&D activities may be, it will not be total. There are in fact different advantages and disadvantages linked to both the centralisation and the decentralisation of technological activities. The main advantages of centralisation – basically connected to economies of scale and scope in R&D, control of innovation and linkages with national business and non-business sectors – seem to be increasingly counterbalanced by those associated with decentralisation. From the investor's perspective, the latter can be summarised in terms of the linkages between innovatory activity and local production, markets, suppliers and clients, and the exploitation of technological fields of excellence in host countries (Pearce and Singh, 1992; Howells and Wood, 1993; Miller, 1994). All these factors acquire a greater or lesser importance depending on the country, on the type of firm, on the products and on the technologies involved.

The empirical evidence on the share of innovation generated outside the home country of the MNE is mixed (Cantwell, 1995; Patel and Pavitt, 1991, 1994 and their chapter in this volume). However, although foreign subsidiaries of MNEs would appear to be primarily involved in the production of goods and services, data on patents registered in the US seem to indicate a slow but significant trend towards increasing shares of innovation generated outside the home country of the parent companies. The possible effects of this tendency on national economies are both direct and indirect (Dunning, 1992). The amount of innovation generated *ex novo* by foreign affiliates of MNEs – which includes also their demand and cost linkages with indigenous suppliers and customers and their impact on local market structure – minus the amount of 'diverted' innovation (i.e., that which would have been generated in the absence of MNEs), gives the net 'technology creation' effect. Therefore, MNEs technological globalisation may enhance the nation's innovative capacity, as much as, in the wrong circumstances, it may weaken it.

Cumulative causation mechanisms might thus occur, giving rise to vicious and virtuous circles which, again, will depend on the sectoral points of strength and weakness in both the home and the host economies. Moreover, it has been pointed out that the increasing number of networks established by MNEs, while boosting decentralisation through inter-border corporate integration of technological activities within the MNE, can further promote the advantages to agglomeration through inter-firm sectoral integration within national boundaries (Cantwell ed., 1994). The 'competitive bidding' to attract high value added FDI and MNEs research activity is likely to become tougher, both between 'higher-order' locations across developed economies, and between 'lower-order' centres, the latter increasingly threatened by the emerging competitors from less-developed countries and regions. The risk of regional inequalities might thus increase also within countries, as 'centres of excellence' would be further encouraged, while backward regions would be further undermined by the strategies and policies of MNEs.

It should be noted that the economic convergence found at a national level is much more questionable when considered at the level of regions. An increasing number of studies have recently addressed this issue, focusing in particular on the EU regions (see, for example, Neven and Gouyette, 1994; Quah, 1996; Fagerberg and Verspagen, 1996; Fagerberg, Verspagen and Caniëls, 1997). It turns out that the process of convergence in GDP across the EU regions, which was observed during most of the post-war period up to the 1970s, is far from stable and, even accounting for differences in industrial structure, it tends to slow down in the later part of the 1980s. Furthermore, the reversal in the trend towards convergence has occurred despite the presence of substantial differences in GDP per capita across European regions. By taking into account differences in innovative capabilities across the EU regions – even more pronounced than at country level – it has been shown that they account for a good deal in explaining the diverging trend in economic growth (Fagerberg and Verspagen, 1996). The consequences of technological globalisation of multinational enterprises on indigenous innovative capacity might thus further exacerbate the disparities between the Northern and the Southern regions of the EU.

Global technological collaboration

As pointed out earlier, the business sector has been increasingly involved in global strategic technology alliances. The most frequently cited motivations are the so-called 'push' factors (Howells, 1997a), namely alliances established principally in order to cope with the complexity of the new, increasingly knowledge-intensive, technological paradigms and to share the risks and costs associated with innovative activity (Katz and Ordover, 1990; Baumol, 1992). What marks these collaborations is that the firms involved maintain distinct ownership structures, while explicitly agreeing to exchange and/or generate, bilaterally or multilaterally, information and techno-scientific knowledge.[2] The 'pull' factors cover the attractiveness of external sources of expertise over internal technological assets, and the desire to improve the scope of in-house scientific and technological competence.

The propensity of firms to collaborate, which emerged first on local rather than globalised markets (Becattini ed., 1987; Becattini and Rullani, 1993), surprised many of those who had studied the economics of the firm in mainstream textbooks. In fact, firms are willing to share with other, often competing, firms a factor strategic to their own competitiveness such as technological competence, far more than it is generally assumed. It emerged quite early on that such collaborations were not limited to the national level but that they went beyond national boundaries (Chesnais, 1988; Vaccà and Zanfei, 1989; Dunning and Gugler, 1992).

Collaborations are all the more advantageous among firms which do not compete in the same products and/or markets. Firms with similar technological knowledge can in practice have very different products, just as firms with similar products and technologies can be active on different markets due to either geographical location or the portion of demand they cater for. An aeronautical firm and a car manufacturer may have an interest in sharing common knowledge on engines without having to compete in the same final markets. In the same manner, two firms in the telecommunications sector having national public enterprises as their clients, could find it convenient to coordinate some research projects aimed at the reduction of costs and the planning of new products. It can be argued, therefore, that the notion of competition, although not directly implied by the third category of our taxonomy, shows a two-way link with that of collaboration. Cooperative agreements are nonetheless a source of comparative advantage, besides the traditional country/firm-specific technological competence: they occur, in fact, to a much greater extent in industries in which competition is more pronounced – i.e., in the most recent technological sectors, such as biotechnology, information technology and new materials (National Science Foundation, 1996). Technological collaborations take place mainly in sectors characterised by oligopolistic and/or monopolistic competition, and they are based on high product differentiation and/or market diversification. Collaboration is therefore becoming a key determinant of competitiveness, which, in its turn, requires increasing efforts to innovate.

Strategic agreements between firms do not exhaust the phenomenon of global collaboration. As referred to above, the academic world collaborates globally. To the extent that the academic world has an influence on industry, its globalisation acts as a vehicle for the diffusion of knowledge and technological innovation.

It has been noted that the intensification of academic collaborations has been particularly boosted by regional economic integration processes. The highest increase in the shares of internationally co-authored articles during the 1980s and the 1990s was registered by the EU countries, showing around 50 per cent of co-authorships as international, mainly intra-area (National Science Foundation, 1996). This seems to support the view that knowledge processes crucially depend on cultural features whose similarities are more likely to be found within the same macro-region. This emerges also by looking at other indicators, such as the international flows of researchers and foreign students enrolled in higher education. For instance, the huge increase of inflows recently experienced by Japan has mainly occurred from within the Asiatic region, as well as patterns of stricter collaborations are found among the members of the Asian and Pacific Economic Cooperation (APEC).

As long as they do not harm competition and consumer's interests, it is likely that technological alliances and scientific collaboration will contribute substantially to strengthening the innovation base of national and regional economies and to spur technological convergence across countries.

Implications for public policy

Up to this point we have analysed the globalisation of innovation mainly from the viewpoint of the impact on the national economies. But globalisation processes, in the field of technology and innovation, constitute also a challenge for public policy, just as they do when they affect other spheres of economic and social life. In particular governments, which represent the other category of actors and exercise well-defined powers on a certain territory, find that their choices are limited by processes they do not entirely control (Holland, 1987; Held, 1991).

The obstacles globalisation poses to government policies are all the stronger in the technological sphere, owing to the relative ease with which knowledge can be transferred across countries. Statements of the type 'Nasa research programmes favour Japanese firms', or 'American universities train the managers of competing countries' or even 'foreign firms are appropriating the national technological heritage', have become commonplace.[3] These preoccupations are linked to governmental action and they inevitably allude to certain political choices. They prompt the following questions: is there any sense in financing great research programmes benefiting all world firms with national resources? Would limiting the access of foreign students be an effective way of preserving technological advantages? Should foreign firms be encouraged or discouraged from investing in R&D in the country?

Two different tendencies have emerged from the current debate on innovation policies. On the one hand, there are those maintaining that government policies aimed at reinforcing a country's technological competence are irrelevant, given that resources employed would not necessarily lead to a national advantage (Ohmae, 1990). This 'technoliberal' vision is implicitly based on the assumption that knowledge and technology can be geographically transferred without much difficulty and that firms' innovating activity does not require the externalities produced by state action. On the other hand, there are those who consider that public-sector intervention is necessary to better equip countries to face technological change and increased globalisation. This view gains support from the approach based on national innovation systems (Lundvall ed., 1992; Nelson ed., 1993; Freeman, 1995; Archibugi and Michie eds., 1997b).

The specific argument we put forward here is that public policies play a different role in each of the three categories of the globalisation of innovation we previously outlined. As we emphasised in section 3, each of the three categories has a very different impact on national economies. Governments will have different interests in each of the three globalisation types and this will lead them to opt for different strategies. In each case, either cooperation or competition will prevail. Is it possible to identify the advantages and drawbacks of each type from the interested country's viewpoint and, where possible, analyse the policies which could reinforce their economic and social utility? More specifically, which of these policies are to the advantage of some countries and to the detriment of others and which are advantageous all round? To what extent do the interests of a country coincide with those of its firms?

Let us start by assuming that it is, in fact, advantageous for a country to promote high technological intensity in its territory. This would allow for higher wages, for demand for a more qualified labour force and, in the long run, for higher growth rates of value added and employment. In other words, technological activities generate a set of externalities benefiting the whole productive system. It is perhaps unnecessary to convince governments about the importance of promoting and attracting technological activities on the territory they control. Public administrations have engaged in the attempt to make the greatest variety of arts and crafts flourish in their country for centuries. There has always been a current of thought attempting to promote the development and wealth of nations through interventions favouring science and technology, although it has been more active in political rather than in academic circles.

Table 12.4 lists the main policy aims with respect to the three globalisation categories and mentions the available instruments, which will be discussed more extensively in the following sections. We emphasise that we have favoured reference to the larger category of public policy rather than

Table 12.4. *Public policies' targets and instruments for the globalisation of innovation*

Categories		Targets	Instruments
International exploitation of national innovations	Inflows	Achieving lower foreign dependency and filling technology gaps. Increasing learning.	Incentives for national infant industries. Promoting collaborations between national firms and leading firms in the field. Incentives for selected FDI in the country.
		Obtaining competitive supply prices.	Negotiations on imports with the firms of other countries.
	Outflows	Supporting national firms to appropriate their innovations. Preserving and developing competitive advantages in high-tech industries.	Export incentives for high-tech industries. Property rights negotiations. Public support for basic research and technology dissemination. Ensuring fair competition. Reinvesting profits in new innovative projects of international scope.
Global generation of innovations by MNEs	Inflows	Enhancing national technological capabilities.	Providing real incentives for the location of new innovative activities with foreign capital. Upgrading S&T infrastructures and institutions.
		Keeping control on foreign capital.	Monitoring the technological strategies and location choices of MNEs.
	Outflows	Strengthening the competitive position of national firms.	Assessment of the need of home-based MNEs to invest abroad in R&D and innovative activities.

| Global techno-scientific collaborations | Scientific | Upgrading the scientific competence of the nation. | Scientific exchange programmes. Incentives for international scientific projects. Participation in international S&T organisations. |
| | Techno-industrial | Allowing the country to become a junction of technical and industrial information. Applying knowledge to production. | Developing infrastructures for techno-collaborations (scientific parks, consortia, etc.). Promoting University/industry linkages. Participation in international organisations for technical and industrial collaborations. |

the more limiting terms of innovation policy, industrial policy or even economic policy. In fact, it will become clear that in many cases the most appropriate policies are to be found in such diverse areas as those of training, education or public administration.

International exploitation of technology

This type of globalisation is the oldest among the types considered here and does not need a radical rethinking of the theories and policies applied to it. Furthermore, this form has the greatest quantitative relevance and presents the most sustained growth rates. It is thus logical that governments have focused their attention on it. It is also the type which directly evokes the rivalry among countries as every country has an interest in maximising the exploitation of its own competence and symmetrically minimising the costs associated with the acquisition of others' competence.

It is advantageous for a country to sell its own products in foreign markets and, as noted above, the advantage becomes even greater if competitiveness is based on sophisticated technological knowledge rather than price. In fact, the former allows the application of profit margins which are difficult to sustain in areas in which technological barriers to entry are very low. Thus, the preoccupation of political advisors with providing support for industries exporting goods of high technological opportunity seems well founded (Tyson, 1992; Scherer, 1992). It is certainly not by chance that governments provide support for the competitiveness of national firms by favouring their innovation programmes, so much so that technological policies are increasingly being merged with commercial policies (Caldwell and Moore eds., 1992; Mowery, 1995).

There are some general policies which must be implemented to enable national firms to maximise the exploitation of their technological competence in foreign markets too. Apart from the availability of informational networks such as the BBC or CNN, incentives to export, real services supplied abroad and decent diplomatic offices, all favour the access of a country's firms to foreign markets. These policies do not favour specific sectors only and can be applied as much to shoes as they can to semiconductors. It should be remembered that innovation plays a crucial role in all industries, not only in those commonly defined as high-tech. However, many countries have started becoming more selective and are gearing their energy and resources towards the support of the most innovative goods and services on foreign markets. Besides, as pointed out in section 3, the success of national firms in competing in global markets will depend increasingly on policies aimed at monitoring and regulating inflows and outflows of embodied and disembodied technology. For example, the need for governments to have some degree of control over the quality of inward and outward FDI is becoming much more pressing in a context of increased globalisation. The proactive strategy implemented by Asian economies, which applied the technology imported through inward FDI in production to empower the domestic industrial and innovative base, is often reported as an example of the national capacity to build a 'sustainable competitive advantage' (Sugden and Thomas, 1994).

Firms have an interest in preserving their technological advantage and in preventing competitors from imitating successful innovations. They implement various strategies aiming to reveal their competence as little as possible, as this allows them to obtain a revenue now and to mortgage one for the future. Governments concur to help national firms preserve and extend their technological advantages. A frequently quoted case is the English Parliament's prohibition of the export of machinery and even of the emigration of artisans up to 1842 in order to prevent Continental Europe from acquiring the technological competence which made English firms the most competitive in the world (Landes, 1969; Bruland, 1989). Such policies, although better disguised, are implemented in many countries to this day. Symmetrically, it is in the importing country's interest to attempt to facilitate the assimilation of knowledge thus enabling the emancipation from the dependence on suppliers. This suggests that, for example, the provision of support for firms which are active in certain industries or the provision of structures, such as the creation of advanced University programmes, allow the country to acquire the knowledge necessary for production. It is certainly significant that the policies proposed by Fredrich List (1841) to enable Germany to compete on equal grounds with Great Britain in the mid nineteenth century are recommended today for developing countries (Freeman, 1995; Bell and Pavitt, 1997).

Contrary to what was happening at the beginning of the nineteenth century and in the first post-war period, the modern world is not characterised by a solid and generalised technological supremacy of a single country. During the *pax* Britannica and the *pax* Americana, both England and the United States had a political, economic and technological hegemony. In the modern world the division of labour is not such that a single country has a marked advantage in all the high-tech industries (Nelson and Wright, 1992). This constrains all industrialised countries, including the larger ones, to select the technological areas in which they intend obtaining a share in the global markets and those in which they intend relying on imports. This observation is corroborated by three facts: (1) Technological competence is very different among developed countries. This is reflected both in the sectoral distribution of their innovations (Archibugi and Pianta, 1992) and in their international commercial specialisation profiles (Amendola *et al.*,

1997). (2) As stated earlier, the differences in each country's technological competence have increased (Archibugi and Pianta, 1992, 1994). (3) The place occupied by a country in technological and commercial specialisation tends to remain constant over time (Cantwell, 1989; Amendola *et al.*, 1997).

Hence, one of the factors allowing a country successfully to exploit its technological competence in foreign markets is the careful selection of the sectors on which it chooses to focus, given its existing competence. The latter, however, reflects the cumulative pattern of national production and skills acquired over time, which itself limits the scope of search for new opportunities. In a world in which the international exploitation of technology is growing, weaknesses in certain technological sectors do not constitute a problem for a country, as long as they are offset by equal strengths. Japan, for example, is not present in certain high-tech sectors (it had to abandon aeronautics in the post-war period and it never entered the nuclear sector) and has concentrated instead on other sectors such as motor vehicles and electronics.

However, Japan's negotiating position is strong even in the sectors in which it is absent as it is 'covered' by the advantages of its leading industries. Thus, it does not appear to be vulnerable to the blackmail of competing countries. Therefore, the problem is not so much to know how to do everything as it is to have enough merchandise to exchange in order to be able to negotiate from an equal standing. Furthermore, in a multipolar world, the greatest risk faced by a country is its inability to find markets for internally generated products rather than to see the imports of certain technologically strategic goods refused.

However, the absence of national 'strongholds' in at least some industries with higher technological opportunities can weaken the competitive position of a country and notably reduce wage levels, employment rates, professional qualifications, and total economic welfare (Freeman and Soete, 1994). Are there ways to identify the best technological and commercial specialisation for a country? Many analyses have focused on international trade classified according to the technological intensity of products,[4] showing, as we already noted, that production and international trade shares of high-tech products are growing. This indicates that a country specialising in such sectors will be operating in expanding markets. Other analyses have explicitly considered the sectoral growth rates of innovation generation (cf. the works based on patents by Meliciani and Simonetti, 1996; Breschi and Mancusi, 1997). They show that the rapidly growing sectors and the high-tech ones coincide. They have also allowed for the identification of the high growth sectors with the lowest technological barriers to entry. Various countries have promoted more complex and accurate studies of technological forecasting,[5] and in many cases these are explicitly connected to the industrial policy strategies to be implemented in order to reinforce the competitive position of national firms on foreign markets.

However, it is certainly neither easy, nor often possible, to 'move' a country's specialisation towards different sectors, especially if they are the ones with more sophisticated technological competence. Success in fields requiring a high technological competence is risky in the first place, because technological and economic uncertainty increases with the complexity of the required competence. The Italian case illustrates many 'false starts' in sectors deemed strategic (steel, petrochemicals, aeronautics). A large amount of resources was invested in such sectors without the Italian industry ever managing to take off beyond the mere necessity to satisfy, and even then only partially, the internal market.

Indeed, there are various actions which may help strengthen the competitiveness of national firms in high-tech industries, such as: public support of basic research and research infrastructure, which actually affects all sectors of the economy; tougher competition policies, which stimulate innovativeness by increasing rivalry in the domestic market, especially in the most 'sensitive' sectors (such as strategic or emerging high-tech sectors); reinforcement of technological dissemination and participation mechanisms, particularly as far as small and medium firms are concerned; support both to pre-competitive R&D in new strategic sectors and to market-oriented R&D in already existing technological advantages. An international system marked by increasing exchange and in which the competition for the exploitation of innovations is growing does not require technological autarchy, but directs countries towards specialisation in fields with high innovation intensity. In other words, it requires them to have desirable goods in order to negotiate from an equal standing.

Global generation of technology

We have already discussed the importance of multinationals in generating innovations. The size of these enterprises influences countries' actions in more than one way, to the extent that the term meso-economy was coined (Holland, 1987) to describe the range of action of their operations and the constraints they impose on national macroeconomic policies.

As regards this form of globalisation, governments have to deal, in practice, with 'national firms with multinational operations' (Hu, 1992), as the title of the successful study suggests. In this case, what are the interests a government must pursue? On the one hand, it is faced with national enterprises which were founded, grew and became competitive thanks to the resources of the national economy and now need to decentralise their technological activities to other countries in order to expand their business scope and maintain their competitiveness. However, as we have seen, from the point of view of the country, this relocation might be damaging, to the extent that the internal market loses technological opportunities. On the other hand, the same national government finds foreign firms (and as such with preferential ties with foreign governments) which intend to reinforce their own position through investments in the country. This implies the influx of new capital and technology for the host country and often the creation of qualified employment, but could also imply the weakening of national firms. Governments have to accept that the long-run strategic intentions of the foreign firms may be often uncertain.

The difficulty for a government in identifying the best interests of its own country is suggested by the variety of different positions both in theory and in practice. Some governments, inspired perhaps by the sceptics of globalisation (Patel and Pavitt, 1991; Hu, 1992) exclude the subsidiaries of multinationals from eligibility for R&D subsidies. Other governments, converted perhaps to the idea that ownership does not matter, offer specific incentives to attract foreign capital. One of the most explicit supporters of this vision, the former US labour secretary Robert Reich (1991, p. 301), argued that 'rather than increase the profitability of corporations flying its flag, or enlarge the worldwide holdings of its citizens, a nation's economic role is to improve its own citizens' standard of living by enhancing the value of what they contribute to the world economy. The concern over national "competitiveness" is often misplaced. It is not what we own that counts: it is what we do.' Yet skills and capabilities associated with foreign investments are arguably of growing importance, whilst ownership has become less relevant: learning curve advantages are mainly people- and institution-embodied and local firms may benefit from global corporations investing in innovation and local human capital (Sharp and Pavitt, 1993).

Public policies should attempt to distinguish between investments directed towards the creation of technological capacity in a country from those of simple acquisition. The creation of additional technological competence is always advantageous for a country, but a government should have instruments to defend national firms exposed to predatory acquisitions by foreign capital. In many cases, multinationals have an interest in acquiring foreign competitors and then merge, reduce or even liquidate the subsidiary's R&D laboratories. Although such strategies may be justified from the firm's point of view, they can impoverish the technological basis of a country. It is for such cases that an industrial policy aimed at protecting the 'family jewels' – which are the most technologically active firms and, precisely for this reason, the ones most exposed to the appetites of their foreign competitors – is necessary.

Beyond individual cases, governments should observe the aggregate and, even more, the sectoral flows of investments with high technological content entering and exiting the country, in order to assess the extent to which their country offers the appropriate environment for the development of innovative projects. If outflows exceed inflows, the reasons for this should be identified. These may include an inadequate domestic infrastructure, excessive institutional rigidities, the absence of adequate interlocutors in the Universities and public research centres. Each of these factors can be dealt with through appropriate public policies. Indeed, as reported in table 12.4, all the above factors apply both to inward and outward flows. The quality of local science and technology infrastructure, as well as that of institutional relations, also help attract and expand new technological activities from abroad. It is thus suggested that the aim of public policy is not to maximise the values of nationally owned assets, but rather to stimulate high value-added activities of local contexts and communities.

Moreover, governments should not only look at the ways through which national competitiveness can be enhanced *vis à vis* foreign rivals. It is becoming increasingly important also to consider the distribution of the costs and benefits of globalisation within national borders, and the potential gap between private and social returns to innovative activity. As we have suggested in section 3, the global generation of innovation by MNEs might give rise to more dramatic imbalances, as they occur in national environments which are supposed to be – at least in principle – more economically and socially homogeneous than the international one. The link between 'global' and 'local' needs to be shaped by government action. As Hirst and Thompson have properly remarked, 'the nation state is central to this process of "suturing": the policies and practices of states in distributing power upwards to the international level and downwards to sub-national agencies are the sutures that will hold the system of governance together. Without such explicit policies to close gaps in governance and elaborate a division of labour in regulation, vital capacities will be lost' (1996, p. 184).

Global technological collaboration

Unlike the other types of globalisation this type does not necessarily impose competition between countries. On the contrary, it is mainly characterised by a positive sum game in which participant economic agents can all gain. This, of course, does not mean that the advantages received by participants are identical: it is probable that in each cooperative agreement some firms gain more than others. These, however, are considerations that go beyond the functions of public administration. What governments should be concerned about is instead to ensure an adequate level of competition in the domestic market. In fact, the degree to which such agreements on technological cooperation are collusive and thus detrimental to internal competition and consumers or, on the contrary, offer generalised advantages because they act as a tool for the diffusion of knowledge which would otherwise remain localised, is still controversial and needs more careful evaluation.

Governments can help their firms to participate in this form of international integration, putting them in a position to enter the virtuous circle which from collaboration leads to learning and from learning to innovation. This can be assisted through inter-governmental agreements as well as through international organisations. In Europe, some such schemes were implemented via the Eureka project and, in more stable form, through the various framework-programmes promoted by the European Commission. What rendered these schemes particularly effective, was that they brought about a competition (through a public competition and an evaluation based on merit of the applications presented for funding) of a variety of projects involving partners from more than one country. This allowed the selection of the projects of the greatest technical and scientific interest among the cooperation proposals. The prevalent 'pull' factor thus is represented by policies and incentives to join collaborative research and technical projects implemented by the EU institutions. The participation rates in such projects varies considerably across countries. Evidence has been provided about trends towards geographical clusters of collaborations (Lichtenberg, 1994). Therefore, it seems central to reinforce the participation mechanisms, encouraging the access of small and medium enterprises and giving everyone the same amount of information on the procedures and modalities to join such international collaborative schemes.

However, beyond the institutional agreements – whether bilateral or multilateral – public administration has the task of creating an infrastructure in its own territory and sustaining domestic technological collaboration and education, rendering the country attractive for cooperation. It is clear that the greater its technical and scientific potential the more a country will be an attractive partner. Developing as well as developed countries can be attractive partners if they have an adequate infrastructure, including communication networks, qualified research personnel, a widespread knowledge of international languages, etc. Furthermore, firms from advanced countries will have an incentive to collaborate in countries with expanding markets. Yet providing a strong infrastructure is certainly a prerequisite for international collaboration, but it is not sufficient as long as technological performances can also be explained in terms of 'institutional failure' (Abramovitz, 1986). As noted earlier, the modernisation of institutions in charge of the diffusion of science and technology is essential, as the lack of appropriate relations between education systems and industry or financial systems and the business sector can provide a serious drawback to the development of scientific and technical collaborations.

In the long run it seems that this is the type of globalisation that can reinforce a country's scientific and technological potential and, therefore, its competitive performance. It can allow a country to become an information crossroads and thus to acquire expertise in a wide range of technologies. Spillovers and knowledge transfer through this form of technological globalisation can indeed be substantially wide, especially when collaboration involves the partnership of different actors – namely governments, other institutions and the business sector – indirectly affecting competitive performances. Thus, there is a strong case for public policy to provide incentives for the development of such international cooperation.

Conclusions

In this chapter we have discussed the process of globalisation of innovation, who the participating subjects are and, on the basis of the possible impact globalisation might have on national economies, the role of public policy. We considered a taxonomy which deconstructs the phenomenon into three categories: exploitation, generation and collaboration. The most diffuse type of globalisation is the international exploitation of innovation developed on a national basis. It is understandable that this type of globalisation is quantitatively the most prominent given that it is also the oldest one. However, the most significant fact is that this type has a higher growth rate than the other two.

The global generation of innovation by multinational enterprises is achieving a certain quantitative relevance, although much less significant than is often stated. The effects of such a trend towards the increased global generation of innovation on national and local systems are, moreover, rather uncertain. Both virtuous circles and vicious cycles of cumulative causation may occur, spurring or weakening national and local innovative capacity and affecting economic and technological convergence across and within national boundaries.

Finally, during the last 20 years, a third type of globalisation has developed, represented by the cooperative strategic arrangements among firms for innovative projects. As in the case of the first, this type of globalisation is more prominent in sectors with higher technological opportunity. Although it is difficult to quantify the economic value associated with this type, it has shown sustained growth.

We have also suggested that a single strategy to deal with the three different types of globalisation does not exist, neither from a firm's nor from a government's point of view. These are three different processes and, although they partly overlap, they should be treated separately.

It is, however, important to emphasise that none of the three categories in this taxonomy renders public policy obsolete. On the contrary, a far wider range of public policies than those currently practiced in the majority of countries are desirable to best exploit the opportunities associated with the globalisation of innovation.

Notes

This paper has been prepared for the expert group of the European Technology Assessment Network on 'Technology Policy in the Context of Internationalisation of R&D and Innovation: How to Strengthen Europe's Competitive Advantage in Technology', European Technology Assessment Network, European Commission. The authors are grateful to Mario Pianta, Jonathan Michie and Giovanna Vertova for their valuable comments and constructive discussions. Simona Iammarino gratefully acknowledges the financial support of the European Commission, under the TMR Marie Curie Research Training Programme (Contract No. ERBFM-BICT961062).

1   Some examples of virtuous and vicious circles connected with inward and outward foreign direct investment are given in Cantwell (1987), Cantwell and Dunning (1991), Howells and Michie eds. (1997).
2   Mowery (1992, p. 211) defines an international collaborative venture as 'interfirm collaboration in product development, manufacture, or marketing that spans national boundaries, is not based on arm's-length market transactions and includes substantial and continual contributions by partners of capital, technology or other assets'.
3   These are recurrent echoes on the specialised press. See, for example, 'Foreign passports, US doctorates', *Issues in Science and Technology*, Spring 1991, 86–7: 'Foreign R&D in the United States', *IEEE Spectrum*, November 1994, 26–30: 'High-tech jobs all over the map', *Business Week*, 19 December 1994, 42–47.
4   Different methodologies to identify the sectors with high technological opportunity have been applied by Guerrieri and Milana (1995), Grupp (1995), Amendola and Perrucci eds. (1995).
5   For a review of the studies made and of the methods used, cf. Martin (1995).

References

Abramovitz, M. 1986. Catching up, forging ahead and falling behind, *Journal of Economic History*, 46: 299–313.
Amendola, G., Guerrieri, P. and Padoan, P. C. 1997. International patterns of technological accumulation and trade, in Archibugi and Michie (eds.) 1997b.
Amendola, G. and Perrucci, A. (eds.) 1995. *L'Italia nella Competizione Tecnologica Internazionale*, Milan, Franco Angeli.
Amin, A. and Tomaney, J. (eds.) 1995. *Behind the Myth of European Union*, London, Routledge.

Archibugi, D. and Iammarino, S. 1998. Innovation and globalisation: evidence and implications, mimeo.

Archibugi, D. and Imperatori, G. (eds.) 1997. *Economia Globale e Innovazione*, Rome, Donzelli editore.

Archibugi, D. and Michie, J. 1995. The globalisation of technology: a new taxonomy, *Cambridge Journal of Economics*, 19: 121–40. Reprinted in Archibugi and Michie (eds.) 1997a.

1997. Technological globalisation or national systems of innovation?, in Archibugi and Michie (eds.) 1997a.

Archibugi, D. and Michie, J. (eds.) 1997a. *Technology, Globalisation, and Economic Performance*, Cambridge, Cambridge University Press.

1997b. *Trade, Growth and Technical Change*, Cambridge, Cambridge University Press.

Archibugi, D. and Pianta, M. 1992. *The Technological Specialisation of Advanced Countries. A Report to the EEC on International Science and Technology Activities*, Boston, Kluwer.

1994. Aggregate convergence and sectoral specialization in innovation, *Journal of Evolutionary Economics*, 4: 17–33.

Barnet, R. J. and Cavanagh, J. 1994. *Global Dreams. Imperial Corporations and the New World Order*, New York, Simon & Schuster.

Baumol, W. J. 1992. Horizontal collusion and innovation, *Economic Journal,* 102: 129–37.

Becattini, G. (ed.) 1987. *Mercato e Forze Locali*, Bologna, Il Mulino.

Becattini, G. and Rullani, E. 1993. Sistema locale e mercato globale, *Economia e Politica Industriale,* 84: 25–48.

Bell, M. and Pavitt, K. 1997. Technological accumulation and industrial growth: contrasts between developed and developing countries, in Archibugi and Michie (eds.) 1997a.

Brecher, J. and Costello, T. 1994. *Global Village or Global Pillage: Economic Reconstruction from the Bottom Up,* New York, Boston, MA, South End Press.

Breschi, S. and Mancusi, M. C. 1997. Il modello di specializzazione tecnologica dell'Italia: Un'analisi basata sui brevetti europei, in Archibugi and Imperatori (eds.).

Bruland, K. 1989. *British Technology and European Industrialization*, Cambridge, Cambridge University Press.

Caldwell Harris, M. and Moore, G. E. (eds.) 1992. *Linking Trade and Technology Policies*, Washington, DC, National Academy Press.

Cantwell, J. A. 1987. The reorganization of European industries after integration: Selected evidence on the role of multinational enterprise activities, *Journal of Common Market Studies*, 26: 127–51.

1989. *Technological Innovation and the Multinational Corporation*, Oxford, Basil Blackwell.

1995. The globalisation of technology: What remains of the product cycle model?, *Cambridge Journal of Economics*, 19: 155–74. Reprinted in Archibugi and Michie (eds.) 1997a.

Cantwell, J. A. (ed.) 1994. *Transnational Corporations and Innovatory Activities*,

London, Routledge, United Nations Library on Transnational Corporations, vol. 17.

Cantwell, J. A. and Dunning, J. H. 1991. MNEs, technology and the competitiveness of European industries, in Faulhaber and Tamburini (eds.).

Chesnais, F. 1988. Technical co-operation agreements between firms, *Science Technology Industry Review*, 4: 57–119.

1994. *La Mondialisation du Capital*, Paris, Syros.

Dasgupta, P. and David, P. 1994. Toward a new economics of science, *Research Policy*, 23: 487–521.

Dodgson, M. 1993. *Technological Collaboration in Industry*, London, Routledge.

Dunning, J. H. 1992. *The Globalization of Business*, London, Routledge.

1993. *Multinational Enterprises and the Global Economy*, Workingham, Addison-Wesley.

Dunning, J. H. and Gugler, P. 1992. Technology based cross-border alliances, Discussion Papers in International Investment & Business Studies, 163, University of Reading.

Dunning, J. H. and Narula, R. 1994. The R&D activities of foreign firms in the U.S., Discussion Papers in International Investment & Business Studies, 189, University of Reading.

Fagerberg, J. 1994. Technology and international differences in growth rates, *Journal of Economic Literature*, 32: 1147–75.

1996. Technology and competitiveness, *Oxford Review of Economic Policy*, 12: 39–51.

Fagerberg, J. and Verspagen, B. 1996. Heading for divergence? Regional growth in Europe reconsidered, *Journal of Common Market Studies*, 34: 431–48.

Fagerberg, J., Verspagen, B. and Caniëls, M. 1997. Technology gaps, growth and unemployment across European regions, MERIT, University of Maastricht (mimeo).

Faulhaber, G. R. and Tamburini, G. (eds.) 1991. *European Economic Integration. The Role of Technology*, London, Kluwer.

Freeman, C. 1995. The national system of innovation in historical perspective, *Cambridge Journal of Economics*, 19: 5–24. Reprinted in Archibugi and Michie (eds.) 1997a.

Freeman, C. and Soete, L. 1994. *Work for All or Mass Unemployment?* London, Pinter.

Freeman, C. and Soete, L. (eds.) 1990. *New Explorations in the Economics of Technical Change*, London, Pinter Publishers.

Granstrand O., Håkanson, L. and Sjölander, S. (eds.) 1992. *Technology Management and International Business. Internationalization of R&D and Technology*, Chichester, Wiley.

Grossman, G. M. and Helpman, E. 1991. *Innovation and Growth in the Global Economy*, Cambridge, MA, MIT Press.

Grupp, H. 1995. Science, high-technology and the competitiveness of EU countries, *Cambridge Journal of Economics*, 19: 209–23.

Guerrieri, P. 1997. The changing world trading environment, technological capability and the competitiveness of the European industry, Paper presented at the

Conference on 'Technology, Economic Integration, and Social Cohesion', Wien, 24–5 January.

Guerrieri, P. and Milana, C. 1995. Changes and trends in the world trade in high-technology products, *Cambridge Journal of Economics*, 19: 225–42. Reprinted in Archibugi and Michie (eds.) 1997b.

Hagedoorn, J. and Schakenraad, J. 1993. Strategic technology partnering and international corporate strategies, in Hughes (ed.).

Held, D. 1991. Democracy, the nation-state and the global system, *Economy and Society*, 20: 138–72.

Hirst, P. and Thompson, G. 1996. *Globalization in Question*, Cambridge, Polity Press.

Holland, S. 1987. *The Global Economy*, London, Weidenfeld and Nicolson.

Howells, J. 1997a. Research and development externalisation, outsourcing and contract research, paper presented at the Conference on 'Collaboration & Competition in R&D and Innovation Programmes: Lessons for the Public and Business Sectors', Cambridge, 9–11 June.

Howells, J. 1997b. The globalisation of research and technological innovation: A new agenda?, in Howells and Michie (eds.) 1997.

Howells, J. and Michie, J. (eds.) 1997. *Technology, Innovation and Competitiveness*, Aldershot, Edward Elgar.

Howells, J. and Wood, M. 1993. *The Globalisation of Production and Technology*, London, Belhaven Press.

Hu, Y. S. 1992. Global or stateless corporations are national firms with international operations, *California Management Review*, 34: 107–26.

Hughes, K. (ed.) 1993. *European Competitiveness*, Cambridge, Cambridge University Press.

Iammarino, S. and Michie, J. 1997. The political economy of the globalisation of technology – some implications for competition and collaboration, paper presented at the Conference on 'Collaboration and Competition in R&D and Innovation Programmes', Cambridge, 9–11 June.

Kaldor, N. 1981. The role of increasing returns, technical progress and cumulative causation in the theory of international trade and economic growth, *Economie appliquée*, 34: 593–617.

Katz, M. L. and Ordover, J. A. 1990. R&D Cooperation and competition, *Brookings Papers on Economic Activity,* Microeconomics, 20: 137–203.

Kitson, M. and Michie, J. 1998. The political economy of globalisation, in this volume.

Lall, S. 1979. The international allocation of research activity by US multinationals, *Oxford Bulletin of Economics and Statistics*, 41: 313–31.

Landes, D. 1969. *The Unbound Prometheus. Technological and Industrial Development in Western Europe from 1750 to the Present*, Cambridge, Cambridge University Press.

Lichtenberg, F. R. 1994. R&D Collaboration and specialization in the European Community, CIBER Working Paper, 1, University of Columbia, New York.

List, F. 1841. *The National System of Political Economy*, English translation, London, Longman & Co, 1885.

Lucas, R. E. Jr. 1988. On the mechanism of economic development, *Journal of Monetary Economics*, 22: 3–42.

Lundvall, B.-Å. (ed.) 1992. *National Systems of Innovation*, London, Pinter Publishers.

Mansfied, E., Teece, D. and Romeo, A. 1979. Overseas research and development by US-based firms, *Economica*, 46: 187–96.

Mariotti, S. 1993. Internazionalizzazione e fattori tecnologici nell'industria italiana, *Economia e politica industriale*, 20: 229–49.

Martin, B. 1995. *Technology Foresight: A Review of Recent Government Exercises*, OECD, Working Group on Innovation and Technology Policy, Paris.

Meliciani, V. and Simonetti, R. 1996. *Specialization in Areas of Strong Technological Opportunity and Economic Growth*, Science Policy Research Unit, University of Sussex, Brighton.

Michie, J. and Grieve Smith, J. (eds.) 1995. *Managing the Global Economy*, Oxford, Oxford University Press.

Miller, R. 1994. Global R&D networks and large-scale innovations: The case of the automobile industry, *Research Policy*, 23: 27–46.

Molero, J. 1997. Patterns of internationalization of Spanish innovatory firms, *Research Policy*, forthcoming.

Mowery, D. 1992. International collaborative ventures and US firms' technology strategy, in Granstrand, Håkanson and Sjölander (eds.).

1995. The practice of technology policy, in Stoneman (ed.).

Mytelka, L. K. (ed.) 1991. *Strategic Partnership. States, Firms and International Competition*, London, Pinter Publishers.

National Science Foundation 1996. *Science and Engineering Indicators 1996*, Washington DC, US Government Printing Office.

Nelson, R. (ed.) 1993. *National Systems of Innovation*, New York, Oxford University Press.

Nelson, R. and Wright, G. 1992. The rise and fall of American technological leadership: The postwar era in historical perspective, *Journal of Economic Literature*, 30: 1931–64.

Neven, D. J. and Gouyette, C. 1994. Regional convergence in the European Community, CEPR Discussion Paper, 914, February.

Ohmae, K. 1990. *The Borderless World: Management Lessons in the New Logic of the Global Market Place*, London, Collins.

Patel, P. and Pavitt, K. 1991. Large firms in the production of the world's technology: An important case of non-globalisation, *Journal of International Business Studies*, 22: 1–21.

1994. National innovation systems: Why they are important and how they might be measured and compared, *Economic Innovation and New Technology*, 3: 77–95.

Pearce, R. D. and Singh, S. 1992. *Globalizing Research and Development*, London, Macmillan.

Perraton, J., Goldblatt, D., Held, D. and McGrew, A. 1997. The globalisation of economic activity, *New Political Economy*, 2: 257–77.

Pianta, M. (ed.) 1989. *L'economia globale*, Rome, Edizioni Lavoro.

Quah, D. T. 1996. Regional convergence clusters across Europe, CEP-LSE Discussion Papers, 274, February.

Reich, R. 1991. *The Work of Nations*, London, Simon & Schuster.

Ruigrok, W. and van Tulder, R. 1995. *The Logic of International Restructuring*, London, Routledge.

Scherer, F. M. 1992. *International High-Technology Competition*, London, Harvard University Press.

Sharp, M. and Pavitt, K. 1993. Technology policy in the 1990s: Old trends and new realities, *Journal of Common Market Studies*, 31: 129–51.

Stoneman, P. (ed.) 1995. *Handbook of the Economics of Innovation and Technological Change*, Oxford, Blackwell.

Stopford, J. and Strange, S. 1991. *Rival States, Rival Firms. Competition for World Market Shares*, Cambridge, Cambridge University Press.

Strange, S. 1988. *States and Markets*, London, Pinter Publishers.

Sugden, R. and Thomas, R. 1994. Inward Investment in Western Europe: Objectives, Research Centre for Industrial Strategy, University of Birmingham, mimeo.

Thirlwall, A. P. 1979. The balance of payments constraint as an explanation of international growth rate differences, *Banca Nazionale del Lavoro Quarterly Review*, 32: 45–53.

Tyson, L. D. 1992. *Who's Bashing Whom? Trade Conflict in High-Technology Industries*, Washington DC, Institute for International Economics.

Vaccà, S. and Zanfei, A. 1989. L'impresa globale come sistema aperto a rapporti di cooperazione, *Economia e politica industriale*, 64.

Vertova, G. 1997. Similarities in advanced countries' technological performance in the twentieth century, Discussion Papers in Economics and Management, 363, University of Reading.

Young, S. and Hood, N. 1995. Attracting, managing and developing inward investment in the single market, in Amin and Tomaney (eds.).

Zanfei, A. 1996. L'organizzazione internazionale delle attività innovative, *Economia e Politica Industriale*, n. 90: 217–57.

Index

Abbott, S. 129
Abernathy, W. 107
Abramovitz, M. 176, 264
academic collaboration 246, 253–4
Ackoff, R. L. 82
affiliation 228
agglomeration 79–81, 84, 186
Ajami, R. A. 186
Alder, P. 84
Alderman, N. 80
Allen, T. J. 78, 82, 83
alliance capitalism 185
alliances 185, 212, 214, 215, 220, 245–8
Almeida, P. 186, 237
Amable, B. 40, 43, 50
Amendola, G. 259, 260
Amin, A. 77, 79, 80, 81, 86
Andersen, J. B. 120–35
Andersen, S. E. 7, 9
Andreasen, L. 42
Antonelli, C. 5
Applebaum, E. 51
Appold, S. J. 81
appropriability argument 225, 230–1, 233
Arcangeli, F. 84
Archibugi, D. 1–13, 36, 50, 57, 59, 70, 140,
    155, 172, 176, 178, 238, 242–66
Arrow, K. J. 22, 24, 84, 101, 125, 230
Ashby, W. R. 82
Asheim, B. 85
Audretsch, D. 235, 237
Aydalot, P. 79

Baker, A. G. 82
Barnet, R. J. 242
Barre, R. 12, 40, 50
Barrera, M. P. 229
Baumol, W. J. 252
Becattini, G. 73, 79, 253

Bell, M. 259
Bellon, B. 86
Bhagwati, J. 169
Bianchi, P. 72
Birch, D. 123
Birkinshaw, J. 187, 212
Blair, Tony 163
Boulding, K. E. 4, 82
Boyer, R. 40, 43, 50
Breschi, J. 242, 260
Bretton Woods 167–8
Britton, J. 77
Broeck, J. Vanden 185
Bruland, K. 259
Brusco, S. 73, 79
burns, A. F. 79
business angels 130–2
Bygrave, W. D. 128, 133

Caldwell Harris, M. 258
Camagni, R. 84
Caniëls, M. 252
Cantwell, J. A. 11, 40, 97, 172, 186, 187,
    225–39, 250, 260
capability
    learning 19
    social 177
    tacit 231, 236–7
capital
    institutional 132
    markets 177–8
    see also venture capital
Carlsson, B. 2, 3, 4, 8, 28, 71
Carlton, D. L. 69
Casson, M. 97
catching-up 60–1
Cavanagh, J. 242
Caves, R. 185
Chandler, A. 107

Chang, S. J. 186
Carles, D. 72
Chesnais, F. 12, 38, 76, 242, 246, 253
Clark, J. 50
Clement, K. 128
Clinton, President W. J. 19
Coclanis, P. A. 69
Cohen, W. M. 234
collaboration
  academic 246, 253–4
  private sector 245–6, 252–4, 263–5
Cooke, P. 86
Coriat, B. 42, 43
corporations *see* firms; multinational
  enterprises
Costello, T. 242
Crafts, N. F. R. 177
cumulative causation 175, 251

Dahmen, E. 39
Dalton, D. H. 187
David, P. A. 6, 75, 76
Davies, A. 155
D'Cruz, J. R. 186
de Bernis 39
de Tocqeville, A. 102
Dearlove, J. 73
DeBresson, C. 6
demand, new 51
development blocks 39
Dodgson, M. 246
Dollar, D. 36
Dosi, G. 4, 35–45, 121
Dunning, J. H. 11–12, 184–222, 245, 251,
  253

East Asia 143–4
economic convergence 36, 250, 252
economic divergence 248
economic growth
  and globalisation of technology 49,
    56–7
  and shocks 174–5
  and trade 166–7
economic structure 49, 51
Edquist, C. 3, 4, 6, 52, 139, 149
education
  adult 27
  policy 30
  system 26–7, 113, 233, 236
  see also training
EFTA 168–9
Ehrnberg, E. 8
Eichengreen, B. 177
employment 20, 42–4, 53, 57–60
  MNEs 207–9, 212, 214

enterprises *see* firms; multinational
  enterprises
European paradox 42–3
European Union 143, 168–9
  Eureka 264
  trade specialisation 146–54
Evangelista, R. 51, 52

Fabiani, S. 36
Fagen, R. E. 4, 82
Fagerberg, J. 36, 248, 250, 252
Feldman, M. P. 235, 237
Feller, I. 69, 83–4
Ferrier 39
financial systems 104–7, 114
  deregulation 122
  globalisation 123
firms
  capabilities 35, 42–3
  interactions between 78, 239
  modes of governance 42
  modes of learning 41–2
  organisational forms 35, 42–3
  performance 35
  response to environment 8, 77
  rivalry 108, 206, 210
  strategies 35, 42–3
Firn, J. R. 74, 77
Florence, P. S. 79
Foray, D. 6, 75, 76
foreign direct investment 220, 245
  changing nature of 184–5
  importance attached to 212, 215
  mergers and acquisitions 185
  and nation-specific assets 11–12
  public policy for 259
  rise in 140–1
  and trade 250
  see also multinational enterprises
France 69, 133–4, 150–1
free-rider problem 101
Freeman, C. 2–4, 36, 38, 50, 67, 70–1, 101,
    121, 139, 176, 238, 255, 259, 260
Frost, T. 237
Fusfield, A. R. 83

Galli, R. 6, 7
Garnier 74
Gassler, H. 8
Gatson, R. J. 131
Germany 126–9, 150–1, 170–1
Gershenkron 39
Gertler, M. 85
Gibbons, M. 104
globalisation
  capital markets 177–8

globalisation (*cont.*)
  definition 9, 178
  economic trends 165–71
  effect on trading environment 140–4
  increase in 228
  and local distribution 263
  of R&D 85–6
  and specialisation 139, 238
  state role under 163–80, 225
  and system of innovation 10–12
  of technology 49–62, 171–4, 178
  see also globalisation of innovation
globalisation of innovation 238
  collaboration 245–6, 252–4, 263–5
  exploitation 245, 248, 250, 258–61,
    265
  generation 245, 251–2, 261–3, 265
  impact on national economies 246–54
  and public policy 254–65
  taxonomy 243–6
Glyn, A. 177
Gourevitch, P. 149
Gouyette, C. 252
Grieve Smith, J. 10, 242
Grossman, G. M. 248
Guerrieri, P. 139–57, 9, 12
Gugler, P. 253

Hagedoorn, J. 172, 185, 229, 245
Hägerstrand, T. 78
Hall, A. D. 4, 82
Hamilton 39
Hansen, N. 85
Harrison, B. 79, 80
Harrison, R. 124, 131
Harrod, R. 174–5
Hassink, R. 72
Hay, M. 129
Hayes, R. 107
Held, D. 254
Helpman, E. 248
Henderson, R. 235, 237
Henriksson, R. H. G. 28
Hermer, J. 131, 132
Hicks, D. 103, 114, 235
Hirst, P. 73, 163, 165, 263
Hodgson, G. 5
Hodson, C. 187
Holland, S. 254, 261
Hood, N. 187, 212
Howells, J. 1–13, 67–87, 173, 251, 252
Hu, Y.-S. 83, 94, 112, 245, 261
Hund, J. M. 79

Iammarino, S. 242–66, 10
imitation 233–4

income distribution 20, 26, 31
industrial policy 121, 176
  principles for 27–9
  see also public policy; state; technology
    policy
industrial taxonomy 144–5
industry specialisation
  core/periphery 74–5
  regional 73–4
information 19
  flows 78
  market failure 125–6
  technology 21, 111
  see also knowledge
innovation
  capturing returns to 229–35
  definition 3–4, 229
  diffusion 54
  and imitation 233–4
  investment-based 54–7
  localised search 83
  process and product 51–62
  and profits 226–9
  R&D-based 54–7
  see also globalisation of innovation;
    national systems of innovation; R&D;
    regional system of innovation; system
    of innovation; technology
institutions 39–40, 42, 71
  convergence 120
  creation of 237
  effective capacity 77
  ensemble of 73
  evolutionary change 121
  rigidity 122
  rules 121
invention, localised 83–4
Irwin, D. 169
Isard, W. 79
Ishizuka, T. 235
Italy 152–3

Jacobsson, S. 8
Jaffe, A. 103, 235, 237
Japan 148–9, 170–1, 190
Jefferson, M. 83
Johnson, B. 5, 84
Johnston, R. 104

Kaldor, N. 174, 248
Katz, M. L. 252
Katzenstein, P. 122
Keck, O. 106, 115
Keeble, D. 77, 79
Keen, P. 235
Kim, W. S. 186

Kindleberger, C. 170
Kitschelt, H. 72
Kitson, M. 163–80, 246
Klevorick, A. K. 230
Kluth, M. F. 120–35
knowledge 19
    accumulation 39, 43
    capital 185
    flows 78, 230
    infrastructure 77
    local 36–8, 84
    market 22
    as public good 101–3, 230–3
    reproduction 40
    sharing 84
    sticky 40
    tacit 23, 40, 84
    transfer 23
    see also information
Kogut, B. 186, 237
Krugman, P. R. 39
Kuemmerle, W. 186, 189, 210
Kumar, N. 187

Lall, S. 237
Landes, D. 259
Lawson, Nigel 163
learning
    capability 19
    localised 83–4
    organisational 44
    public policy for 232–3
    role of 5
    social process 20, 23–4, 28
learning economy 20–2, 24
    pure market in 25–6
Levin, R. C. 230
Levinthal, D. 234
Levy, J. D. 133
Lewis, A. 165
licences 245
Lichtenberg, F. R. 264
Lichtenburg, R. M. 79
linkages
    local 206, 235
    regional 78
    sectoral 39, 146
List, F. 38, 259
Lloyd, P. J. 168–9
localisation 79–81, 83–5
lock-in 85
Lucas, R. E. 248
Lundan, S. 187, 193
Lundvall, B.-A. 2–7, 9–11, 19–33, 38–9, 50, 54, 70–1, 76, 81–2, 84, 101, 139, 155, 255
Lyn, E. O. 186

McKelvey, M. 6, 70, 81
MacPherson, A. 83
Maddison, A. 165, 169, 170, 171
Malecki, E. J. 69, 74, 77, 78
management systems 107
Mancusi, M. C. 260
Mansfield, E. 85, 232
Marchall, A. 73–4
market size 250
Markusen, A. 79
Marshall, A. 79, 79–8
Marshall, R. 77
Marx, K. 102, 226, 228, 231
Mason, C. 124, 131
Mayer, C. 107
Meliciani, V. 260
Metcalfe, J. S. 67, 172, 176
Michie, J. 1–13, 36, 50, 155, 163–80, 238, 242–4, 246, 250, 255
Milana, C. 147
Miller, R. 251
Moore, G. E. 258
More, R. A. 84
Mowery, D. C. 234
multinational enterprises 172–3, 184
    activities in host countries 185–7
    affiliations 228
    alliances 228–9
    asset and employment 207–9, 212, 214
    in Europe, Japan and US 190
    home base 185, 210–11, 217
    inter-firm rivalry 206
    policy implications 220
    questionnaire 187–93
    R&D 186–7, 190–2, 209–10, 251
    relationship with state 239, 261–3
    role 12
    specialisation 228
    technological intensity 205–10
    technology feedback 193
    trade 212, 214, 215
    see also foreign direct investment
multinationality, degree of 193, 205, 207, 212, 215, 219–20
Mytelka, L. K. 246, 234

Naes Gjerding, A. 29
NAFTA 143, 168
Narin, F. 103, 114
Narula, N. 187
Nash, P. A. 69, 77
national system of innovation 237–9
    definitions 38, 67, 70–1
    dominance of 99–100
    key features 100–10
    non-convergence 94, 113–14

national system of innovation (*cont.*)
  persistence 40–1, 56–7, 68
  political economy of 121–2
  two dimensions 3
Neary, I. 2, 70, 72, 73
Nelson, R. R. 2–3, 36, 38–9, 42, 50, 70–1,
    76, 101, 139, 149, 176, 229–31, 238,
    255, 259, 321
networking 132
Neven, D. J. 252
Newton, K. 103
Niosi, J. 86
Nye, M. J. 69
Nyholm, J. 29

Oakey, R. P. 69, 77
Ohmae, K. 139, 163, 242, 255
Oman, C. 143
Ordover, J. A. 252
Orsenigo, L. 121

Paget, K. M. 73
Papannastassiou, M. 186
Patel, P. 8–10, 12, 36, 39–40, 94–116, 172,
    190, 238, 245, 248, 251, 262
patents 95–6, 173, 245
Pavitt, K. 6, 8–10, 12, 36, 39–40, 84, 94–116,
    144, 190, 237–8, 245, 248, 251, 259,
    262
Pearce, R. D. 186, 187, 251
Perani, G. 51
Perraton, J. 242
Perroux, F. 39, 79
Petit, P. 51
pharmaceuticals 206, 208
Phelps, N. A. 77
Pianta, M. 8, 36, 49–62, 70, 140, 238, 248,
    259, 260
Pini, P. 51
Piscitello, L. 186
planned economies 25
politics 122
Porter, M. E. 86, 94, 96, 101, 108, 149, 154,
    155, 185, 193, 206
Prais, S. 103
Prakker, F. 124
Pred, A. R. 75, 84
productivity and wages 227
profits
  erosion of 228–9
  and innovation 226–9
  and wage costs 226–8
public policy
  convergence and stability 174
  and globalisation of innovation
    254–65

on knowledge creation 232
on specialisation 259–61
see also industrial policy; state;
    technology policy
pure market economy 25

Quah, D. T. 252

R&D
  basic research 101–3
  business-funded 104
  centralised and decentralised 173–4,
    251
  corporate expenditure on 106–7
  face-to-face contact 85–6
  globalisation of 85–6
  non-globalised 96–8, 111–12
  outside home base 186–7, 190–2, 212
  public research 235
  returns on 108, 235–6
  uncertainty of outcome 230
  underinvestment 236
  see also innovation; technology
regional competitiveness 42–4
regional problem 85
regional system of innovation
  bottom-up perspective 77–85
  France 69
  and globalisation 85–6
  governance 72–3
  Scotland 68
  top–down perspective 70–7
regionalism 142–3, 168–9, 178
Reich, R. 262
research see R&D
Ricardo, D. 227, 228
Ricks, D. A. 186
Ring, P. S. 85
risk 84–5
  assessment 128, 132
Roberts, N. J. 79
Robins, K. 79, 80, 81
Rosenberg, N. 3, 71, 84, 176, 231, 234,
    238
Rothwell, R. 98
Rugman, A. M. 185, 186
Ruigrok, W. 242
Rullani, E. 253

Sanna-Randaccio, F. 228
Santarelli, E. 7
Saviotti, P. 5, 6, 9
Schakenraad, J. 172, 229, 245
Scherer, F. M. 6, 142, 258
Schettkat, R. 51
Schmandt, J. 72, 73

Schumpeter, J. A. 226
Schwartz, M. 232
Serapico, M. G. 187
Serra, Count 39
Setterfield, M. 175
Sharp, M. 114, 262
Shonfield, A. 122
Simonetti, R. 260
Singh, S. 186, 187, 251
Sjoholm, F. 154
skills 103–4, 113
Smith, A. 38, 112, 226, 227, 231
Smith, K. 75
social capabilities 177
social cohesion 20, 23–4
Soete, L. 36, 40, 50, 139, 260
Soskice, D. 40, 121
Spain 152–3
specialisation *see* trade specialisation
spillovers 101, 231
Stankiewicz, R. 3, 4, 8, 71
state
    monitoring technology flows 258–9,
        262–3
    relationship with MNC 239, 261–3
    to ensure competition 112–13
    under globalisation 163–80, 225, 238
    venture capital provision 133–4
    see also industrial policy; public policy;
        technology policy
Stephan, P. E. 235
Stopford, J. 246
Storper, M. 79, 86
Strange, S. 246
Sugden, R. 259
Sunley, P. 79, 80
Svensson, K. 126
Sweden 150, 152–3
Sweet, S. 235
system of innovation
    basic minima 81–2
    boundaries 10–12
    characteristics of 4–6
    definitions 3
    empirical analysis of 8, 9
    European 114–15
    firms response to 8
    flows and links 6–8
    historical perspective 68–70
    location-related heterogeneity 36–8
    origin of 2
    role of learning 5
    sectoral 2, 71–2
    see also national system of innovation;
        regional system of innovation
systems nest 75

Tassey, G. 75
Taylor, M. J. 78, 81, 83
technological accumulation 110
technological advantage 108–9
technological capacity 144
technological change
    acceleration of 142
    and basic research 102
    evolutionary 231–2
    internationalised 28
    nature and direction 50
technological globalisation 49–62, 171–4,
        178
technological systems 2
technology, *see also* innovation; R&D
technology policy 61–2, 176, 235–9
    institution building 121
    knowledge-based 29–30
    principles for 27–9
    supply side 29
    see also industrial policy; public policy;
        state
technology transfer 127–8
Teece, D. J. 104, 235
Teubal, M. 6, 7
Thatcher, Margaret 24
Thirwall, A. P. 248
Thomas, M. D. 79
Thomas, R. 259
Thompson, C. 74
Thompson, G. 73, 163, 165, 263
Thompson, W. R. 79
Thorngren, B. 74
Thrift, N. 77
Thwaites, A. T. 69, 77
Timmons, J. A. 128, 133
Tornqvist, G. 74, 78
Townroe, P. M. 79
trade 212, 214, 215
    and economic growth 166–7
    and FDI 250
    geographic concentration 169
    growth of 141–2
    imbalance 227, 228
    structure 141–2
trade specialisation 238, 248
    convergence 144
    data 155–7
    EU 146–54
    France 150–1
    Germany 150–1
    and globalisation 139, 154–5
    Italy 152–3
    Japan 148–9
    public policy 259–61
    and technological capacity 144

trade specialisation (*cont.*)
  USA 148–9
training 29, 113, 233, 236
  see also education
Trajtenberg, M. 235, 237
trust 23–4
Tucker, Rev. 39
Tylecote, A. 140, 154
Tyson, L. D. 258

Ulvenblad, P. O. 126
uncertainty 84–5, 230
United Kingdom
  nineteenth century 259
  as leading nation 169–70
  pharmaceutical industry 70
  trade specialisation 150–1
  venture capital 130–3
United States 148–9, 169–71, 190
Urata, S. 144
user–producer relations 39

Vaccà, S. 253
van Tulder, R. 242
venture capital 120
  business angels 130–2
  classification 124
  France 133–4
  Germany 126–9
  intermediaries 130
  operating principles 123–4
  period of investment 124

recipients 129
state role 133–4
United Kingdom 130–3
Verbeke, A. 184
Vernon, R. 79, 185
Verspagen, B. 36, 252
Vertova, G. 250
Vivarelli, M. 52
Von Bertalanffy, L. 82
Von Hippel, E. 83

wages and productivity 227
Wagner, S. 232
Walker, W. 106
Walras, L. 39
Walsh, V. M. 82
Weber, A. 79
Wells, J. 165
Wes, M. 165
Westling, H. 29
Wiig, H. 85
Williamson, O. E. 126
Winter, S. 42, 229, 230–1, 238, 321
Wolff, E. N. 36
Wood, M. 80, 85, 173, 251
Wood, P. 68
Wright, G. 259
Wymbs, C. 184–222, 11, 12

Zanfei, A. 253
Zysman, J. 40, 122